Designs of Social Research

Designs of Social Research

D.K. Lal Das

RAWAT PUBLICATIONS
Jaipur • New Delhi • Bangalore • Hyderabad • Guwahati • Kolkata

ISBN 81-7033-984-7 (HB)
ISBN 81-7033-985-5 (PB)

Reprinted, 2015

Published by
Prem Rawat for **Rawat Publications**
Satyam Apts., Sector 3, Jawahar Nagar, Jaipur - 302 004 (India)
Phone: 0141 265 1748 / 7006 Fax: 0141 265 1748
E-mail : info@rawatbooks.com
Website: rawatbooks.com

New Delhi Office
4858/24, Ansari Road, Daryaganj, New Delhi 110 002
Phone: 011-23263290

Also at *Bangalore, Hyderabad, Guwahati* and *Kolkata*

Typeset by Rawat Computers, Jaipur
Printed at Chaman Enterprises, New Delhi

Contents

Preface

As a teacher of social work research at graduate and post-graduate levels and a supervisor of Ph.D. dissertations for over two decades, I have spent a great deal of time searching for a suitable text on designs of social research for my students and research scholars. It became increasingly evident that most research books describe design of research as a plan of study, generally vague and tentative. Many authors have expressed that the design of research has to undergo many changes and modifications as the study progresses and insights into it deepen. As a result, every researcher ends up with a research design of his own having his own methodological strategies.

However, I am of the view that since a research design is a scientific model, it has to be logical and systematic so that it can help researchers to execute the research project.

In preparing this text on designs of social research, my intent, therefore, is to help social science students, research scholars and educators to learn about the crucial stage of social research—development of research design.

A research design includes the details about the problem, the objectives, research questions, area of study (population), sampling plan, and methodology and techniques of data collection and analysis. In fact, the research design spells out in considerable detail what occur in the following steps of the research process. It also reflects the dimensions of research designs.

In other words, a design of social research aims at helping the researcher to prepare a scientific model—logical and systematic—so that it can help them to execute the research project.

Keeping in view the above objectives, the design of social research has a unique role to play in enabling the students, research scholars as well as educators to execute research projects.

It is against this background, this book deals with the subject in a very specific way, that is, while in general it describes the basics of social research, its focus remains on the designs of social research. As such, the book contains two parts, namely, (a) basics of social research, and (b) designs of social research. Part I includes the basics of social research such as scientific approach, basic elements of social research, measurement in social research and analysis of social data. The major contents of Part II of the book include meaning and dimensions of research designs, exploratory research designs, descriptive research designs, experimental research designs, pre-experimental research designs, quasi-experimental research designs, action research designs, evaluation research designs, intervention research designs and survey research designs. In a nutshell, the salient features of the book are as under:

(1) Each chapter includes illustrations from practice, which discuss how research designs can be developed. In this way, I have emphasized the need of development of designs in social research.
(2) In Part-I, basics of social research have been presented in very concise form. The purpose is to reduce the material that has minimal or no relevance to research designs.
(3) Part-II is written exclusively for designs of social research for students, scholars and educators, who are concerned about scientific social research.

Designs of Social Research Curriculum in Social Science Research

Curriculum of designs of social research in social sciences has traditionally been modelled keeping in view the textbooks on social science research published in early 50's or late 60's. This is most probably the reason why goals/purposes of social research—

exploratory, descriptive, or explanatory research—are taught as the design of social research in many schools/universities. As such, students/research scholars largely view their researches either exploratory or descriptive and draw conclusions from the research findings through the process of deductive reasoning. Seldom do they try to test the interventions or evaluate the outcome of their interventions. The experimental research course offered to social science students has hardly any relevance to practice. As a consequence, students/scholars fail to do experiments. Most of them develop a notion that they have nothing to do with experimental research.

The Emerging Need

Social science research curriculum needs to be redesigned to enable it to emerge from shadowy existence and occupy an equal place with other disciplines. While redesigning the curriculum, exploratory, descriptive or explanatory research should be perceived as goals of social research. Research designs like experimental, intervention, action and survey need to be given due weightage in the curriculum of social science research. Besides, practical examples need to be identified to merge with theory. It is evident from the above discussion that the curriculum of social science research needs change in its focus, especially in the areas of research design, so that the research becomes relevant and useful for social science students and scholars.

Stimulating Research in Social Work

Social science educators have to realize that it is on them that the primary responsibility of expanding the horizons of social research devolves. The present emphasis on teaching research designs must be dispensed with detailed discussion with suitable examples of experimental, intervention, action and survey research.

The perspectives of research designs can provide a framework for teaching designs of social research. Most of the knowledge used by social science educators lacks a strong empirical basis—an unavoidable limitation of profession that deals with the elusive complexities of psychological and social phenomena. Social science educators can make use of scientific orientation in motivating students/scholars to go for empirical testing of the various knowledge bases of social sciences—theories, principles and concepts taught in the theory classes. Research will provide empirically grounded knowledge, which in turn can make a significant change in the attitude of the students/scholars and educators towards social science research.

Most social science students study research for only one reason—it is a compulsory requirement for the degree. Many students wonder why research courses are required for social sciences when there is so much to learn about how to understand people. It is imperative for social science educators, who teach research courses, to convince students that social research is a problem-solving method too and it seeks to accomplish the same humanistic goals as does social sciences. For this, social science educators have to use appropriate illustrations geared specifically to social science from the fieldwork experiences of the students.

Finally, the book will help the reader to understand research methods and also utilize them for social science research.

Acknowledgements

First of all, I would like to express my gratitude to Mr. Pranit Rawat, Managing Director, Rawat Publications, for his initiative to bring out a book on *Designs of Social Research.*

I thank all research scholars and post-graduate students whom I have been supervising for their dissertations over the years. They may not be aware of the fact that their queries have helped me a lot to organize my thoughts, which are now presented through this text. I especially want to express my gratitude and appreciation to Mrs. T. Saraswati, who has gone through my earlier book on social research thoroughly and has shared her views, which has helped me to organize my thoughts in this book. I am extremely thankful to her.

My colleagues at R.M. College of Social Work have generously shared their perspectives on teaching social research designs and offered their consistent support while I was writing the book. I especially want to express my gratitude and appreciation to Mrs. Vanila Bhaskaran, who, in spite of her indisposition, not only did proofreading meticulously but also read the whole typescript and offered valuable suggestions on some of the chapters of this text. I express my gratitude to Mr. A. Ravindra Chary and Mr. Hari Babu, also my colleagues, who readily and promptly made available the books and journals whenever I needed.

There are also many other people who have contributed to this project in a number of ways.

A special word of thanks must be given to Mrs. Iyesha who typed the manuscript and fed the typedscripts into computer and helped to get "hard" and "soft" copies of the book.

Two of my colleagues, Dr. (Mrs.) Anna Mathew and Mrs. Mrudula, approached me and asked me if I can join them in an intervention research project and help them to use single-subject design of social research and bring out a research paper. I agreed to be a co-researcher in the project supervised by Dr. (Mrs.) Anna Mathew. The research paper is an excellent example of an intervention research project using single-subject design of social research. I have included an abridged version of the research paper in this book. I take this opportunity to appreciate the pioneering effort of my colleagues.

I am thankful to Dr. (Mrs.) B. Vijayalaksmi, Dr. B. Devi Prasad and Dr. K. Vishweswar Rao for permitting me to reproduce an abridged form of their article 'Trends in Articles' published in *The Indian Journal of Social Work*, 1971-1990.

Finally, I acknowledge the support of Pushpa, my wife, who understood, with great patience, my working with computer for long hours and even on holidays, which was unavoidable. I thank my family members—Hemendra, Rathindra, Sneha and Kalpana—for their salient support. Finally, I acknowledge the innocent queries of my grandchildren, Harsh, Yash and Eshant—"For whom I am working so hard?", "How they are going to be benefited?", "Would it be simple to understand?" and a "great suggestion"—"Don't give difficult questions in the exercise!" which created an atmosphere that helped me to complete the project more meaningfully than it would have been without their "queries".

Hyderabad **D.K. Lal Das**
October 2005

I

Basics of Social Research

1

The Scientific Approach

Man has always been interested in the facts and events that have been taking place around him. He has been exploring different sources of evidence concerning the facts and events to acquire reliable knowledge about the various aspects of human experience. However, it was observed that personal bias influenced the selection of sources of evidences and that care was not exercised to examine the authenticity of the evidences provided by these sources. The result was inconsistency in the explanation of the same facts and events time and again. Hence, to acquire reliable knowledge, scientists, thinkers and philosophers have used various methods.

Among the various methods, the method of science is perhaps the most commonly used method of knowing or fixing beliefs. This is because more dependable knowledge is attained through science as it ultimately appeals to evidence and propositions are subjected to empirical tests.

The scientific approach has one characteristic that no other method of attaining knowledge has, i.e., objectivity. There is a well-conceived self-control mechanism all along the way to the scientific knowledge. This mechanism is so designed that it not only controls and verifies the scientist's activities and conclusions but it also keeps the scientist away from his personal beliefs, perceptions, biases, values, attitudes and emotions. Thus, the approach helps the scientist to attain objectivity.

To what extent is the scientific approach useful in studying the problems of society? How can we acquire reliable knowledge about the various aspects of human experience? To be more specific, how can the scientific approach be of value in understanding social phenomena? In response to these questions, our approach would be first, to understand the meaning of science and then to examine the scientific approach, its assumptions and aims and finally to take a close look at the approach to find out how it can help social scientists to understand social phenomena.

Meaning of Science

The word 'science' is derived from the Latin word 'scienta', which means "to know". Throughout history, people have been very keen to acquire knowledge by using various methods. However, it was felt necessary to evolve a method by which individual thinking has no effect on the conclusions. In other words, the method should be such that the ultimate conclusion of every man is the same. Endeavours to acquire knowledge, which involved such methods, came to be known as science.

The term 'science' has been defined in different ways. To some, science means an objective investigation of empirical phenomena; to others, denotes an accumulation of systematic knowledge; to still others, it means all knowledge collected by means of the scientific methodology. Nevertheless, whatever may be the way of defining, science is united by its methodology. Hence, it would be easier to understand science if we first consider science as a method of approach, and then discuss its aims and functions.

A method is a system of explicit rules and procedures. Thus, an approach to acquire knowledge, which follows certain explicit rules and procedures, is science. Further, the results—the acquired knowledge—are evaluated in the light of the method. The process of study, which involves these steps, is science.

Aims of Science

The ultimate aim of science is to produce an accumulating body of reliable knowledge, which enables us to understand the world in which we live and its ways. First, a science describes the various phenomena that interest us such as: What was the population growth rate of our country in the last decade? Description of a phenomenon is followed by explanation. Explanation answers the question: Why is there a higher rate of population growth in underdeveloped countries than in developed countries? In other words, the scientist first describes the situation and then explains it. The explanation of situation brings meaning to the description. Finally, science contributes to the body of knowledge by way of prediction. Prediction means making inferences from the facts. For example, if the present conditions continue, the population of the country will cross 1,000 million, by the end of this decade. It is true that the scientists rarely make absolute predictions; instead, they infer in terms of probabilities. The final step of science: prediction has been referred to as one of "the most desirable fruits of scientific labour".

What is Research?

When we observe certain objects or phenomena, we are often unaware of our biases, we do not question them and so we attribute our observations entirely to the objects or phenomena being observed. In this process, it is possible to arrive at right decision on the basis of wrong reasons or vice versa. This questions the process of observation. Was the observation error free? Every method of knowing has certain limitations. While observing, are we aware of our limitations? Any study to create new knowledge or aims to increase existing fund of knowledge—may it be through observation or by some other methods—is called research, if it takes into account the biases, the errors and limitations. As such, research may be described as systematic and critical investigation of phenomena towards increasing the stream of knowledge.

Scientific Research

Science aims at description, explanation and understanding of various objects or phenomena in nature and research involves special endeavours to systematic and critical investigation. Thus, towards increasing the stream of knowledge, now, it is easier to define scientific research. We may define scientific research as a systematic and critical investigation about the natural phenomena to describe, explain and finally to understand the relations among them.

Scientific Method

It is obvious that it would be impossible to comprehend the nature and content of research without an appreciation of a method. The method used in scientific research is usually designated as scientific method. According to George Lundberg (1946), scientific method consists of three basic steps: systematic observation, classification and interpretation of data. Through these steps, scientific method brings about not only verifiability of the facts, but also it lays the confidence in the validity of conclusions.

The definition requires some more explanations. First, when Lundberg (1946) says that scientific method is systematic observation, he means in effect, the scientific investigation is not ordered, it aims only at discovering facts as they actually are and not as they are desired to be and as such the investigators can have critical confidence in their conclusions. Second, the scientific method is concerned with 'classes of objects' not 'individual objects' specifically universality and predictability are other features of scientific method. The method makes it possible to predict about a phenomenon with sufficient accuracy.

Use of Scientific Method in Social Sciences

Social sciences primarily deal with human behaviour, which is, by and large, complex and dynamic in nature. One cannot, therefore, investigate under guided conditions as in natural and physical sciences. This creates many problems to the researcher such as the problems of subjectivity and individualistic generalizations etc.

The problems arising out of the nature and content of social sciences do not seriously diminish the importance of scientific method for social scientists. Notwithstanding the inherent defects of social sciences, scientific method can be acceptable with its own limitations for the study of social phenomena so far, as it helps to arrive at valid generalizations.

Approaches to Social Research

A problem can be studied with different approaches. A researcher may take into consideration the phenomenon as a whole and describe it as it exists or may wish to analyze it by its components in measurable or quantifiable terms. The former approach is termed as qualitative approach and the latter is known as quantitative approach. These are further described as under:

Qualitative Approach

In some situations it is difficult to analyze a phenomenon into various components or variables, which can be measured in quantified terms. In such cases, the researcher takes into consideration the phenomenon as a whole and assumes that there is some quality in the phenomenon in its entirety. When the researcher attempts to retain the totality of a phenomenon while verifying propositions regarding it, he adopts a qualitative approach. This approach describes the experiences of people in depth and permits the researcher to record and understand people thoroughly in their own perceptions. Qualitative approach helps us to examine the nature of human behaviour and experience and social conditions. It also permits the researcher to study selected issues, cases or events in depth. While using this approach, the researcher seeks to capture what people have to say in their own words.

Qualitative approach takes into consideration 'detailed descriptions' of situations, events, people, interactions and observed behaviours. These data are also available in the form of 'direct quotations' from people about their experiences, attitudes, beliefs and thoughts. Data in qualitative approach are collected through direct observations, participant observations, in-depth interviewing, case studies, recorded documents, open-ended questionnaires and journals.

The validity and reliability of qualitative data depends to a great extent on the methodological skills, sensitivity and integrity of the researcher. Systematic and rigorous observation involves far more than just being present and looking around. Skilful interviewing involves much more than just asking questions. Content analysis requires considerably more insights into the data than reading to see what's there. Thus, generating useful, credible qualitative findings through observation, interviewing and content analysis requires discipline, knowledge, training, practice, creativity and hard work (Patton, 1990: II).

Quantitative Approach

Quantitative approach focuses on objective and standardized means of inquiry and application of statistical analysis for attainment of objectivity and generalizations. Quantitative researchers use interview, questionnaire and structured observation as major methods to collect data. Quantitative approach uses standardized measures that fit diverse opinions and experiences into predetermined response categories. This approach measures the reactions of a large number of individuals to a limited set of questions, thus facilitating comparison and analysis of data with the help of close-ended questionnaires, attitude scales, rating scales and postal surveys.

Qualitative Approach versus Quantitative Approach

For quite sometime the qualitative-quantitative debate has persisted in the field of social research. It has been more of a philosophical debate than that of research practices. Qualitative methods have been the subject of considerable controversy among social scientists. The philosophical and theoretical perspectives, which undergrid qualitative approach, include phenomenology, naturalistic behaviourism and the socio-cultural context of social interaction. This method estimates validity, reliability and objectivity of a social situation and tries to project the empirical social world as it actually exists to those under investigation, rather than as the researcher imagines it to be.

In recent years, however, the debate has softened. A consensus has gradually emerged that the important challenge is to match appropriate methods to research questions and not to advocate any single methodological approach for all research situations. Both qualitative and quantitative data can be collected for/under the same studies.

Research Process

In social research a deductive approach is commonly used, that is, hypotheses are derived from a theory. Variables in the hypothesis are operationally defined and data are collected based on the operational definitions. In short, social research (basic research) moves from the abstract to concrete. Theories serve to integrate and explain the observation (data) by researchers.

The research process is the paradigm of research project. In a research project, there are various scientific activities in which researcher engages him in order to produce knowledge. Although each research project is unique in some ways, all projects, regardless of the phenomenon being studied, involve, by and large, some common activities. Each of these activities is interdependent. The research process is thus the system of these interrelated activities. The various activities are conveniently grouped into six stages as shown below in Figure 1.

Thus, a research process involves six interdependent stages. The researcher usually enters the research process at stage I. However, when he enters stage II, he has to draw on past studies to

Figure 1
Stages of Research Process

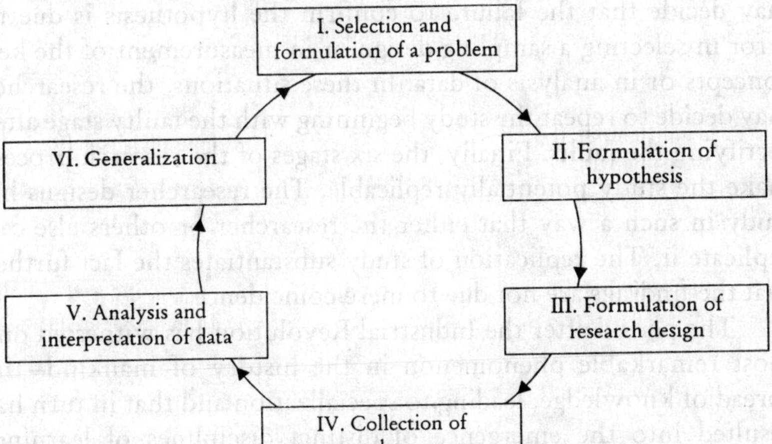

formulate his hypothesis. Similarly, to select a research design, the researcher has to keep in mind the problem and the hypothesis. A researcher, who has no knowledge of how to collect and analyze data, may find himself unable to formulate a testable hypothesis, or formulate a research design. This brief discussion on the research process makes it very clear that each of these six stages of research process are dependent upon others.

The research process is also cyclic in nature. In fact, the research process is not complete at the stage VI. The process leads to two situations. The first situation may be that the data did not support or partially support the hypothesis. In this situation, the researcher must return to the stage I. He, then, may decide to reformulate the problem and hypothesis and then list it exactly as before. In the second situation, that is, even if the research is successful and the findings of stage VI confirm the hypothesis of stage II, it is advisable to repeat the study preferably with a different sample as to reconfirm the findings. This will also support the contention that the hypothesis cannot be rejected. The exact repetition of a study is called *replication.*

Another characteristic feature of the research process is *self-correction*. In the situation, when the data did not support or only partially support the hypothesis and the researcher has sufficient reasons to decide that the hypothesis is adequate, then he may decide that the failure to confirm the hypothesis is due to error in selecting a sampling design or in measurement of the key concepts or in analysis of data. In these situations, the researcher may decide to repeat the study beginning with the faulty stage after rectifying the faults. Finally, the six stages of the research process make the study potentially replicable. The researcher designs his study in such a way that either the researcher or others else can replicate it. The replication of study substantiates the fact further that the findings are not due to mere coincidence.

The period after the Industrial Revolution has witnessed one most remarkable phenomenon in the history of mankind—the spread of knowledge, leading to specialization and that in turn has resulted into the emergence of distinct disciplines of learning. Science of society encompassing man's social life, commonly known as *social sciences,* has acquired a prominent place in the contemporary disciplines of learning. Today, the social sciences are a recognized stream of knowledge. This has been a result of advances in individual social science disciplines. Research has been an integral part of academic pursuits in social sciences in the past. Social sciences have marched on to the present form with the help of constant research and investigation. Natural and exact sciences have been able to develop advance methodology of research and succeeded in reaching the highest order of accuracy and precision and hence the greater depths of knowledge.

Social sciences adopted the methods of researches used in natural and exact sciences. But they could not achieve the order of accuracy and precision similar to the physical sciences basically because of the problems of control, measurement and quantitative analysis of social data, which is very much heterogeneous and complex in nature. The researchers in social sciences also differ from the researchers in general. It would not be inappropriate to use the term 'social research' to cover all scientific enquiries conducted in the field of social and behavioural sciences.

Nature of Social Research

The object of social research is clearly the discovery of causal relationships in human behaviour. It is generally acknowledged that in human behaviour, as much as in natural phenomena, a large degree of measurable and predictable sets of associations occur. Social research, then, like research in physical and natural sciences, seeks to establish, measure, and analyze these associations in all their variety and intensity (Thomas, 1968: 294). Social research, however, assumes a distinct character of its own in a significant measure when it comes to the application of scientific process, characteristics of research in natural and physical sciences, to social phenomena. Unlike physical and natural sciences, in social research, the objects are conscious and active human beings. The individual behaviour of the objects, whether it is free or determined, makes the social research really a difficult job. Further, the researcher and object being similar, the scope of an objective approach in social research is limited to a considerable extent.

Social research concerns with social data, which are much more complex than that of the physical data. The basis of all social interactions, whether it is a large complex group or a small cohesive group, is expectations of behaviour, which in turn is result of many factors. The complex nature of social data reduces the power of exact prediction in social research. Most of the subject matter of social research is qualitative and does not admit quantitative measurement. It is more so, because social phenomena are known only symbolically through concepts or terms representing such phenomena.

In social research, it is difficult to segregate the cause and effect. It is because many a time the cause is also the effect, hence, it makes no sense to say which is the cause and which is the effect. The above exposition makes it very clear that the social data typically pose certain problems when it comes to measurement, precision and prediction in social research.

Basic Presumptions of Social Research

The problems posed by the nature of social data are not in any way insurmountable. The limitations, which appear to preclude the application of scientific process in social research, derive from our unfamiliarity with social data rather than from the nature of the social data themselves.

Social research presumes that the applicability of scientific process in the study of social phenomena is possible because of the following situations (Galtung, 1970):

(1) It is presumed that all social interaction follows some kind of natural law. Social phenomena are social actions. Therefore, it is possible to make studies of social phenomena.

(2) It is presumed that the social phenomena follow certain definite trends at least in the short period. Thus, it is possible to predict with quite a high degree of accuracy the social behaviour.

(3) Social data are complex to us, because our knowledge of them is inadequate and we have not been able to develop tools of study, which can explain them in more simple way.

(4) In social research we presume that it is possible by stratification or classification of social data on the basis of certain traits or properties, to ensure fairly high degree of internal homogeneity within each stratum. Thus, valid generalization based on conclusions of a social inquiry is possible.

(5) It is presumed that the various characteristics in nature are uniformly distributed and hence, social interaction follows certain definite order. Therefore, it is presumed that similar cause produces similar result under similar circumstances. As such, it is possible to find out the effects from the cause(s) or cause from the effect.

Planning a Research Project

The approaches discussed above provide with guidelines by which we can develop a research plan, select techniques to collect data, interpret them and arrive at generalizations.

In this section, we will learn how to plan a research project. The plan consists of every details of a research project. It helps a researcher in many ways. First of all, it gives a complete picture of the whole research process he/she needs to undergo if he/she is interested in studying a phenomenon. A well-prepared research plan also helps to make time and budget estimate. Finally, a plan of research project enables a researcher to monitor his/her research project. Sometimes, the purpose of developing a research plan is to try to obtain a grant to cover the expenses of the research project. Whether or not we are applying for a grant, developing research plan is useful. Steps in planning a research project are described as under:

Step 1: Identification of a Research Problem

The first step in planning a research project is the identification of a suitable problem. In each area/field of social sciences innumerable problems exist. The choice of a suitable problem is one of the most difficult tasks for a researcher, especially if he/she is a beginner.

There are many sources to which a researcher may go to identify a research problem. Once you decide to take up a problem for a research study, immediately, you need to evaluate the proposed problem in the light of your competence, possible difficulties, availability of data, financial and field constraints, and limitations of time. After evaluating the problem, you have to make it a specific problem. Let us assume that you have chosen the problem of street children. To undertake a research study on this problem, you have to narrow it down to specific research problem. You may make it specific by saying that you would like to study the psychosocial problems of street children with specific reference to a slum.

It is very commonly experienced in social sciences in general and social work in particular, that students respond to this assignment by drawing a total blank. Other students grasp eagerly onto a topic, such as the causes of delinquency, and rush off with total confidence that they are about to solve this enduring problem. It is very obvious that in each case, the student will be having difficulty in formulating a research problem. In the first case, the difficulty is in locating a problem to investigate, whereas in the second, it is in formulating a problem sufficiently specific that it is amenable to scientific research. This problem is not unique to students. Every student researcher must grapple with the issue of problem formulation. Because it is the initial step and provides the basis for the complete research project, problem formulation is of crucial importance. Many potentially serious research problems can be avoided—or at least minimized—by careful process of problem formulation. Thus, we will present below the major issues to be considered in problem formulation, beginning with how to select a problem on which to conduct research:

Selecting a Research Problem

The first hurdle confronting a researcher is to select a topic that is appropriate for scientific inquiry. Actually, this is not as difficult as it may first appear because the social world around us is literally full of unanswered questions. Selecting a problem calls for some creativity and imagination, but there are also a number of sources you can look for inspiration. Some of the more common sources of research problems are discussed here.

Personal Interest

A researcher often selects a research topic simply because he/she has an interest in some aspect of human behaviour, possibly owing to some personal experience. A researcher might, for example, be interested in the problem of alcoholics because he/she has been experiencing the ill-effects of it in his/her family. Truancy or delinquency might be the focus of research attention because of contact with some youngsters in trouble in the neighbourhood. A research study generally focuses on behaviour that is unique and thus compelling to some.

A researcher who selects a topic out of his/her personal interest must be careful to demonstrate the scientific worth of his/her projects. The goals of scientific research are to describe, explain, predict and evaluate. The aim of a research study should be to advance the knowledge, not just satisfy personal curiosity. A researcher who chooses a topic based on his/her personal interest—especially if it deals with some unusual aspect of human behaviour—should be prepared for the possibility that others will fail to see the worth of that research.

Social Problems

To identify a topic for a research study, you need to look through the daily newspaper, where you can read about the many social problems that our society faces. Problems such as crime, delinquency, poverty, pollution, overpopulation, drug abuse, alcoholism, mental illness, sexual deviance, discrimination, exploitation and oppression have all been popular sources of topics for social research. A number of journals such as *The Indian Journal of Social Work, Social Welfare, Social Change*, etc., communicate the results of scientific investigations into current social problems.

Within each of these broad categories of social problems, there is a range of issues that can be studied. Many studies, for example, focus on the origin of a problem. Others are concerned with the effects and consequences these problems have for individuals, groups and society. Still others deal with the impact of social programmes and other intervention efforts intended to ameliorate these problems. People associated with non-governmental organizations, who are routinely involved with many of these problems, can find opportunities for research that are directly related to their professional activities.

Step 2: Define the Research Topic

Once a research problem has been identified, the research topic needs to be defined. In this stage of research the overall plan for the research project must be set out in logical order to see if it makes sense.

Your research topic should be defined in such a way that it is clearly understood. If you are studying, say for example, alcoholism, you need to put your research question into a framework which suggests that you are very clear and specific about the problem of alcohol consumption and abuse. In short, topics of research must be grounded in some already-known factual information, which is used to introduce the topic and from which the research question will emerge.

Step 3: Review of Existing Literature

Reviewing the existing literature relevant to the topic you want to study is the next step in planning a research project. Social research topics are usually embedded in so many different kinds of literature that the researcher must be careful into selecting the best literature to examine. While many researchers collect every material which has some linkages with the topic, you need to keep the central theme of your topic in mind to guide you through your search of the literature in the field. It is also important to examine different types of literature where relevant inferences are drawn from scientific data interpretations. It would be very useful if research findings from studies using various methods are critically examined.

For preparing a research plan, you should refer to the significant findings you have gathered. This will help you to raise questions or guide you to decide your area and unit of study. You must be able to draw out these findings from the studies and summarize them in such a way that someone unfamiliar with study can easily grasp their meaning and importance. To do this, you should look at the background literature review sections, which generally come at the beginning of published research articles. Most of these reviews are very condensed; they extract a few salient points from numerous studies, summarizing them in a way that is relevant to the study in question.

Step 4: Clarification of Concepts and their Measurement

In a study, a set of concepts is used to explain the phenomenon. These concepts need clarifications with reference to the particular topic. Through the clarifications and discussion of the concepts, a research model is developed at this stage. Precision in conceptualization is critical in the social sciences, and it is not easy to achieve. Concepts like alcoholism, autonomy and juvenile delinquency may all seem to be familiar terms. However, the precise meanings you attach to these concepts must be defined and clarified, and then an appropriate way to measure concepts must be found or devised.

In the research plan, a clear definition of the main concept(s) is most essential. It is also essential to discuss the process of measurement of the concepts. Besides, you should also touch upon the potential problems in measuring the concepts. These include two critical issues: *validity*, that is, whether the measurement of a concept in fact produces a result that truly represents what the concept is supposed to mean; and *reliability*, that is, whether the measurement would lead to same results, whenever it is repeated, that one could have some confidence in the results.

Step 5: Identification of Objectives of the Study

Once the problem, the theoretical background, the clarification of concepts, and the major methods of data collection have been explained, it is time to address the aim and objectives of the study.

At this stage, you are required to present the aim and objectives of the study in brief to justify your study in terms of both its rationale and the implications that it might raise. But, in a proposal, the study design must be presented before the rationale. Here, it is important to note that rationale for doing the project will be accomplished only if the study is done well. Preparing a plan of your study will show that you have devised a plan to study your problem that seems feasible; you reinforce the sense that the aim and objectives of the study will be achieved. The value of the study lies not only in what it alone will produce, but also in how it may add to or challenge other research in the area.

Step 6: Formulation of Hypotheses

A common strategy in scientific study is to move from a general theory to a specific researchable problem. A part of this exercise is to develop hypotheses, which are testable statements of presumed relationships between two or more concepts. Hypotheses state what we expect to find rather than what has already been determined to exist. For example, we might hypothesize that the acceptance of the use of alcohol among adolescents' peers will lead to increased likelihood that the adolescents will consume alcohol.

Step 7: Operationalization of Concepts and Development of Research Instruments

Once you are settled with the concepts for your study, you need to operationalize the concepts so that you can develop your measuring instruments such as questionnaire. In a survey, the questionnaire is nothing but concepts in operational form. In an experiment, the operationalization of the independent variable (concept) is the actual stimulus. In field studies, this process of operationalization occurs in a very different manner. It is often carried out after the field notes have been collected. After that the researcher may find evidence that suggests certain meanings, at which time the process of conceptualizations is carried out. To test whether you are correct, you may go back to the field to see if another instance of this operationalized concept occurs.

It is always advisable to use more than one indicator for better measurement of the concept. This will strengthen your study.

Step 8: Selection of Method of Data Collection

There are three primary means of data collection, namely, observation, interview and questionnaire. You will learn about these methods in subsequent units of this book. In these units the methods are explained in details so that you can use them to design and carry out a study based on questionnaires or interviews, and in field studies using different types of observation techniques. It also describes different forms of what might be called data collection procedures for using secondary data.

While preparing the research plan, you must describe how you will collect primary data. In case you are planning to use secondary data, you must mention which sources of available data you will actually use. You may also very briefly discuss about issues of access to the data. It is important for a researcher to see that he/she must be able to get the data he/she proposes. If you anticipate problems in securing the proposed data, these should be discussed and possible alternative sources of data might be suggested. Most researchers propose to use one source of data, yet you may propose few more sources through which you may also collect data from other sources to widen their scope.

Step 9: Selection of Sample

The selection of sample whom you will study depends on many factors and it is not possible to take into account all. However, there are some factors, which affect the selection of the sample to a great extent. We will discuss a few of them. The homogeneity or heterogeneity of the universe is one such factor, which affects the sample selection procedure to a great extent. For example, if you are interested in studying medical students, which is a very homogeneous group, even a very small sample will be representative of the universe whereas if you plan to study a college having arts, science and commerce faculties, you may have to chose a very large sample and even then you may not have confidence to say that your sample is representative.

You may be interested in generalizing your findings to others beyond those studied. When probability samples are used, it is possible to determine how representative your sample is of the population who might have got into your study. Sampling plans may be very simple or complex. When the rules of probability are not followed and you merely select a sample of subjects who seem to fulfil the needs of your study, you have a non-probability sample. For many studies, such a sample is sufficient; and for some, it is the best that can be achieved. Whatever the design of your sample, it needs to be explained in detail in your research plan. It should be so precise that someone else could generate a similar sample by following your procedures. Remember that even if you select a representative sample, you have to be very careful in making generalizations.

Step 10: Collection of Data

There are different methods of data collection. Each method of data collection has its special concerns, which need to be considered fully before doing the study. This is why, pretesting is so valuable, because it helps you to find and address potential problems before they enter your study and cause bigger problems.

The plans for collecting data should be described carefully. In a field study, it is always more difficult to be precise, and you may need to make changes once you enter the field. Nevertheless, it is better to have a clear plan that can be changed as you move forward. For an experiment, data collection procedures can usually be described very precisely. This is also true of a survey. Surveys using mailed questionnaire tend to have multiple stages in the data collection procedure to increase the response rate. If you are using secondary data, you need to describe at this stage how you will collect the data.

Step 11: Processing of Data

Once the data are collected, they must be processed. If the responses are in qualitative terms, you have to prepare a code book where you have to give numbers for the qualitative responses. This is very much essential if you wish to process your data through computer. If they are field notes, they must be organized and categorized in a proper manner.

In the research plan, a concise statement may be included to address this subject. It may describe what type of computer facility is available, what possible sources of assistance are available, and what efforts are being made to increase accuracy in the handling of the data. There are now some technological advances in data gathering which speed the process from data gathering to data entry. An example is the SPSS (Statistical Package for Social Sciences) now becoming quite common in social research.

Step 12: Analysis of Data

We need to plan how we will analyze the data. It is advisable to prepare a plan of analysis of data spelling out the various applications of statistical tests carefully while the study is being designed. It is better to have a planned strategy that can be adapted than to end up with piles of data for which you have no organized plan.

You are also required to explain how you are planning to compare or contrast different variables, for example, men with women, one rehabilitation programme with another, length of time spent in an organization by the attitude of employees towards the new incentive introduced recently, and the like.

In addition, you need to consider which statistical tests you plan to apply to evaluate the association/differences between the variables. For example, if you propose to measure correlation between the variables to test whether there are significant correlations between them, you have to select an appropriate test that could get the result you need.

Step 13: Presenting the Results

At the end of the study, you have to present the results of the study in the form of a report. While preparing a research report, you have to follow a number of writing conventions. These conventions are commonly known as research formats.

The steps discussed above are presented in a flow chart form on the next page to help the learners to comprehend the complete research process quickly.

The steps in a research process as shown above should not lead to the impression that the process is linear in nature. In fact,

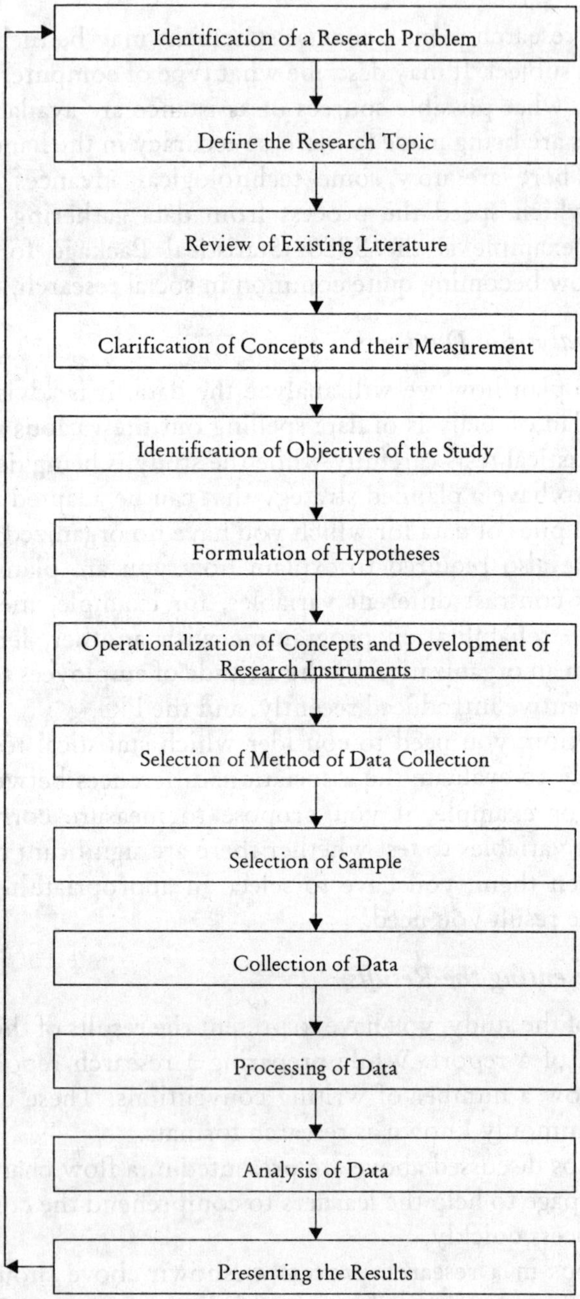
Identification of a Research Problem
Define the Research Topic
Review of Existing Literature
Clarification of Concepts and their Measurement
Identification of Objectives of the Study
Formulation of Hypotheses
Operationalization of Concepts and Development of Research Instruments
Selection of Method of Data Collection
Selection of Sample
Collection of Data
Processing of Data
Analysis of Data
Presenting the Results

the research process is not complete at the stage 13. There are two possibilities: The first may be that the data did not support or partially support the hypothesis. In this situation the researcher must return to the step 1. He/she, then, may decide to reformulate the problem and hypothesis and then test it exactly as before. In the second possibility, that is, even if the research is successful and the findings of step 13 confirm the hypothesis formulated at step 6, it is advisable to repeat the study preferably with a different sample as to reconfirm the findings. This will also support the contention that the hypothesis cannot be rejected. The exact repetition of a study is called *replication*.

Another characteristic feature of the research process is *self-correction*. In a situation, when the data did not support or only partially support the hypothesis and the researcher has sufficient reasons to decide that the hypothesis is adequate, then, he may decide that the failure to confirm the hypothesis is due to error in selecting a sample or in measurement of the key variables/concepts or in analysis of data. In these circumstances, the researcher may decide to repeat the study beginning with the faulty step after rectifying the faults. Finally, the steps of the research process make the study potentially replicable. The researcher designs his/her study in such a way that either the researcher or anybody other than him/her can replicate it. The replication of study substantiates the fact further that the findings are not due to mere coincidence.

Organization of the Book

This book is about designs of social research—the third stage of the research process. A research design is the strategy that guides the researcher throughout the process of research. With this view in mind, this book is organized in two parts. Part I has five chapters. Chapter 1 discusses about the scientific approach, the research process, scientific method and nature of social research. Chapter 2 covers the basic elements of social research, namely, concepts, constructs, fact, theory and hypothesis. Chapter 3 deals with the concept of measurement, and various levels of measurement. Chapters 4 covers common techniques of data analysis like univariate and bivariate analysis, which are used in most of the social research designs. Chapter 5 discusses some advanced techniques of data analysis, namely, trivariate or multivariate analysis, which is an essential component of experimental research designs.

Part II of this book is devoted to the various designs of social research. Chapter 6 discusses about three dimensions of social research, namely, research designs by purpose of a study, research designs by its intended use and research designs indicating the effects of time. Chapter 7 covers the logic of causal inference and various experimental research designs. Chapter 8 deals with pre- and quasi-experimental research designs. Chapter 9 is devoted to intervention research designs. Chapters 10, 11, and 12 discuss various social research designs like action research designs, evaluation research designs and survey research designs. Chapter 13 discusses the qualitative research designs. The last chapter deals with the evaluation of research project.

Important Terms for Review

- Predictability
- Objectivity
- Universality
- Verifiability
- Replication
- Science
- Research
- Social Phenomena
- Scientific Research
- Scientific Method
- Research Process
- Nature of Social Research
- Presumptions of Social Research

Further Readings

Bailey, Kenneth D., *Methods of Social Research*, London: The Free Press, 1978.

Baker, L. Therese, *Doing Social Research*, New York: McGraw Hill, 1988.

Black, James A. and Champion, Dean J., *Methods and Issues in Social Research*, New York: John Wiley, 1976.

Broadbeck, May (ed.), *Readings in the Philosophy of Science*, New York: The MacMillan, 1968.

Galtung, John, *Theory and Methods of Social Research*, London: George Allen and Unwin, 1970.

—, "Theory and Methods of Social Research: A Plea for Pluralism" in Yen, Else (ed.), *Comparative Methodology Theory and Practice in International Research*, London, 1978.

Goode, W.J. and Hatt, P.K., *Methods of Social Research*, New York: McGraw Hill, 1952.

Kerlinger, Fred R., *Foundations of Behavioural Research*, Delhi: Surjeet Publications, 1964.

Kidder, Louise H., *Research Methods in Social Relations*, New York: Holt, 1981.

Kothari, L.R., *Research Methodology*, New Delhi: Vishwa Prakashan, 1985.

Lal Das, D.K., *Practice of Social Research: Social Work Perspective*, Jaipur: Rawat Publications, 2000.

Lundberg, G.A., *Social Research*, New York: Longman, 1946.

Mohsin, S.M., *Research Methods in Behavioural Sciences*, Orient and Longman Limited, Calcutta, 1984.

Monette, Duane R. et. al., *Applied Social Research: Tool for the Human Services*, Chicago: Holt, 1986.

Nachmias, D. and Nachmias, C., *Research Methods in the Social Sciences*, New York: St. Martins Press, 1981.

Patton, M.Q., Qualitative Evaluation and Research Methods (2nd edn.) Sage: New Delhi, 1980.

Punch, K.F., *Introduction to Social Research*, New Delhi: Sage, 1998.

Thomas, P.T., "Social Research" in *Encyclopaedia of Social Work India*, New Delhi: Government of India, 1977.

Wilkinson, T.S. and Bhandarkar, P.L., *Methodology and Techniques of Social Research*, Bombay: Himalaya Publishing, 1977.

Review Questions

1. What is a scientific approach?
2. What are the characteristic features of scientific approach?
3. What is quantitative approach in social research?
4. What is qualitative approach in social research?
5. How we can establish the validity and reliability of qualitative data?

6. What kinds of research topics are appropriate for qualitative approach of social research methodology?
7. What is a scientific research?
8. Discuss the possibilities and limitations of use of scientific method in social research.
9. Discuss in brief the process of social research.
10. What is the nature of social research?
11. Discuss the basic presumptions of social research.
12. Differentiate between the terms 'concept' and 'construct'.
13. Why it is necessary to plan a research project?
14. List out at least three advantages of a research plan.
15. Differentiate between processing and analysis of data.

2

Basic Elements of Social Research

Social scientists conduct research on two distinct but interrelated levels: conceptual-theoretical and observational-empirical. More precisely, social researches involve a constant interplay of two processes: theory construction and theory testing. For example, it is a fact that in the last 100 years social mobility has increased. This fact is not merely based on random observation, but is an empirically verified statement about phenomena. This involves both a scientific observation and a predetermined conceptual-theoretical framework by which the observation is guided. In this chapter, the conceptual theoretical level of social research has been explained with the help of the basic elements, such as concepts, constructs, variables, relations/associations hypothesis, facts and theory.

Concepts and Constructs

There are innumerable phenomena in nature, but the systematic character of scientific study limits the area of research to a few phenomena. In fact, it is impossible, if not absurd, to study the whole phenomenon. Thus, instead of studying whole phenomenon, science deals with only certain aspects of phenomenon dealing with the realities which we experience in our day-to-day lives, such as 'mass', 'weight', 'power', etc. The process of separating any phenomenon from all that is connected with it is an act of abstraction (Goode and Hatt, 1952: 41).

A concept is an abstraction representing objects, such as 'water', 'glass', 'gold' etc. Concept may be a property of an object, or a phenomenon. For example, 'mass', 'weight' and 'density' are properties of objects. These concepts are frequently used by physical scientists. Concepts such as 'village', 'rural', 'urban', 'family' and 'house' are common among social scientists.

Concepts are terms or words which we can point to an object, the term or word represents. For example, when we say 'house', we can point to an object, the word represents. We can also measure the area on which it exists, the height, width and thickness of walls and such other dimensions of the house. There are many similar terms such as 'tree', 'temple', 'book', 'chalk', and so on for which we can point out numerous objects and measure their dimensions.

Every scientific description has developed its unique set of concepts for communicating its research findings. The importance of concepts in scientific investigation may be gauged from the fact that the conceptual-theoretical system of science is very often referred to as a conceptual system.

Concepts are used to stand for the phenomena or aspects of phenomena under study. It should be kept in mind that we use concepts as symbols of the phenomena we are studying and it is really these phenomena which we interrelate to one another. Researchers, many a time, confuse the concept with the phenomenon it is supposed to symbolize and treat concept as though they are the phenomenon themselves. This confusion leads to the fallacy of reification—to the error of treating abstraction as actual phenomenon.

A construct is a deliberately adopted concept having an added meaning for a specific purpose. Let us take an example—'achievement' as a concept. It is an abstraction formed from the observation of certain characteristics of achievers and non-achievers. Achievement, as a construct, is defined in such a way that it serves two distinct purposes. One, a construct can be related to other constructs in various ways which will serve as the theoretical framework of the research. For example, we can say that achievement is in part a function of motivation. Two, achievement as a construct is so consciously and deliberately defined and specified that it can be observed and measured.

A construct of more interest to social researchers is 'social status'. It is an abstraction formed from the observation of certain traits of individuals. These traits are associated with the position of individuals in the society, which are ascertained by certain indicators such as level of education, social group, and recognition by the society, etc. The assessment of various indicators put together and expressed in a word 'social status'.

Some other examples of constructs are 'race', 'religion', 'intelligence', etc. Constructs do not have objects to point out. These terms are abstraction from the observation. Hence, we first define these terms, and then we respond to the definitions instead of observable characteristics.

The first set of terms—the terms which have direct empirical referents—are referred to as concepts, whereas the second set of terms have no direct empirical referents and are referred to as constructs. Though the terms 'concept' and 'construct' have almost similar meanings, yet there is a significant difference.

Fact and Theory

In the context of social research fact simply means some phenomenon that has been observed. Scientific research aims at systematic description of observed facts and of their relations. It also aims at understanding the nature and interpreting the observed facts and relations. This involves the reduction of observed facts and their relations into a limited number of general statements that account for the observed facts and their relations. These general statements embody a theory (Mohsin, 1984: 4).

There is little agreement among social scientists on what theory is. For example, according to Goode and Hatt (1952), a theory refers to the relationship between facts or the ordering of them in some meaningful ways, whereas to Kerlinger (1973), a theory is a set of interrelated constructs (concepts), definitions and propositions that present a systematic view of phenomena by specifying relations among variables, with the purpose of explaining and predicting the phenomena.

There are many more explanations of what a theory is. Despite the disagreement, there are certain common points in almost all the explanations. Keeping this in view we can understand a theory as a systematic explanation for the observed facts and their interrelations.

Variable

A variable is an empirical property that takes two or more values. In other words, if a property can change in value or kind, it can be regarded as variable (Nachmias and Nachmias, 1998: 1). For example, gender is a variable because it can be assigned two values: male or female. Similarly, marital status is a variable because it can take on the values of unmarried, married, divorced or widowed. When a variable has only two values, it is termed as dichotomous variable.

Dependent and Independent Variables

In most of the cases researchers focus on cause-effect relationships and start with an effect, then search for its causes. The variable which represents the cause, is termed as independent variable. The variable that is the effect or is the result or outcome of another variable is the dependent variable. In other words, the variable expected to explain change in the dependent variable is referred to as the independent variable. The independent variable is also known as explanatory variable. Independent variable is considered as the presumed cause of changes in the values of dependent variable. Process-wise, the dependent variable is the expected outcome of the independent variable. Independent variable and dependent variable are also termed as predictor and criterion variables respectively.

Control Variables

The variable, which is used to examine the possibility that an empirically observed association between an independent variable and dependent variable is spurious, is known as control variable. An association that can be explained by control variables is termed as spurious association.

Continuous and Discrete Variables

A variable is called continuous if does not have a minimal size. In other words, we can say that the values of continuous variables are arbitrarily fixed. For example, time is a continuous variable, since one may decide to measure it in days, hours, minutes, seconds, one-millionth of a second, and so on. Similarly, the length of an object may be 8.50 centimetre long, or it may be 85 millimetre long.

Unlike continuous variables, the value of discrete variables is a fixed quantity. For example, the number of children per family is a discrete variable because it may be 3 or 4, but not 3.24 or 4.67.

Relation/Association

The term 'relation/association' in social research signifies the relations/associations between two or more variables. When we say that variable X and variable Y are related/associated, we mean that they vary together. In other words, when we say that the variables are related/associated, we mean that there are something common to both variables. For example, if we say that salary and job satisfaction are related/associated, we mean that the two variables vary together; for example, employee with higher salary will have higher level of job satisfaction.

Rosenberg (1968) made an important distinction between two kinds of relationship. The one is a stimulus-response relationship, characterized by an independent variable, which is external, specific and well-defined, with a dependent variable being a particular response to it. For example, relationship between reward and satisfaction or between advertisement and consumption patterns is of the stimulus-response type. The second type is between property (usually some background characteristics) and dispositions, such as attitudes, values and orientations. Examples are the relations between social class and political tolerance or between race and prejudice.

Hypothesis

Once we have formulated the problem for research, we proceed to formulate tentative solutions or answers to it. These proposed answers or solutions constitute the hypothesis, which we need to test on the basis of facts, which are to be collected in the course of our fieldwork. Thus, the term 'hypothesis' can be defined as a proposition or tentative solutions or answers or generalizations, which are yet to be tested.

Sometimes, a hypothesis it may be implicit, for, in absence of it we cannot effectively go ahead with the investigation. We would not know what facts to look for and what relations or order to search for among them. Thus, hypotheses guide the researcher through bewildering jungle of facts to see and select only those that are relevant to the problems.

Collection of facts merely for the sake of collecting them will yield no fruits. To achieve fruitful results, one should collect such facts as are debatable. The only difference between gathering data without a hypothesis and gathering them with one is that, in the latter case, we deliberately recognize our limitations and reduce fallibility. Moreover, we have greater concentration of attention on particular aspects. A hypothesis helps us to see the kind of data that must be collected in order to answer the research question, and the way in which they should be organized most efficiently.

Sources of Hypothesis

Available literature is considered as the major source of hypothesis. While reviewing the literature, a researcher comes across various theories and assumptions. These theories and assumptions form the bases of several hypotheses. Personal experiences, the socialization process and learning experiences are some other sources of hypothesis. On the basis of personal experiences, a researcher may be able to generate hypothesis. Many a time views peculiar to persons and causal observations help a researcher to formulate hypotheses.

Findings of other study are often a source of valuable hypotheses. A researcher on the basis of the findings of other studies may hypothesize that the similar causal relationship between a set of variables will hold good in his present study too.

Theories are, in fact, a seedbed of hypotheses. Many hypotheses stem from a body of theory, which the outcome of logical deductions of theories. Theories represent what are known. A logical deduction from these theories constitutes which must be true if the theories are true.

Characteristics of Usable Hypothesis

The chief characteristic of a usable hypothesis is that it must be empirically testable. This means when a researcher formulates his hypothesis, he must be aware of the instruments available to measure the variables included in the hypothesis. This is also because of the fact that unless a researcher is aware of the available tools for measurement, he will not be able to test his hypothesis empirically. Conversely, hypotheses must not be moral judgments because it would be impracticable to measure the variables in the hypotheses. Finally, the hypotheses are required to be conceptually clear and as far as possible specific.

Research Hypothesis

The hypothesis derived from theories is termed as *research hypothesis* or working hypothesis. The researcher, who wishes to study a social phenomenon, looks for various theories about the social phenomenon, because theories explain the nature of things or events. Thus, these explanations are regarded as suppositions or tentative statements about reality until they are verified to the researcher's satisfaction. These suppositions or statements identified by the researchers for testing are known as research hypothesis and conventionally symbolized as H_1. Examples of research hypotheses are: the females visit cinema oftener than the males or broken homes lead to juvenile delinquency.

Null Hypothesis

For the purpose of testing a research hypothesis, a researcher formulates the corollary of it that is a *null hypothesis*. It is, in one way, the reverse of research hypothesis, which refutes or denies the relationship expressed in research hypothesis. In other words, a null hypothesis states that there is no difference or relationship between variables. Null hypotheses are conventionally symbolized as H_0. Let us consider the research hypothesis discussed above:

H_1 The females visit cinema oftener than the males.

H_2 Broken homes lead to juvenile delinquency.

The null hypotheses for these research hypotheses would be:

H_0 The females and males do not differ in respect of the frequency of visiting cinema.

H_0 There is no relationship between broken homes and juvenile delinquency.

Conventionally, null hypothesis is tested in research because it is ordinarily more exact, and is easy to disprove. Statistical techniques are better adopted to test a null hypothesis.

Steps in Testing Hypothesis

Step 1: State the research hypothesis

H_1 There is a significant difference between under-graduate and post-graduate students with regard to their reading habits.

Step 2: Formulate the null hypothesis

H_o There is no significant difference between under-graduate and post-graduate students with regard to their reading habits.

Step 3: Choose a statistical test

Let us suppose that we have decided to use t-test statistic to test if there is no significant difference between the variables considered in the research hypothesis.

Step 4: Specify a significance level

Further, we suppose that we would like to test our hypothesis at .05 level of significance.

Step 5: Compute the statistical test

In this step, the researcher has to compute t-test (for computation of t-test readers are advised to refer any standard book on statistics). On computation of the test, let us say that the test yielded a value of 6.78, df = 9.

Step 6: Reject/accept the H_o

Since the calculated value of t-test is more than the critical value we reject the null hypothesis (for rules of acceptance/rejection of null hypothesis readers are advised to refer any standard book on statistics).

Step 7: Draw the inference, i.e., accept/reject H_1

We accept the research hypothesis because the null hypothesis has been rejected. Hence, we can infer that there is a significant difference between undergraduate and post-graduate students with regard to their reading habits.

Type I and Type II Errors

Unlike physical sciences, in social sciences, we do not find propositions that indicate certainty. In real world, almost all the propositions, generally, indicate some sort of probabilities. Thus, instead of stating that if A is true, B must follow, we say only if A is true, B will probably also be true.

We thus admit the possibility that B may be false even if A is true. Thus, if we reject A whenever B is false, we also run the risk of making error that of rejecting a true research hypothesis (H_1). We refer to this kind of error as type I or α error.

Otherwise, if we fail to reject (accept) A when B is true, we again run the risk of making an error, since A may actually be false. Accepting a false research hypothesis (H_1) is referred to as type II or β error.

Examples

1. Most members will conform to societal norm (A).
2. It is a norm of society not to steal.
3. B is a member of society.

Inferences

I. B will probably not steal. Therefore, if A is true B will probably also be true. But if B does steal, we reject A with some risk of type I error (since A may be true, B being one of the few dishonest members).

II. If we fail to reject A when B is true, we run a risk of making an error since A may actually be false, i.e., failing to reject a false H_1, is referred to as a type II or β error.

In social research inferences drawn from the sample are applied to the population from which the sample is drawn. The following statements help us to understand type I and type II errors with reference to the sample and population:

Type I error: Populations differ when in fact they are alike.

Type II error: Two populations are alike when in fact they differ.

Type I and II errors are shown diagrammatically as below:

	Population Realities: Difference	Population Realities: No Difference
Research Conclusions (drawn on the basis of sample) Reject H_O (there is difference) →	CORRECT DECISION	TYPE I ERROR
Accept H_O (there is difference) →	TYPE II ERROR	CORRECT DECISION

When we test hypothesis, we do not study the entire population; instead, we study a part of it. As such, we can never prove if the null hypothesis is true or false. What we try to prove is whether the sample results are sufficiently likely or unlikely to justify the decision to accept or to reject the null hypothesis.

The null hypothesis can be either true or false. A researcher has a choice of either rejecting or accepting the hypothesis. Hence, there are four possibilities as presented below:

Case 1. The null hypothesis is true and it is rejected.

Case 2. The null hypothesis is true and it is accepted.

Case 3. The null hypothesis is false and it is rejected.

Case 4. The null hypothesis is false and it is accepted.

In the first case, a null hypothesis is rejected when it is true. This decision is an error. This error—the rejection of true hypothesis—is termed as a type I error. In the second case, there is no error because the researcher accepts a hypothesis, which is true. The same is with the third case, there is no error in decision because a hypothesis is false and it is rejected. But, the decision in the fourth case is an error, that is, a false hypothesis is accepted. Accepting false hypothesis is known as a type II error.

Important Terms for Review

- Concept
- Construct
- Fact
- Theory
- Variable
- Conceptual System
- Reification
- Fallacy of Reification
- Referent
- Empirical Referent
- Hypothesis
- Research Hypothesis
- Null Hypothesis
- Significance Level
- Type I & Type II Errors

Further Readings

Bailey, Kenneth D., *Methods of Social Research*, London: The Free Press, 1978.

Baker, L. Therese, *Doing Social Research,* New York: McGraw Hill, 1988.

Black, James A. and Champion, Dean J., *Methods and Issues in Social Research,* New York: John Wiley, 1976.

Galtung, John, *Theory and Methods of Social Research,* London: George Allen and Unwin, 1970.

Goode, W.J. and Hatt, P.K., *Methods of Social Research,* New York: McGraw Hill, 1952.

Kerlinger, Fred R., *Foundations of Behavioral Research,* Delhi: Surjeet Publications, 1964.

Kidder, Louise H., *Research Methods in Social Relations,* New York: Holt, 1981.

Kothari, L.R., *Research Methodology,* New Delhi: Vishwa Prakashan, 1985.

Lal Das, D.K., *Practice of Social Research: Social Work Perspective*, Jaipur: Rawat Publications. 2000.

Mohsin, S.M., *Research Methods in Behavioural Sciences*, Orient and Longman Limited, Calcutta, 1984.

Monette, Duane R. et. al., *Applied Social Research: Tool for the Human Services*, Chicago: Holt, 1986.

Nachmias, D. and Nachmias, C., *Research Methods in the Social Sciences*, New York: St. Martins Press, 1981.

Rosenberg, Morris, *The Logic of Survey Analysis*, New York: Basic Books, 1968.

Wilkinson, T.S. and Bhandarkar, P.L., *Methodology and Techniques of Social Research*, Bombay: Himalayan, 1977.

Review Questions

1. What is a 'concept'? Differentiate 'concept' from 'construct'.
2. What is a hypothesis? Identify some hypotheses from your own experience.
3. What are the various sources of hypothesis? Discuss the utility of a null hypothesis in the process of testing hypothesis.
4. What is a theory?
5. What is the relationship between theory and research?
6. What is the relationship between theory and hypothesis?
7. What are some criteria that must be met before a hypothesis can be tested?
8. Differentiate between research hypothesis and null hypothesis.
9. What is an alternate hypothesis?
10. Discuss some functions of statistical hypothesis.
11. Differentiate between type I error and type II error in test of hypothesis.

3

Measurement in Social Research

We use many measures in our daily lives. For example, we often measure our weight to see how well our diet is working. We use a thermometer to find out our body temperature. We check fuel metre to be sure to reach our destination. As we drive, we watch the speedometer so that we must not lose our control of the cart. Measurements of weight, temperature, fuel and speed are concerned with the physical world. Such precise, well-developed measures, which use in daily life, are fundamental in the natural sciences.

We also measure the non-physical world in everyday life, but usually in less exact terms. We are measuring when we say that a treatment is excellent, that Rakesh is really smart, that Karan has negative attitude towards life, that Mohan is really prejudiced, or "a lot of violence" are imprecise, vague, or intuitive measures. We also measure when we judge how well we like a particular dress or food or a song or a painting.

We, thus, measure physical objects as well as non-physical objects. By and large, measurement in social research is concerned with concepts, constructs and variables. Consequently, measurement in social research is relatively complex and demanding task, especially so when it concerns constructs.

Concept of Measurement

The concept of measurement refers to the process of describing abstract concepts in terms of specific indicators by assigning numbers to these indicators in accordance with rules. It is easy to assign numbers in respect of properties of objects, but it is really difficult in respect of constructs. For instance, measuring 'achievement', 'motivation', 'social status' or 'marital adjustments' is obviously more difficult than measuring 'income', 'chronological age' or 'level of education' of an individual. In other words, while concepts like 'income', 'chronological age' or 'level of education' can be measured directly, constructs like 'achievement', 'motivation', 'social status' or 'marital adjustments' have to be measured indirectly. Thus, we can expect comparatively higher level of accuracy in measuring concepts than in the case of constructs.

In social research measurement of social phenomena has become an essential prerequisite because of a number of reasons. One of the important reasons for measuring social phenomena is to allow the researcher the opportunity of using these phenomena in hypotheses to determine the effects of a set of variables on others (Black and Champion, 1976: 170).

Let us consider the following hypothesis: "the boys who are lower in their self-esteem will tend to become chronic absentees than the boys with higher self-esteem (a social psychological component of personality)". Testing of this hypothesis needs a formal theoretical scheme where 'self-esteem' would be related systematically to 'absenteeism' in a causal fashion. One part of the testing process would consist of determining rank of absentees of the boys from the school attendance records. We would match those boys with another group of boys randomly, selected from the same school who are regular in attending their classes. To ensure comparable samples of 'absentees' and 'regulars', the groups could be matched according to several other characteristics such as age, sex, year of education, socio-economic background, education and occupation of parents and others.

Other part of testing of hypothesis requires assessment of socio-psychological variable 'self-esteem'. How do we determine that a particular boy who is a chronic 'absentee' or 'regular' has more or less this trait than the others? We cannot test the hypothesis mentioned above, until and unless we can quantify the variable 'self-esteem'. To test the hypothesis, it is essential that the variable 'self-esteem' must be measured empirically. We must be able to say that boys vary according to this variable, and furthermore, we should specify the degree to which each boy possesses this variable. Only then, we would be able to test our hypothesis. Measurement allows the researcher the opportunity of using variables in hypothesis to determine their effects on others.

Monette et al (1986) define measurement as a process of describing abstract concepts in terms of specific indicators by the assignment of numbers or other symbols to this indicator in accordance with rules.

In a very broad sense, measurement determines whether a variable is present or absent. But, in practice, measurement is more complex process, which involves operations to determine the extent to which a variable is present or absent. Let us consider the following examples:

A social researcher, who is working with street children, interviews a child by asking following questions:

1.	Do you save money?	Yes/No
2.	If yes, how much?	Rs.______per day
3.	"Child labour in our country must be banned."	Strongly Agree/Agree/ Undecided/Disagree/ Strongly Disagree

The above three questions attempt to measure some of the aspects of street children. The first question measures one aspect by determining the presence or absence of a characteristic 'saving habit' among street children. The second one tries to measure in a more specific way involving the amount saved which tries to determine the degree of intensity of saving. Finally, a reaction or comment to a statement is in a sequence of responses, which in turn can be converted into scores and would measure the phenomena in question more specifically.

The concepts, constructs and variables—the basic elements of social research—cannot be normally observed directly. While concepts such as income, saving, type of house, nativity etc. can be observed and hence measurement is not very difficult whereas mental retardation, poverty, anxiety, depression, social class and the like cannot be seen but only measured through some indicators. For example, we can see a child who is being abused. But, what about other physical abuses, which might not have been reported by a child. We cannot observe all such abuses. However, we can examine him/her physically or we can gather some information from his/her parents/guardian's behaviour towards him/her. On physical examination we may notice bruises on his/her back or fractured leg. On inquiry we may come to know that he/she is slapped by parents/guardian now and then or he/she is uncared or neglected. All these things are indicators of child abuse—a variable not the actual properties of the variable itself. This example also suggests us that there can be more than one indicator of a variable. The simple indicator or a variable is treated as 'item'. A set of items used to qualify a variable is commonly known as 'scale'. For example, attitude scales consciously involve asking a person a set of questions or items and then aggregating their responses into a single score that represent their attitude on an issue.

Levels of Measurement

Social phenomena can be measured in various ways, such as by asking questions or noting behaviour/observation. Measurement also differs from one and another in terms of levels of measurement. Levels of measurement refer to a set of rules that define permissible mathematical functions that can be performed on numbers/scores produced by a measure. There are four levels of measurement, namely, nominal, ordinal, interval and ratio.

Nominal Level of Measurement

Nominal level of measurement is the lowest and most simple level of measurement. When a variable is classified into several nominal sub-classes, it is said that the variable in question is measured on a nominal level. For example, the variable, sex, has two nominal sub-classes, male and female. Similarly, religions have many sub-classes, if not infinite, among which are included Hindus, Muslims, Christians and Sikhs.

Numbers assigned to nominal sub-classes at this level of measurement represent serial order only. The numbers do not have mathematical values. Hence, no mathematical function is possible with nominal data. For example, let us consider the classification of nominal data as shown below:

1. Hindu
2. Muslim
3. Christian

In this example, suppose, we add 1 and 2, we will get 3. Which would be equivalent of saying that a Hindu plus a Muslim equals a Christian? This is not true. In other words, 1, 2 and 3 here represent first, categories of respondents who are Hindus, second, categories of respondents who are Muslims and third, categories of respondents belonging to Christianity. Another example of nominal level of measurement is getting information about marital status in the following format:

Marital Status:	1. Unmarried	( )
	2. Married	( )
	3. Divorcee	( )
	4. Widow	( )

Ordinal Level of Measurement

When the relative positions of objects or persons with respect to some characteristics are defined, measurements are possible on ordinal levels. The fundamental requirement of an ordinal level of measurement is that one be able to determine the order of positions of objects or persons in terms of characteristics under study. Ordinal level measurements are considered of higher level than nominal level because in addition to being mutually exclusive (feature of nominal level of measurement) the categories have a fixed order. Level of education, for example, constitutes an ordinal variable and measures levels of education on ordinal scales.

The following illustration shows level of education divided into ordinal categories. In ordinal level of measurement, the numbers are used not only to differentiate sub-classes, but also to determine less than or greater than relationship between them. For example, see the responses given to the level of education:

Level of Education:

1. Graduate ( )
2. Intermediate ( )
3. High School ( )
4. Middle School ( )
5. Primary ( )
6. Illiterate ( )

The responses have numbers ranging from 1 to 6 and are designed to identify ordinal differences between levels of education. Each level is assigned a particular number relative to others and it can be determined readily that graduate level of education is higher than intermediate. However, there is no attempt to say that an equal distance will be found between all numbers. We cannot say that the same distance exists between 1 and 2 as exists between 3 and 4.

Interval Level of Measurement

Interval level between the categories of measurement has equal spacing in addition to the characteristics of nominal level (mutually exclusive) and ordinal level (having fixed order). In interval measures the positions are not only ordered either in ascending order (lower, middle and higher) or in descending order (higher, middle and lower) but the intervals of measurement are also equal. In other words, the distance between the positions is equal, such as the degrees of a temperature scales. The examples of true interval scales are Fahrenheit and Celsius temperature scales. The units of measurement of both the scales are degree and are based on equal spacing characteristics of interval level of measurement.

In an interval scale an equal distance between units will be found. That means 2 are same distance from 3 as 6 are from 5 and so on. For example, in thermometer having Celsius as unit of measurement, 60 degrees is 10 degrees more than 50 degrees. However, we cannot compare the ratios of two temperatures. It would be erroneous to infer that 100 degree is twice as hot as 50 degrees. This is because interval scale does not have an absolute zero.

In social science research, we have very few variables, which can be measured at interval level. One such measure that is relevant to social sciences is measurement of intelligence by Intelligent Quotient (IQ) tests. Units of measurement on IQ test are specific and each point on the scale is mutually exclusive. In addition, the distances between IQ scores of 90 and 100 and 100 and 110 are equal. However, since the zero point on the interval scale is arbitrary, we cannot say that a person with an IQ of 130 is twice as intelligent as a person with on IQ of 65.

Ratio Level of Measurement

Income can be measured at ratio level of measurement because it has an absolute zero (no income, at least in money terms, not in term of economic status). Hence, a person with monthly income of Rs. 15,000 has thrice as much as a person earning Rs. 5,000. Most of the function can be performed on data measured on interval scales.

Ratio level of measurement is the highest level of measurement. This has all the characteristics of interval level of measurement except that the zero point is absolute in this case rather than arbitrary as in interval level of measurement. This means the ratio level of measurement contains the characteristics of nominal level of measurement (mutually exclusive), ordinal level of measurement (fixed order) and interval level of measurement (equal spacing, in addition to an absolute zero).

In social science research we rarely come across a situation where ratio level of measurement is warranted mostly because it is really difficult to arrive at absolute zero while measuring a social phenomenon. However, to understand the ratio level of measurement, we will consider the measurement of income with which social researchers are likely to deal with. Though there is considerable controversy on whether no income at all can be considered as absolute zero points of the scale, and whether there is equal spacing between the units, we will consider the measurement of income on this scale for the sake of better understanding.

Since the ratio level of measurement facilitates the equality of ratio, we can make statements like an income of Rs. 30,000 is thrice as much as Rs. 10,000 but only one-third as much as Rs. 90,000. However, one has to keep in mind that income, as ratio measure, is only an indicator of the amount of money available to a person not as the measure of person's socio-economic status. For example, a difference between Rs. 1,00,000 and Rs. 1,10,000 does not necessarily indicate a change in socio-economic status equivalent to that between Rs. 20,000 and Rs. 30,000. It should be finally noted that the variables capable of being measured at high levels are always better than the variables capable of being measured at lower levels.

Thus, while measurement at nominal level is considered as least precise, ratio level of measurement is considered as the most precise level of measurement. As far as possible, the researcher should use the scale that provides the most precise description. Of course, the nature of variables under study is a deciding factor for level of measurement. The levels of measurement, their characteristics, degree of precision and applicability of statistical procedures are summarized below:

Levels of Measurement	*Characteristics*	*Degree of Precision*	*Application of Statistical Procedures*
Nominal	Mutually Exclusive	Very Low	Percentages, Ratios, Proportions
Ordinal	Mutually Exclusive + Order	Low	Median, Quartiles, Deciles, Quartile Deviation, Rank Order Correlation, Gamma
Interval	Mutually Exclusive + Order + Equal Distance	High	Mean, Median, Standard Deviation, Difference of Means, F-tests, Correlations, Regression
Ratio	Mutually Exclusive + Order + Equal Distance + Absolute Zero	Very High	Mean, Median, Standard Deviation, Difference of Means, F-tests, Correlations, Regression

Indicating Level of Measurement

While indicating levels of measurement one important consideration is the selection of variables in accordance with the objectives of the study. Accordingly, the levels of measurement should be selected keeping in mind the availability of tools of data collection. This is very important from the data analysis point of view. Almost all the statistical procedures have been designed in accordance with the levels of measurement of the variables (see Appendix A and Appendix B). As such, the selection of the statistical procedures completely depends upon the levels of measurement of the variables.

Sources of Error

As far as possible, the measurement should be precise and unambiguous. However, this objective is not achieved in total particularly in social sciences. As such, the researcher must be aware of the sources of error in measurement. For example, there are a number of factors, which contribute to errors in measurement of social phenomena. These factors greatly affect the measurement process. The errors come because an individual's behaviour cannot be measured in isolation. Moreover, the behaviour of an individual is reflection of many other factors. Thus, the measurements are bound to differ when we try to measure it in isolation. Errors are also due to situations because varied situations affect the social phenomena in different ways.

Another source of errors may be the instrument itself. For instance, it is possible that the instrument is not uniform. That is, the concepts or constructs may be differently understood by the subjects may be because of ambiguous definition or conceptualization/operationalization.

Errors may come due to coding and tabulation of data and computation of statistics etc. Measurement results are likely to be effected by the application of inappropriate method of data analysis. It may also be due to the use of incorrect statistical procedures.

Problems in Measurement

Some of the important criteria for assessing the acceptability of measures are: (1) reliability, (2) sensitivity, (3) dimensionality, and (4) validity.

Reliability

It refers to the degree to which measures produce the same result over time. Measurement reliability has been defined as 'constant results' when repeated under conditions taken to be constant (Kaplan, 1964).

Sensitivity

It refers to the degree to which measures detect actual difference. When we use a research instrument (scale) we expect that it would consistently separate those who are 'high' on the attitude continuum from those who are 'low'. With item analysis, each item is subjected to a measurement of its sensitivity to separate the 'highs' from the 'lows'.

Dimensionality

Measurement helps the researcher to discriminate respondents on a continuum of values. Dimensionality is a property of a scale which refers to the degree to which measures lie along a single underlying continuum.

Validity

It refers to the degree to which measures reflect the attributes they are supposed to measure. In other words, a measure is said to be valid if it measures accurately the concept that it is intended to measure. There are three types of validity: (i) content validity, (ii) criterion related validity, and (iii) construct validity.

Content validity

It indicates the extent to which a measuring instrument covers the topic under study. If the measuring instrument contains a representative sample of the universe of the content, we say that the instrument has content validity. It is determined by the judgement of the expert. It can also be determined by using a panel of judges.

Criterion-related validity

This measurement of validity is concerned with the ability of an instrument to predict the outcome or estimate the existence of some current condition.

Construct validity

An instrument is said to have construct validity if it confirms to predicted correlation with other available instrument, which is supposed to measure similar construct.

Important Terms for Review

- Abstraction
- Concepts
- Constructs
- Variables
- Concept of Measurement
- Levels of Measurement
- Nominal Level of Measurement
- Ordinal Level of Measurement
- Interval Level of Measurement
- Ratio Level of Measurement
- Reliability
- Sensitivity
- Dimensionality
- Validity
- Sources of Error
- Problems in Measurement

Further Readings

Bailey, Kenneth D., *Methods of Social Research*, London: The Free Press, 1978.

Baker, L. Therese, *Doing Social Research,* New York: McGraw Hill, 1988.

Black, James A. and Champion, Dean J., *Methods and Issues in Social Research,* New York: John Wiley, 1976.

Festinger, L. and Katz. D. (eds.), *Research Methods in the Behavioral Sciences*, New York: The Dryden Press, 1953.

Goode, W.J. and Hat, P.K., *Methods in Social Research,* New York: McGraw Hill, 1952

Kerlinger, Fred R., *Foundations of Behavioral Research,* Delhi: Surjeet Publications, 1964.

Kidder, Louise H., *Research Methods in Social Relations,* New York: Holt, 1981.

Kothari, L.R., *Research Methodology*, New Delhi: Vishwa Prakashan, 1985.

Lal Das, D.K., *Practice of Social Research: Social Work Perspective*, Jaipur: Rawat Publications, 2000.

Miller, D.C., *Handbook of Research Design and Social Measurement,* New York: David McKey Co., 1964.

Mohsin, S.M., Research Methods in Behavioural Sciences, Calcutta: Orient Longman Limited, 1984.

Monette, Duane R. et. al., *Applied Social Research: Tool for the Human Services,* Chicago: Holt, 1986.

Moser, C.A. and Kalton, G., *Survey Methods in Social Investigation,* London: Heinemann Educational Books Harper and Brothers, 1950.

Nachmias, D. and Nachmias, C., *Research Methods in the Social Sciences*, New York: St. Martins press, 1981.

Rubin, Allen and Babbie, E., *Research Methods for Social Work*, Belmont, California, Wadsworth, 1989.

Sellitz, G. et. al., *Research Methods in Social Relations,* New York: Holt. Rinehart and Winston (3rd edition), 1973.

Wilkinson, T.S. and Bhandarkar, P.L., *Methodology and Techniques of Social Research*, Bombay: Himalayan, 1977.

Young, P.V. *Scientific Social Surveys and Research,* Englewood Cliff, N.J. Prentice Hall (4th edition), 1953.

Review Questions

1. What is measurement? Discuss the importance of measurement in social research.
2. What are the various levels of measurement? Elaborate your answer with suitable examples from social research.
3. Differentiate between nominal, ordinal, internal and ratio levels of measurement. Give examples of each levels of measurement.
4. "Some social variables cannot be directly measured and therefore they are not legitimately within the scientific domain." Comment on the statement with examples.
5. What are the problems of measurement of social phenomena?
6. What are some major considerations in deciding the level of measurement of a variable?

4

Analysis of Social Data

In the previous chapter we have discussed measurement in social research. Once data are collected with the help of a questionnaire, the researcher turns his/her focus of attention on its analysis. In this chapter, we will discuss about one of the most important stages of the research process, i.e., data analysis.

A researcher has to make his/her plan for each and every stage of the research process. As such, a good researcher makes a perfect plan of analysis of data. To make the plan of analysis of data, the researcher has to take into consideration the research design (discussed in chapters 6 to 12) of his/her study. It is the design of research which helps the researcher to develop the framework of his/her plan of data analysis.

To some researchers data analysis is not a very serious activity. They feel many a time that data analysis is a job of computer assistants. As a consequence, they have to be contended with the results given by computer assistants which may not help them to achieve their objectives. To avoid such situations, it is essential that data analysis must be planned in advance and instructed to computer assistants accordingly. In this chapter, we will discuss this aspect of social research.

Data Processing

Data processing refers to certain operations such as editing, coding, computing of the scores, preparation of master charts, etc. After collection of filled-in questionnaires, editing of entries therein is not only necessary but also useful in making subsequent steps simpler. Many a time, a researcher or the assistants either miss entries in the questionnaires or enter responses, which are not legible. This sort of discrepancies can be resolved by editing the schedule meticulously. Another problem comes up at the time of tabulation of data when the researcher asks for tabulation of responses from consecutive questions. In cases where data are not *cleaned,* there has to be inconsistency in the tabulations. In the process of editing, the researcher has to be very careful about consecutive questions having 'not applicable' as a response.

Coding of Data

Coding of data involves assigning of symbols (numerical) to each response of the question. The purpose of giving numerical symbols is to translate raw data into numerical data, which may be counted and tabulated. The task of researcher is to give numbers to response carefully. As we have already discussed various types of questions (such as open-end, close-end, matrix, factual, opinion, etc.) in the previous chapter, the coding scheme will vary accordingly. For example, a close-end question may be already coded and hence it has to be just included in the code book, whereas coding of open-end questions involves operations such as classification of major responses and developing a response category of 'others' for responses which were not given frequently. The classification of responses is primarily based on similarities or differences among the responses. Usually, in the case of open-end questions, to classify responses, the researcher looks for major characteristics of the responses and puts it accordingly. In case of attitude scales, the researcher has to keep in mind the direction or weightage of responses. For example, a response 'strongly agree' is coded as '5' the subsequent codes would be in order. Therefore, if there are responses like 'agree', 'undecided', 'disagree' and 'strongly disagree', they have to be coded as 4, 3, 2 and 1. Alternatively, if 'strongly agree' is coded as -2, the subsequent responses would be coded as -1, 0, +1 and +4. The matrix questions have to be coded taking into consideration each cell as one variable. For example, if the column of matrix represents employment status, namely, 'permanent' and 'temporary' and the row represents employers or type of employer, namely, government and private, the first cell would represent a variable 'government-permanent', the second cell would represent 'government-temporary' and so on.

In order to demonstrate the points discussed above, a section of the code book used in the research study referred above is reproduced in Table 4.1.

Table 4.1
Code Book

Q. No	*Var. No.*	*Information Sought*	*Responses*	*Code*	*Column No.*	*Remarks*
		Respondents Number			1-3	
2	1	Age		-	4-5	Actual
3	2	Designation	Worker	1	6	
			Supervisor	2		
			Manager	3		
4	3	Establishment	Public	1	7	
			Private	2		
5	4	Level of Education	Graduate	1	8	
			Intermediate	2		
			High School	3		
			Middle School	4		
			Primary	5		
			Illiterate	6		
			Other	7		
6	5	Marital Status	Married	1	9	
			Unmarried	2		
			Widow	3		
			Divorce	4		
36	35	Nature of Work	Yes	1	10	
			No	2		
	36	Duration of Work	Yes	1	11	
			No	2		
	37	Wages	Yes	1	12	
			No	2		
	38	Promotion	Yes	1	13	
			No	2		
43	42	Attitude of Employer	Agree	1	14	
		Preference for Male Employees	Undecided	2		
			Disagree	3		

Preparing a Master Chart

After a code book is prepared, the data can be transferred either to a master chart or directly to computer through a statistical package. Going through master chart to computer is much more advantageous than entering data directly to computer because one can check the wrong entries in the computer by comparing 'data listing' as a computer output and master chart. Entering data directly to computer is disadvantageous, as there is no way to check wrong entries, which will show inconsistencies in tabulated data at the later stages of tabulation. A sample of master chart prepared in accordance with the code book is presented in Table 4.2.

Data Analysis

The purpose of data analysis is to prepare data as a model where relationships between the variables can be studied. Analysis of data is made with reference to the objectives of the study, hypotheses and research designs. It is also designed to test the hypotheses. Analysis of data involves re-categorization of variables, tabulation, explanation and casual inferences.

The first step in data analysis is a critical examination of the processed data in the form of frequency distribution. This analysis is made with a view to draw meaningful inferences and generalizations.

Re-categorization

The process of categorization in accordance with the objectives and hypotheses of the study is arrived at with the help of frequency distributions. Re-categorization is a process to arrange categories with the help of statistical techniques. This helps the researcher to justify the tabulation. The responses to a statement may be assigned scores or weightage. These scores or weightage are summated and may be re-categorized as 'high', 'medium' and 'low' based on the values of quartiles. The basic principle in the process of categorization or re-categorization is that the categories thus

Table 4.2

Master Chart

Respondent Number				*Variable Labels*									
				Age	*Designation*	*Establishment*	*Level of Education*	*Marital Status*	*Nature of Work*	*Duration of Work*	*Wages*	*Promotions*	*Attitude of Employer*
				Question? Variable/Column Number									
1	2	3	4	5	6	7	8	9	10	11	12	13	14
0	0	1	1	4	1	2	1	2	3	2	3	4	3
0	0	2	2	1	2	3	4	5	6	7	8	9	5
0	0	3	3	3	3	3	4	2	6	7	2	6	
0	0	4	4	5	7	8	9	1	3	5	6	1	1
0	0	5	5	4	5	1	4	2	1	1	4	3	
0	0	6	6	3	1	2	3	4	5	6	3	1	5
0	0	7	7	5	4	5	6	9	7	8	5	2	4
0	0	8	8	1	4	2	5	3	6	3	7	8	9
0	0	9	9	2	2	4	2	6	7	8	2	1	5
0	0	0	0	9	5	6	8	7	9	2	4	4	3
0	0	1	1	2	2	8	4	9	3	4	7	3	8
0	0	2	2	2	5	7	9	5	1	4	2	4	3
0	0	3	3	2	9	4	5	6	7	2	6	9	6
0	0	4	4	2	8	7	9	5	2	4	6	2	3
0	0	5	5	3	5	4	8	7	9	2	4	2	3
0	0	6	6	2	4	8	7	9	5	8	4	5	6
0	0	7	7	8	7	4	9	4	3	4	6	3	4

obtained must be exhaustive and mutually exclusive. In other words, the categories have to be independent and not overlapping.

Tabulation

Tabulation is a process of presenting data in a compact form in such a way as to facilitate comparisons and show the involved relations. In other words, it is an arrangement of data in rows and columns. This also helps the researcher to perform statistical operation on the data to draw inferences. Tabulation can be generally in the form of univariate, bivariate, trivariate or multivariate tables. Accordingly, analysis proceeds in the form of univariate analysis, bivariate analysis and trivariate or multivariate analysis.

Setting up the Analytic Model

Before we begin the analysis of data, we have to look back to the objectives, hypotheses and research design of the study and set up analytic models. These models are diagrammatic presentation of variables and their interrelationships.

To illustrate the process of making analytic model, we will consider a study on the life satisfaction of elderly persons. The major objectives and hypothesis of the study are:

Objectives

1. To assess the extent of life satisfaction among older adults, and the factors determining it.
2. To find out how loneliness, physical and psychological health, social support and spiritual well-being effect life satisfaction in older adults.

Hypothesis

There may be a direct association between physical and psychological health, loneliness, spiritual well-being and life satisfaction of older adults.

From the proposed hypothesis, it is very clear that the life satisfaction among older adults is the dependent variable in the study. Further, the researcher wishes to examine the associations among independent variables—physical and psychological health, loneliness, social support and spiritual well-being—and the dependent variable—life satisfaction. The bivariate associations among dependent and independent variables can be diagrammatically presented as follows:

Bivariate Analytic Models

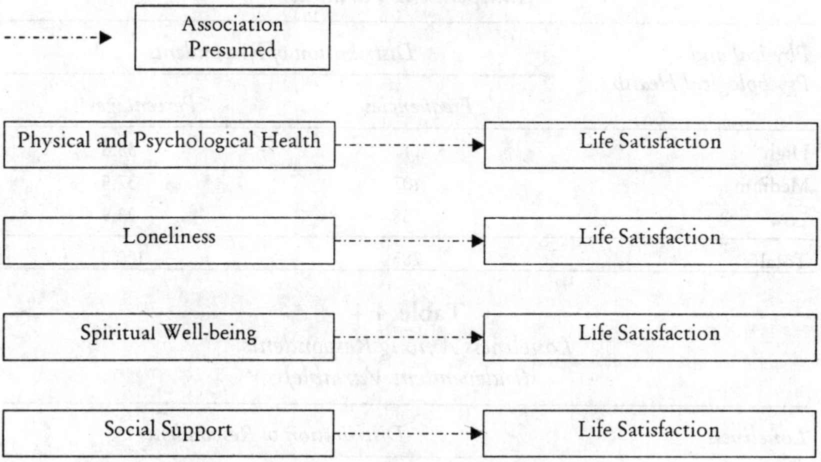

Before we examine the bivariate associations among dependent and independent variables, it is essential to analyze the independent variables and dependent variables using the method of univariate analysis.

Univariate Analysis

Univariate analysis refers to tables, which give data relating to one variable. Univariate tables, which are more commonly known as frequency distribution tables, show how frequently an item repeats. Examples of frequency tables are given below. The distribution may be symmetrical or asymmetrical. The characteristics of the sample, while examining the percentages, further properties of a distribution, can be found out by various measures of central tendencies. However, the researcher is required to decide which is most suited for a particular analysis. To know how much is the variation, the researcher has to calculate measures of dispersion.

Usually, frequency distribution tables are prepared to examine each of the independent and dependent variables. Tables 4.3, 4.4, 4.5 and 4.6 present four independent variables and Table 4.7 one dependent variable.

Table 4.3
Physical and Psychological Health of Respondents (Independent Variable)

Physical and Psychological Health	*Distribution of Respondents*	
	Frequencies	*Percentages*
High	110	38.6
Medium	107	37.5
Low	68	23.9
Total	285	100.0

Table 4.4
Loneliness Among Respondents (Independent Variable)

Loneliness	*Distribution of Respondents*	
	Frequencies	*Percentages*
Low	83	29.1
Medium	136	47.7
High	66	23.2
Total	285	100.0

Table 4.5
Spiritual Well-being Among Respondents (Independent Variable)

Spiritual Well-being	*Distribution of Respondents*	
	Frequencies	*Percentages*
Low	74	26.0
Medium	147	15.6
High	64	22.5
Total	285	100.0

Table 4.6
Social Support of Respondents (Independent Variable)

Social Support	*Distribution of Respondents*	
	Frequencies	*Percentages*
Low	79	27.7
Medium	138	48.4
High	68	23.9
Total	285	100.0

Table 4.7
Life Satisfaction Among Respondents (Dependent Variable)

Life Satisfaction	*Distribution of Respondents*	
	Frequencies	*Percentages*
Low	83	29.1
Medium	142	49.8
High	60	21.1
Total	285	100.0

A frequency distribution of a single variable is the frequency of observation in each category of a variable. For example, an examination of the pattern of response to variable 'physical and psychological health' of the respondents in Table 4.3 would provide a description of the number of respondents who have high, medium and low level of physical and psychological health. The categories of ordinal, interval and ratio variables are arranged in order. Let us consider the frequency distributions (Tables 4.3, 4.4, 4.5, 4.6 and 4.7) which describe four independent variables, viz., physical and psychological health, loneliness, spiritual well-being, social support—and the one dependent variable—life satisfaction of respondents. The tables have four rows: the first three being the categories of variables, which appear in the left hand columns and the right hand columns show the number of observation in each category. The last rows are the totals of all frequencies appearing in tables. To analyze the data, it is necessary to convert the frequencies into figures that can be interpreted meaningfully. Frequencies expressed in comparable numbers are called proportions or percentages. A proportion is obtained by dividing the frequency of a category by the total number of responses in the distribution. Proportions when multiplied by 100 become a percentage. Proportions and percentages permit the comparison of two or more frequency distributions. Note, for instance, while distribution of respondents by 'physical and psychological health' displayed in Table 4.3 clearly shows the predominance of respondents from 'high' whereas a reversed trend is observed in the cases of 'loneliness', 'spiritual well-being', 'social support' and 'life satisfaction' in the distribution of respondents in Tables 4.4, 4.5, 4.6 and 4.7, which indicate that the proportions of respondents with 'low scores' is considerably higher than the respondents with 'high scores'.

Bivariate Analysis

Once we describe the independent and dependent variables we look for bivariate associations among the variables. To know the associations among independent variables—physical and psychological health, loneliness, social support and spiritual well-being—and the dependent variable—life satisfaction, the data pertaining to these variables are cross-tabulated. A bivariate table presents data of two variables with row or column percentages. Bivariate tables with row percentages are shown below:

Table 4.8

Physical and Psychological Health and Life Satisfaction

Physical and Psychological Health	*Life Satisfaction*			*Total*
	High	*Medium*	*Low*	
High	37(33.6)	63 (57.3)	10 (9.1)	110 (100.0)
Medium	22(20.6)	56 (52.3)	29 (27.1)	107 (100.0)
Low	1 (1.5)	23 (33.8)	44 (64.7)	68 (100.0)
Total	60(21.1)	142 (49.8)	83 (29.1)	285 (100.0)

Figures in parentheses show row percentage.

$\chi^2 = 70.397$ df = 4 p = .000 (significant) C = 0.445

Table 4.9
Loneliness and Life Satisfaction

Loneliness	*Life Satisfaction*			*Total*
	High	*Medium*	*Low*	
Low	18(21.7)	51 (61.4)	14 (16.9)	83 (100.0)
Medium	36(26.5)	67 (49.3)	33 (24.3)	136 (100.0)
High	6 (9.1)	24 (36.4)	36 (54.5)	66 (100.0)
Total	60(21.1)	142 (49.8)	83 (29.1)	285 (100.0)

χ^2 = 31.086 df = 4 p =.000 (significant) C = 0.314

Table 4.10
Spiritual Well-being and Life Satisfaction

Spiritual Well-being	*Life Satisfaction*			*Total*
	High	*Medium*	*Low*	
Low	4 (5.4)	34 (45.9)	36 (48.6)	74 (100.0)
Medium	36 24.5)	71 (48.3)	40 (27.2)	147 (100.0)
High	20 31.3)	37 (57.8)	7 (10.9)	64 (100.0)
Total	60 21.1)	142 (49.8)	83 (29.1)	285 (100.0)

χ^2 = 30.843 df = 4 p =.000 (significant) C = 0.312

Table 4.11
Extent of Social Support and Level of Life Satisfaction

Social Support	*Life Satisfaction*			*Total*
	High	*Medium*	*Low*	
Low	8 (10.1)	30 (38.0)	41 (51.9)	79 (100.0)
Medium	25 (18.1)	75 (54.3)	38 (27.5)	138 (100.0)
High	27 (39.7)	37 (54.4)	4 (5.9)	68 (100.0)
Total	60 (21.1)	142 (49.8)	83 (29.1)	285 (100.0)

χ^2 = 46.166 df = 4 p = .000 (significant) C =.139

The association between two variables can be explained either by comparing the percentages of respondents column-wise or row-wise depending upon computation of percentages. If the percentages are calculated row-wise, we compare data column-wise. The association between the variables can also be examined by various statistical techniques depending upon the level of measurement of the data. Since the data are in nominal levels of measurement, the Chi-square test would be more appropriate in this case. Apparently, associations among independent variables—physical and psychological health, loneliness, spiritual well-being, social support—and the dependent variable—life satisfaction are statistically significant and hence the variables are interdependent. Therefore, it may be inferred that older adults have higher level of life satisfaction with higher physical and psychological health, spiritual well-being and social support and lower level of loneliness.

In bivariate analysis the researcher also explains the nature and the degree of association, that is, whether the relationship is positive or negative and it also indicates the degree of association in terms of high, moderate or low. Analysis of the nature of associations clearly shows that except 'loneliness' all other independent variables are positively associated with the dependent variable 'life satisfaction'. In case of 'loneliness' it is observed that the variables are inversely associated. The Coefficients of Contingency (C) show the degree or strength of correlations between the variables. Results show that while correlations among physical and psychological health, loneliness, spiritual well-being and life satisfaction are 'moderate', correlations between social support and life satisfaction is weak.

Results of the bivariate analysis show that the variables are correlated. In other words, we may say that life satisfaction among older adults depends on physical and psychological health, loneliness, spiritual well-being and social support. That means the results are in line with the analytic models presented in the beginning of this chapter. Hence, we can present the associations diagrammatically as shown below:

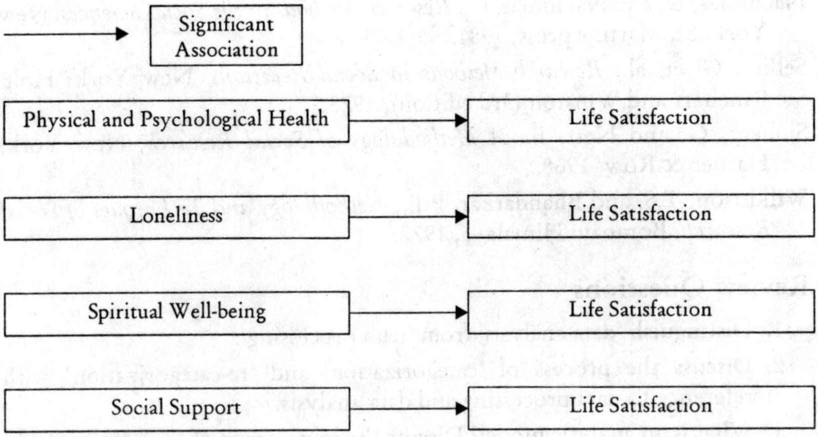

Important Terms for Review

- Data Processing
- Data Analysis
- Re-categorization
- Tabulation
- Analytic Model
- Univariate Analysis
- Bivariate Analysis
- Row Percentage
- Column Percentage

Further Readings

Bailey, Kenneth D., *Methods of Social Research*, London: The Free Press, 1978.

Baker, L. Therese, *Doing Social Research,* New York: McGraw Hill, 1988.

Blalock, Hubert M., *Social Statistics,* New York: McGraw Hill, 1972.

Doby, J.T. et al., *An Introduction to Social Research,* London: Harrisburg Stackpole Co., 1953.

Kerlinger, Fred R., *Foundations of Behavioural Research,* Delhi: Surjeet Publications, 1964.

Lal Das, D.K., *Practice of Social Research: Social Work Perspective*, Jaipur: Rawat Publications, 2000.

Monete, Duane R. et. al., *Applied Social Research: Tool for the Human Services,* Chicago: Holt, 1986.

Nachmias, D. and Nachmias, C., *Research Methods in the Social Sciences*, New York: St. Martins press, 1981.

Sellitz, G. et. al., *Research Methods in Social Relations,* New York: Holt. Rinehart and Winston (3rd edition), 1973.

Sjoberg, G. and Nett, B., *A Methodology of Social Research,* New York: Harper & Row, 1968.

Wilkinson, T.S. and Bhandarkar, P.L., *Methodology and Techniques of Social Research*, Bombay: Himalaya, 1977.

Review Questions

1. Distinguish 'data analysis' from 'data processing'.
2. Discuss the process of 'categorization' and 're-categorization' with reference to data processing and data analysis.
3. What is an analytic model? Discuss the importance of analytic model in data interpretation.
4. Describe the process of examining bivariate associations between variables.

5

Control, Elaboration and Multivariate Analysis

Bivariate analysis of data is the initial step of cause-effect analysis. It is followed by trivariate analysis of data. The purpose of trivariate analysis is to substantiate the findings of bivariate analysis. The bivariate analysis establishes co-variation and its direction. To draw the causal inference, one has to re-examine the bivariate relations by controlling the effect of other variables into the analysis. Suppose one finds a relationship between 'smoking habits' and 'academic performance' of students, that is, those students who smoke frequently have bad academic performance. If we wish to interpret the result at this juncture, we would say that there is a cause-effect relationship between the variables and that increasing/decreasing the frequency of smoking will increase/decrease the academic performance. However, it is also possible that decrease in the academic performance is not due to increase in the frequency of smoking but rather to mental depression. That is students with high level of depression generally smoke more frequently just to get some relief and also mental depression act adversely on academic performance. In other words, the relationship between 'smoking habits' and 'academic performance' is due to the fact that the both the variables are associated with a third variable, i.e., 'mental depression'.

Bivariate relationship may be observed because of two reasons: it may be observed just due to chance, or it may exist due to a third variable which is yet to be revealed. Above all, the change in the dependent variable may be explained by more than one single independent variable. In both the cases, re-examination of the bivariate relationship by controlling the effect of third variable serves the purpose of clarifying and elaborating the original relationship.

Trivariate Analysis

In the preceding chapter we discussed bivariate analysis of data. This chapter deals with the analysis of relationship between more than two variables. Various research designs require trivariate and multivariate analyses of data. It plays a very significant role in drawing inferences.

Trivariate and multivariate analyses serve three important functions in social research; control, elaboration and prediction. Firstly, whenever the experimental control is not possible, trivariate analysis is used to examine the bivariate relationship to see if the relationship is due to the third variable. Secondly, bivariate relationship is clarified by introducing a third variable. Finally, trivariate analysis helps to identify more independent variables to account for the variation in the dependent variable.

Variable as a Control

If the two variables are associated, it is not necessary that there is cause and effect relationship between the two variables. It is essential that the effects of other variables are ruled out as alternative explanation of the relationship. For example, a relationship between 'knee joint pain' and 'amount of rainfall' can probably be accounted for by the variable 'humidity'. Humidity is related to both knee joint pain and amount of rainfall and this joint relationship produces a statistical relationship that has no causal significance. The original bivariate relationship between 'knee joint pain' and 'amount of rainfall' is called 'spurious'. It is mandatory for a researcher to reveal such variables and substantiate the bivariate relationship. It is the basic principle of all research designs and is achieved by a process called 'control'.

In experimental research designs (supra, Chapter 7) the subjects are divided into two groups, viz., experimental group and control group, by using the process of randomization. This assures that all the extraneous variables are controlled and the groups differ only with regard to their exposure to the independent variable. However, it is rather difficult to manipulate groups before the study in quasi-experimental research designs (supra, Chapter 8). As such, statistical techniques are used as method of control in quasi-experimental and survey research designs. The statistical techniques are used during data analysis. There are two methods of statistical control: (1) cross-tabulation, and partial correlation. In the first method data are cross-tabulated and sub-groups are compared. In the second method—partial correlation—a statistical procedure is used to nullify the effects of extraneous variables.

Cross-Tabulation as a Method of Control

In this method, the sample is divided into sub-groups according to the categories of the controlled variable. The variables, which show an association with independent and dependent variables, are selected as control variables. The original bivariate association is re-examined within each sub-group. There are three possibilities: (1) the original bivariate association is not affected by the third variable, (2) the original bivariate association is affected by the third variable and the association is disappeared, and (3) the original bivariate association is partially affected.

While, when a third variable completely accounts for the bivariate association between the independent and dependent variable, the association is referred as spurious whereas if a third variable does not account for the bivariate association between the independent and dependent variable, the association is referred as non-spurious.

Trivariate Analytic Models

The independent variables 'physical and psychological health', 'loneliness', 'spiritual well-being' and 'social support', which have shown association with dependent variable 'life satisfaction', are selected as control variables.

The bivariate associations among dependent and independent variables with a third variable as control can be diagrammatically presented as follows:

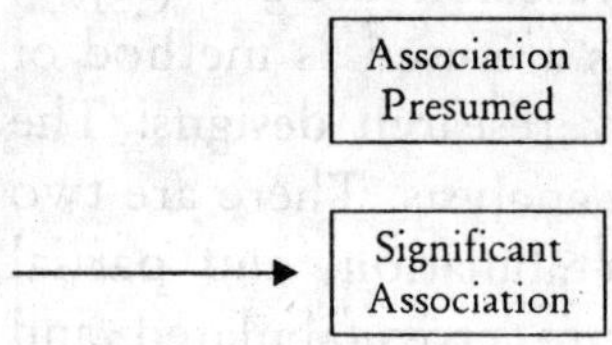

Model 1

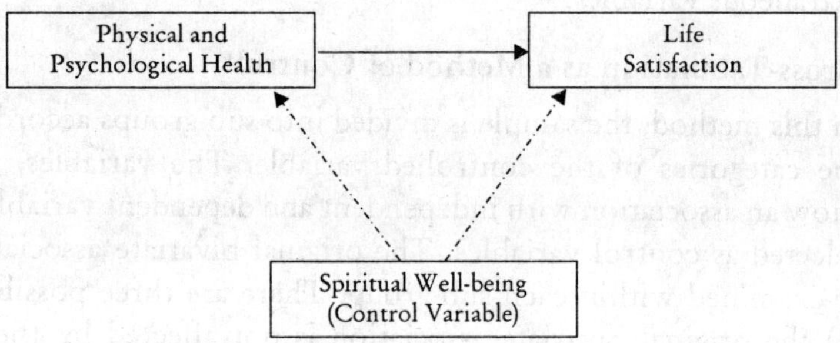

Model 2

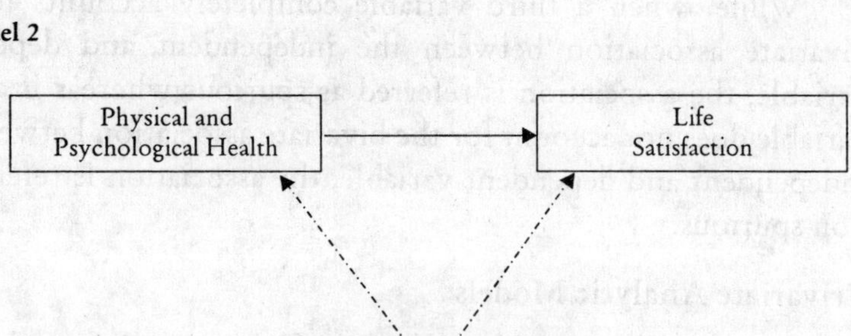

Model 3

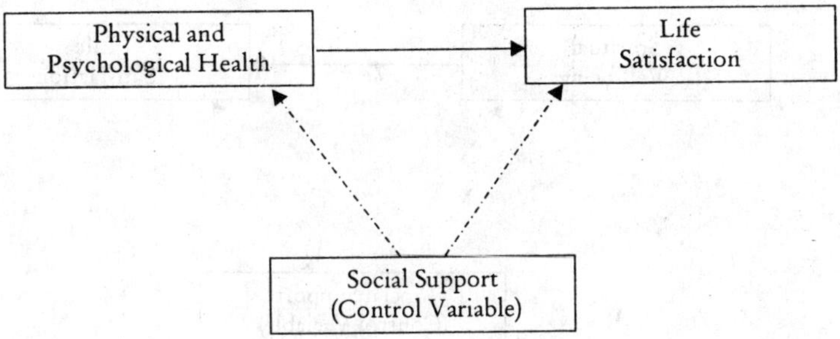

Model 4

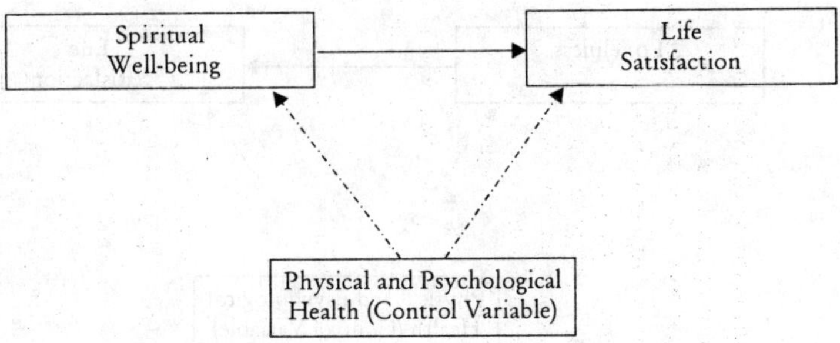

Model 5

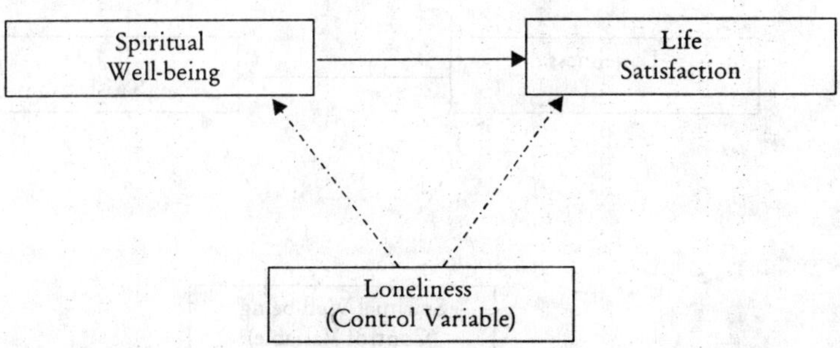

Model 6

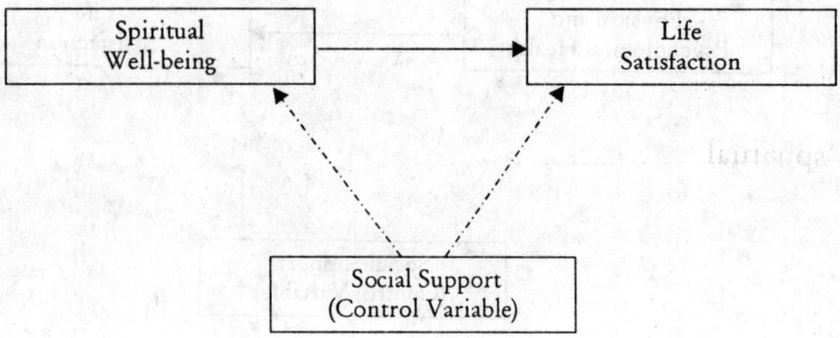

Model 7

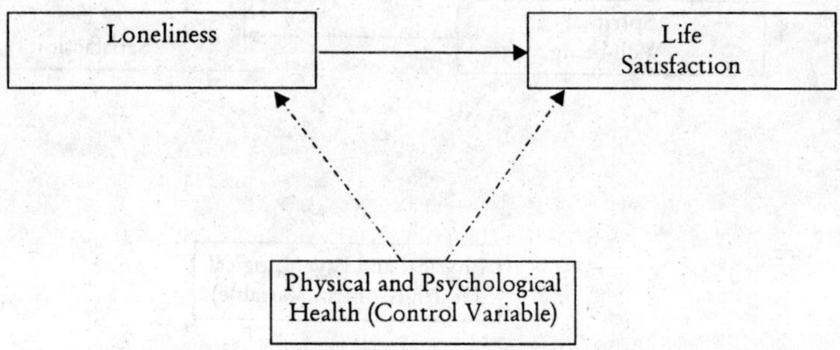

Model 8

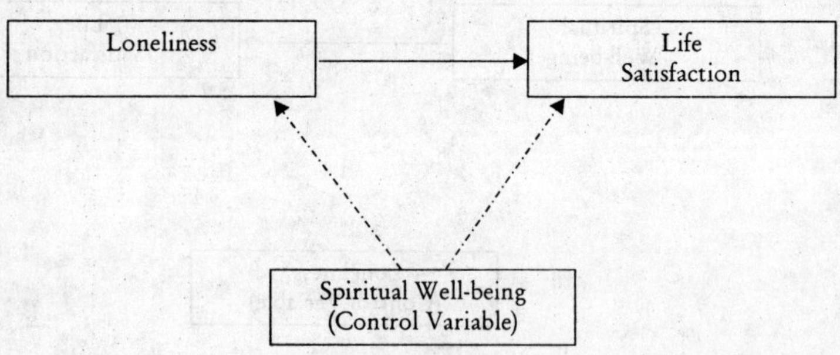

Model 9

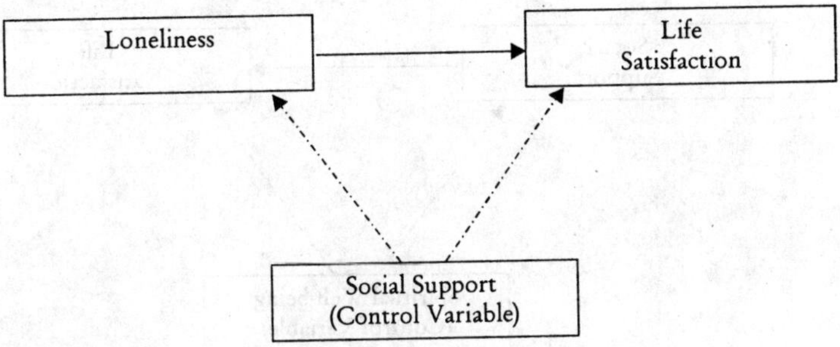

Model 10

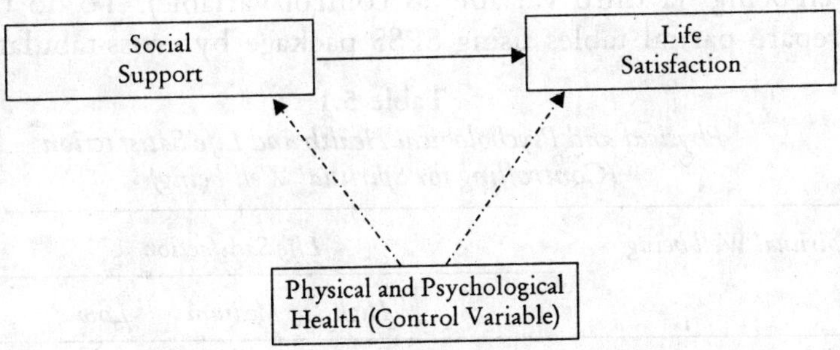

Model 11

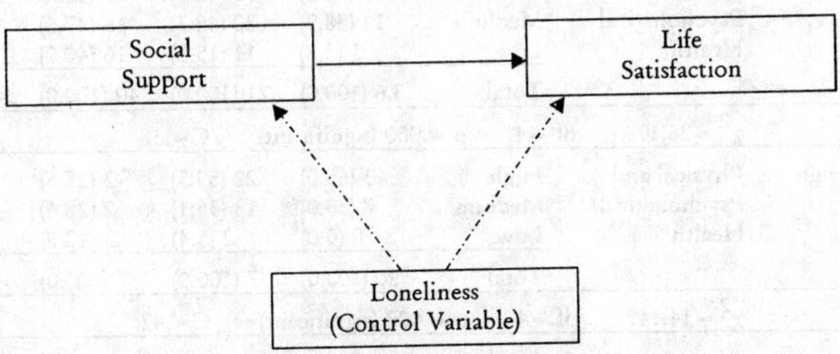

Model 12

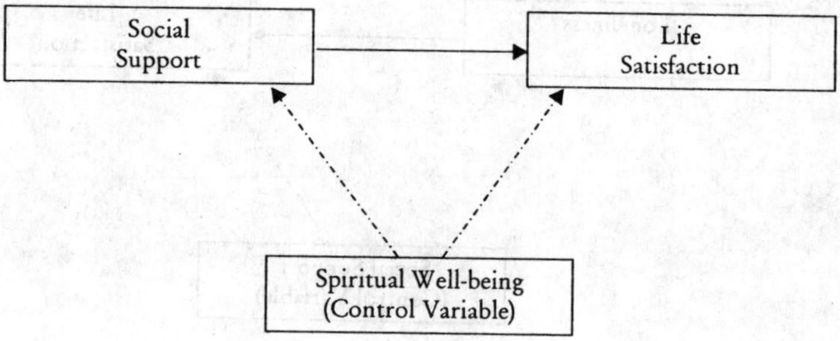

Let us re-examine the bivariate associations between 'physical and psychological health' (independent variable) and' life satisfaction' (dependent variable) controlling the effect of 'spiritual well-being' (a third variable as control variable). To do this we prepare partial tables using SPSS package by cross-tabulation of

Table 5.1

Physical and Psychological Health and Life Satisfaction (Controlling for Spiritual Well-being)

Spiritual Well-being			*Life Satisfaction*			
			High	*Medium*	*Low*	*Total*
Low	Physical and Psychological Health	High	3 (75.0)	11 (32.4)	3 (8.3)	17 (23.0)
		Medium	1 (25.0)	13 (38.2)	8 (22.2)	22 (29.7)
		Low	0 (0.0)	10 (29.4)	25 (69.4)	35 (47.3)
		Total	4 (100.0)	34 (100.0)	36 (100.0)	74 (100.0)
	$\chi^2 = 8.83$	df = 4	p = .001 (significant)	C = .45		
Medium	Physical and Psychological Health	High	21 (58.3)	30 (42.3)	5 (12.5)	56 (38.1)
		Medium	14 (38.9)	30 (42.3)	19 (47.5)	63 (42.9)
		Low	1 (2.8)	11 (15.5)	16 (40.0)	28 (19.0)
		Total	3 6 (100.0)	71 (100.0)	40 (100.0)	147(100.0)
	$\chi^2 = 26.104$	df = 4	p = .000 (significant)	C = .38		
High	Physical and Psychological Health	High	13 (65.0)	22 (59.5)	2 (28.6)	37 (57.8)
		Medium	7 (35.0)	13 (35.1)	2 (28.6)	22 (34.4)
		Low	0 (0.0)	2 (5.4)	3 (42.9)	5 (7.8)
		Total	20 (100.0)	37 (100.0)	7 (100.0)	64 (100.0)
	$\chi^2 = 14.149$	df = 4	p = .007 (significant)	C = .42		

data pertaining to independent and dependent variables and control the effect of a third variable on the original bivariate association. The results of cross-tabulation of data are presented in Table 5.1.

It is observed from the table that the original bivariate association remains unaffected by the third variable, i.e., 'spiritual well-being'. In the total sample as well as in each sub-group of 'spiritual well-being' the proportion of 'life satisfaction' is unchanged. The result shows that the original bivariate association between the two variables is not accounted for by the control variable 'spiritual well-being'. Thus, it may be concluded that 'spiritual well-being' has no effect on the association between 'physical and psychological health' and 'life satisfaction'. In other words, we can infer that the association between 'physical and psychological health' (independent variable) and 'life satisfaction' (dependent variable) is *non-spurious*. The results of the analysis can be diagrammatically shown as under:

Figure 5.1
Non-Spurious Association between Independent and Dependent Variables

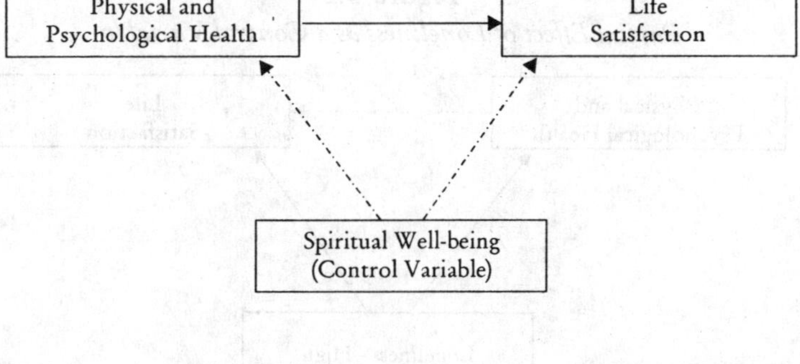

Now, we will re-examine the bivariate association between 'physical and psychological health' and 'life satisfaction' controlling for 'loneliness' as a third variable. Table 5.2 displays partial results:

Table 5.2

Physical and Psychological Health and Life Satisfaction (Controlling for Loneliness)

Loneliness			*Life Satisfaction*			
			High	*Medium*	*Low*	*Total*
Low	Physical and Psychological Health	High	16 (88.9)	33 (64.7)	1 (7.1)	50 (60.2)
		Medium	2 (11.1)	15 (29.4)	6 (42.9)	23 (27.7)
		Low	0 (0.0)	3 (5.9)	7 (50.0)	10 (12.0)
		Total	18 (100.0)	51 (100.0)	14 (100.0)	83 (100.0)
	χ^2 = 32.690	df =4	p =.000 (significant)	C=.539		
Medium	Physical and Psychological Health	High	20 (55.6)	24 (35.8)	5 (15.2)	49 (36.0)
		Medium	16 (44.4)	32 (47.8)	9 (27.3)	57 (41.9)
		Low	0 (0.0)	11 (16.4)	19 (57.6)	30 (22.1)
		Total	36 (100.0)	67 (100.0)	33 (100.0)	136(100.0)
	χ^2 =37.871	df =4	p =.000 (significant)	C=.4726		
High	Physical and Psychological Health	High	1 (16.7)	6 (25.0)	4 (11.1)	11 (16.7)
		Medium	4 (66.7)	9 (37.5)	14 (38.9)	27 (40.9)
		Low	1 (16.7)	9 (37.5)	18 (50.0)	28 (42.4)
		Total	6 (100.0)	24 (100.0)	36 (100.0)	66 (100.0)
	χ^2 =4.306	df =4	p =.366 (not significant)	C=.247		

Figure 5.2

Partial Effect of Loneliness as a Control Variable

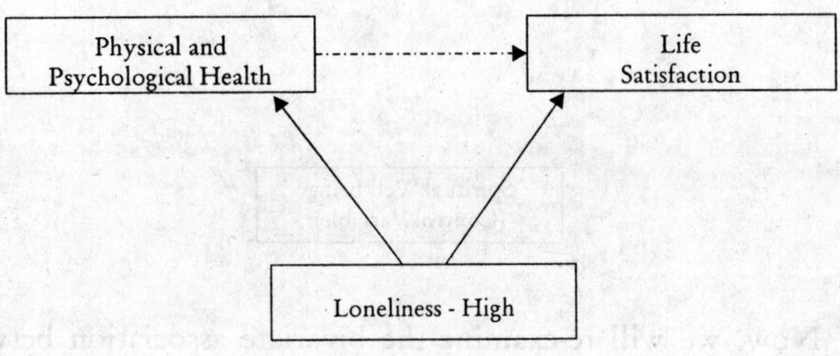

Alternatively,

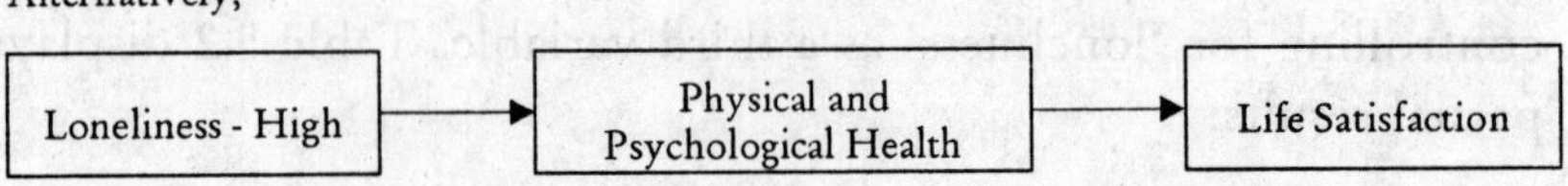

It is evident from the analysis that the original bivariate association is unchanged by the third variable—'loneliness'—in its first two sub-categories, that is, 'low' and 'medium'. In other words, we can say that the original bivariate association is unchanged when 'loneliness' is either 'low' or 'medium'. However, it is found that the original bivariate association is changed when 'loneliness' is 'high'. Therefore, it may be concluded that 'life satisfaction' is independent of 'physical and psychological health' when 'loneliness' is 'high'. To be specific, it may be inferred that in case of 'high' 'loneliness' the 'life satisfaction' is 'low', irrespective of the levels of 'physical and psychological health'. When the effect of third variable is partial, it is called *conditional variable.*

Table 5.3 displays partial results of re-examination of the bivariate association between 'physical and psychological health' and 'life satisfaction' controlling for 'social support' as a third variable.

Table 5.3

Physical and Psychological Health and Life Satisfaction (Controlling for Social Support)

Social Support			*Life Satisfaction*			
			High	*Medium*	*Low*	*Total*
Low	Physical and Psychological Health	High	4 (50.0)	13 (43.3)	1 (2.4)	18 (22.8)
		Medium	4 (50.0)	15 (50.0)	11 (26.8)	30 (38.0)
		Low	0 (0.0)	2 (6.7)	29 (70.7)	31 (39.2)
		Total	8 (100.0)	30 (100.0)	41 (100.0)	79 (100.0)
	$\chi^2 = 40.010$	df = 4	p = .000 (significant)			
Medium	Physical and Psychological Health	High	19 (76.0)	33 (44.0)	6 (15.8)	58 (42.0)
		Medium	6 (24.0)	25 (33.3)	17 (44.7)	48 (34.8)
		Low	0 (0.0)	17 (22.7)	15 (39.5)	32 (23.2)
		Total	25 (100.0)	75 (100.0)	38 (100.0)	138 (100.0)
	$\chi^2 = 25.274$	df = 4	p = .000 (significant)			
High	Physical and Psychological Health	High	14 (51.9)	17 (45.9)	3 (75.0)	34 (50.0)
		Medium	12 (44.4)	16 (43.2)	1 (25.0)	29 (42.6)
		Low	1 (3.7)	4 (10.8)	0 (0.0)	5 (7.4)
		Total	27 (100.0)	37 (100.0)	4 (100.0)	68 (100.0)
	$\chi^2 = 2.341$	df = 4	p = .673 (not significant)			

Figure 5.3
Partial Effect of Social Support as a Control Variable

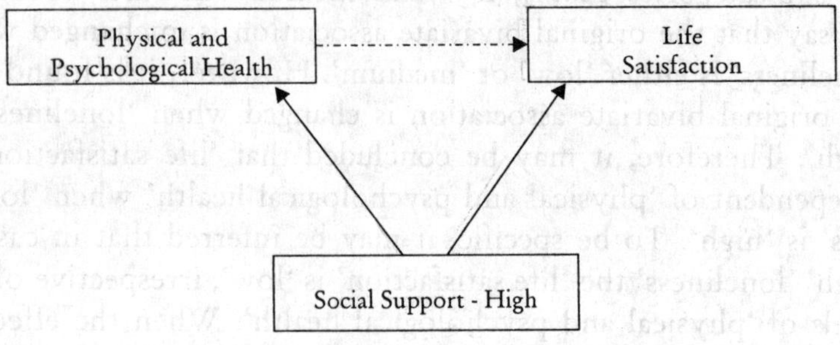

Alternatively,

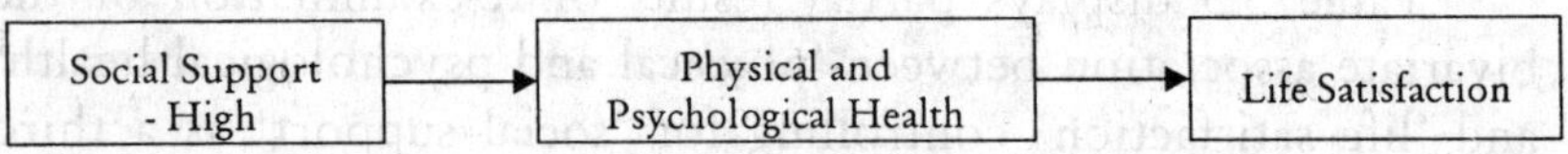

It is observed that the original bivariate association is unchanged by the third variable—'social support'—in its first two sub-categories, that is 'low'—and 'medium'. In other words, we can say that the original bivariate association is unaffected when 'social support' is either 'low' or 'medium'. However, it is found that the original bivariate association is affected when 'social support' is 'high'. Therefore, it may be concluded that 'life satisfaction' is independent of 'physical and psychological health' when 'social support' is 'high'. To be specific, it may be inferred that in case of 'high social support' the 'life satisfaction' will vary irrespective of the levels of 'physical and psychological health'. Hence, 'social supports' appears to be a *conditional variable.*

The second independent variable found to be associated with 'life satisfaction' was 'spiritual well-being'. To examine if the association is non-spurious, we will re-examine the original bivariate association between 'spiritual well-being' and 'life satisfaction' to see the effect of a third variable, i.e., 'physical and psychological health'. Table 5.4 presents the partial results:

Table 5.4
Spiritual Well-being and Life Satisfaction
(Controlling for Physical and Psychological Health)

Physical & Psychological Health			*Life Satisfaction*			
			High	*Medium*	*Low*	*Total*
High	Spiritual Well-being	Low	2 (20.0)	22 (34.9)	13 (35.1)	37 (33.6)
		Medium	5 (50.0)	30 (47.6)	21 (56.8)	56 (50.9)
		High	3 (30.0)	11 (17.5)	3 (8.1)	17 (15.5)
		Total	10 (100.0)	63 (100.0)	37 (100.0)	110 (100.0)
	χ^2 = 3.818	df = 4	p = .431 (not significant)		C = .183	
Medium	Spiritual Well-being	Low	2 (6.9)	13 (23.2)	7 (31.8)	22 (20.6)
		Medium	19 (65.5)	30 (53.6)	14 (63.6)	63 (58.9)
		High	8 (27.6)	13 (23.2)	1 (4.5)	22 (20.6)
		Total	29 (100.0)	56 (100.0)	22 (100.0)	107 (100.0)
	χ^2 = 8.383	df = 4	p = .079 (not significant)		C = .269	
Low	Spiritual Well-being	Low	3 (6.8)	2 (8.7)	0 (0.00)	5 (7.4)
		Medium	16 (36.4)	11 (47.8)	1 (100.0)	28 (41.2)
		High	25 (56.8)	10 (43.5)	0 (0.0)	35 (51.5)
		Total	44 (100.0)	23 (100.0)	1(100.0)	68 (100.0)
	χ^2 = 2.526	df = 4	p = .640 (not significant)		C = .189	

The analysis of data shows that the original bivariate association is affected by the third variable 'physical and psychological health'. In the total sample as well as in each sub-group of 'physical and psychological health' there is no association. The result shows that the original bivariate association is disappeared. That is, the original association between the two variables—'spiritual well-being' and 'life satisfaction'—is completely accounted for by the third variable—'physical and psychological health'. Thus, it may be concluded that the bivariate association between 'spiritual well-being' and 'life satisfaction' was *spurious.* In other words, it may be said that the bivariate association is due to the fact that 'physical and psychological health' affects both the variables, viz., 'spiritual well-being' and 'life satisfaction'. It may be inferred that there is no direct association between 'spiritual well-being' and 'life satisfaction'. They are associated indirectly, i.e., through 'physical and psychological health' (please see the alternative model). The results of the analysis can be diagrammatically shown as under:

Figure 5.4

Spurious Association between Independent and Dependent Variables

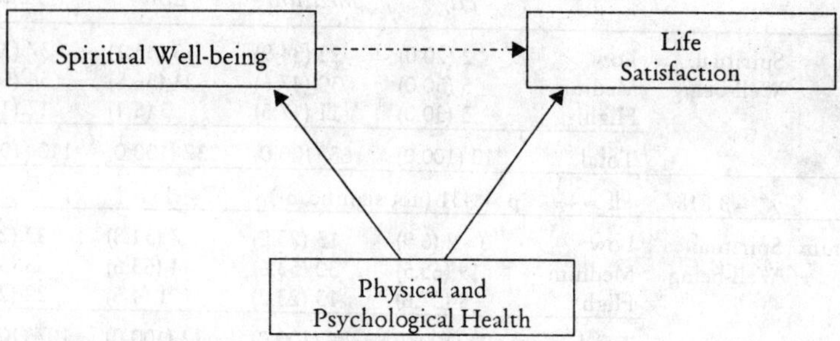

Alternatively,

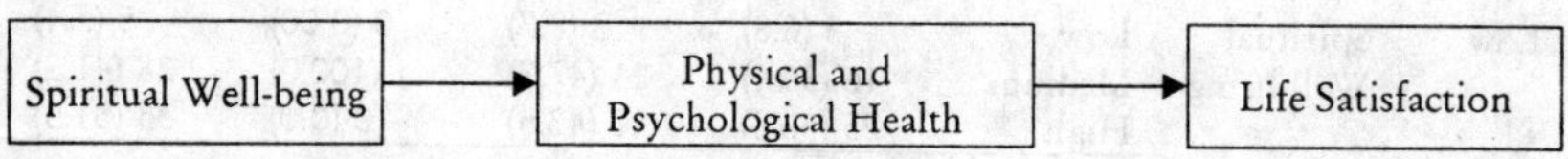

Let us re-examine the bivariate associations between 'spiritual well-being' (independent variable) and 'life satisfaction' (dependent variable) controlling the effect of 'loneliness' (a third variable as control variable). The results of cross-tabulation of data are presented in Table 5.5.

In Table 5.5, it is observed that the original bivariate association remains unaffected by the third variable—loneliness. In the total sample as well as in each sub-group of spiritual well-being the proportion of life satisfaction is unchanged. The result shows that the original bivariate association between the two variables is not accounted for by the control variable—loneliness. Thus, it may be concluded that loneliness has no effect on the association between spiritual well-being and life satisfaction. In other words, we can infer that the association between spiritual well-being (independent variable) and life satisfaction (dependent variable) is genuine (non-spurious). The results of the analysis can be diagrammatically shown in Figure 5.5.

Table 5.5

Spiritual Well-being and Life Satisfaction (Controlling for Loneliness)

Loneliness			*Life Satisfaction*			
			High	*Medium*	*Low*	*Total*
Low	Spiritual Well-being	Low	2 (11.1)	4 (7.8)	5 (35.7)	11 (13.3)
		Medium (84-90)	13 (72.2)	22 (43.1)	8 (57.1)	43 (51.8)
		High	3 (16.7)	25 (49.0)	1 (7.1)	29 (34.9)
		Total	18 (100.0)	51 (100.0)	14 (100.0)	83 (100.0)
	$\chi^2 = 16.493$	df = 4	p = .002 (significant)			
Medium	Spiritual Well-being	Low	2 (5.6)	14 (20.9)	13 (39.4)	29 (21.3)
		Medium	19 (52.8)	42 (62.7)	17 (51.5)	78 (57.4)
		High	15 (41.7)	11 (16.4)	3 (9.1)	29 (21.3)
		Total	36 (100.0)	67 (100.0)	33 (100.0)	136 (100.0)
	$\chi^2 = 19.975$	df = 4	p = .001 (significant)			
High	Spiritual Well-being	Low	0 (0.0)	16 (66.7)	18 (50.0)	34 (51.5)
		Medium	4 (66.7)	7 (29.2)	15 (41.7)	26 (39.4)
		High	2 (33.3)	1 (4.2)	3 (8.3)	6 (9.1)
		Total	6 (100.0)	24 (100.0)	36 (100.0)	66 (100.0)
	$\chi^2 = 10.535$	df = 4	p = .032 (significant)			

Figure 5.5

Non-Spurious Association between Independent and Dependent Variables

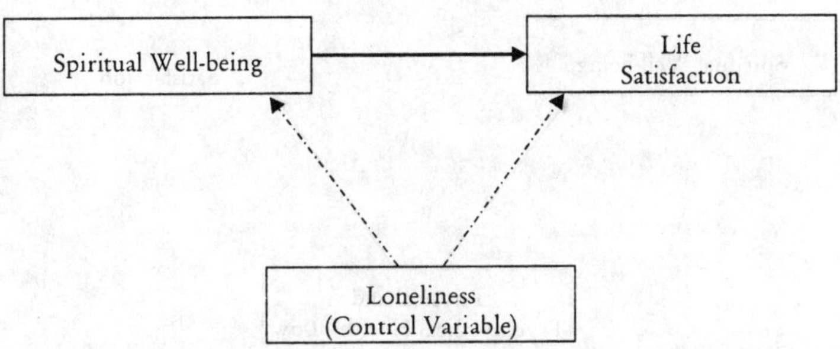

Table 5.6 displays partial results of re-examination of the bivariate association between 'spiritual well-being' and 'life satisfaction' controlling for 'social supports' as a third variable:

Table 5.6
Spiritual Well-being and Life Satisfaction (Controlling for Social Support)

Social Support			*Life Satisfaction*			
			High	*Medium*	*Low*	*Total*
Low	Spiritual Well-being	Low	0 (0.00)	7 (23.3)	18 (43.9)	25 (31.6)
		Medium	4 (50.0)	17 (56.7)	20 (48.8)	41 (51.9)
		High	4 (50.0)	6 (20.0)	3 (7.3)	13 (16.5)
		Total	8 (100.0)	30 (100.0)	41 (100.0)	79 (100.0)
	χ^2 =13.127	df =4	p =.011 (significant)			
Medium	Spiritual Well-being	Low	1 (4.0)	13 (17.3)	17 (44.7)	31 (22.5)
		Medium	19 (76.0)	39 (52.0)	19 (50.0)	77 (55.8)
		High	5 (20.0)	23 (30.7)	2 (5.3)	30 (21.7)
		Total	25 (100.0)	75 (100.0)	38 (100.0)	138 (100.0)
	χ^2 =22.846	df =4	p =.000 (significant)			
High	Spiritual Well-being	Low	3 (11.1)	14 (37.8)	1 (25.0)	18 (26.5)
		Medium	13 (48.1)	15 (40.5)	1 (25.0)	29 (42.6)
		High	11 (40.7)	8 (21.6)	2 (50.00)	21 (30.9)
		Total	27 (100.0)	37 (100.0)	4 (100.0)	68 (100.0)
	χ^2 =7.088	df =4	p =.131 (not significant)			

Figure 5.6
Partial Effect of Physical and Psychological Health as a Control Variable

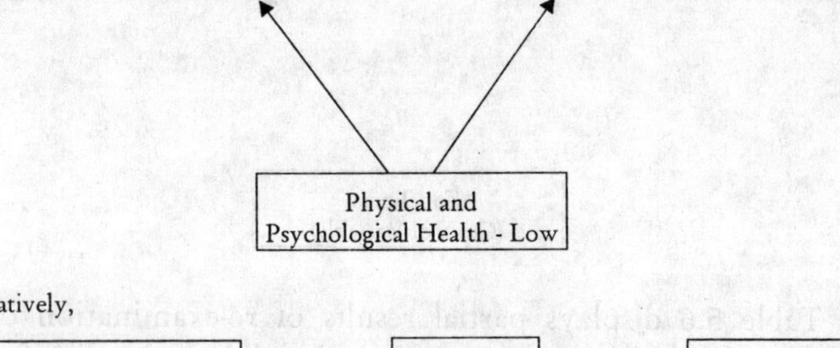

Alternatively,

It is observed that the original bivariate association is unchanged by the third variable—'social support'—in its first two sub-categories, that is, 'low' and 'medium'. In other words, we can say that the original bivariate association is unaffected when 'social support' is either 'low' or 'medium'. However, it is found that the original bivariate association is affected when 'social support' is 'high'. Therefore, it may be concluded that 'life satisfaction' is independent of 'spiritual well-being' when 'social support' is 'high'. To be specific, it may be inferred that in case of 'high social support', the 'life satisfaction' will vary, irrespective of the levels of 'spiritual well-being'. Hence, 'social support' appears to be a *conditional variable.*

'Loneliness' was the third independent variable associated with 'life satisfaction' of older adults. To examine if the association is non-spurious, we will re-examine the original bivariate association between 'loneliness' and 'life satisfaction' by controlling the effect of a third variable, i.e., 'physical and psychological health'. The partial results are presented in Table 5.7 below:

Table 5.7

Loneliness and Life Satisfaction
(Controlling for Physical and Psychological Health)

Physical & Psychological Health			*Life Satisfaction*			
			High	*Medium*	*Low*	*Total*
High	Loneliness	Low	4 (40.0)	6 (9.5)	1 (2.7)	11 (10.0)
		Medium	5 (50.0)	24 (38.1)	20 (54.1)	49 (44.5)
		High	1 (10.0)	33 (52.4)	16 (43.2)	50 (45.5)
		Total	10 (100.0)	63 (100.0)	37 (100.0)	110 (100.0)
	$\chi^2 = 15.861$	df = 4	p = .003 (significant)			
Medium	Loneliness	Low	6 (20.7)	15 (26.8)	2 (9.1)	23 (21.5)
		Medium	9 (31.0)	32 (51.7)	16 (72.7)	57 (53.3)
		High	14 (48.3)	9 (16.1)	4 (18.2)	27 (25.2)
		Total	29 (100.0)	56 (100.0)	22 (100.0)	107 (100.0)
	$\chi^2 = 15.124$	df = 4	p = .004 (significant)			
Low	Loneliness	Low	18 (40.9)	9 (39.1)	1 (100.0)	28 (41.2)
		Medium	19 (43.2)	11 (47.8)	0 (0,00)	30 (44.1)
		High	7 (15.9)	3 (13.0)	0 (0,00)	10 (14.7)
		Total	44 (100.0)	23 (100.0)	1 (100.0)	68 (100.0)
	$\chi^2 = 1.620$	df = 4	p = .805 (not significant)			

The analysis of data shows that the original bivariate association is unchanged by the third variable—'physical and psychological health'—in its first two sub-categories, that is, 'high' and 'medium'. In other words, we can say that the original bivariate association is unaffected when 'physical and psychological health' is either 'high' or 'medium'. However, it is found that the original bivariate association is affected when 'physical and psychological health' is 'low'. Therefore, it may be concluded that life satisfaction is independent of 'loneliness' when 'physical and psychological health' is 'low'. To be specific, it may be inferred that in case of 'low physical and psychological health' the 'life satisfaction' will vary, irrespective of the 'levels of loneliness'. Hence, 'physical and psychological health' appears to be a conditional variable.

Figure 5.7

Partial Effect of Social Support as a Control Variable

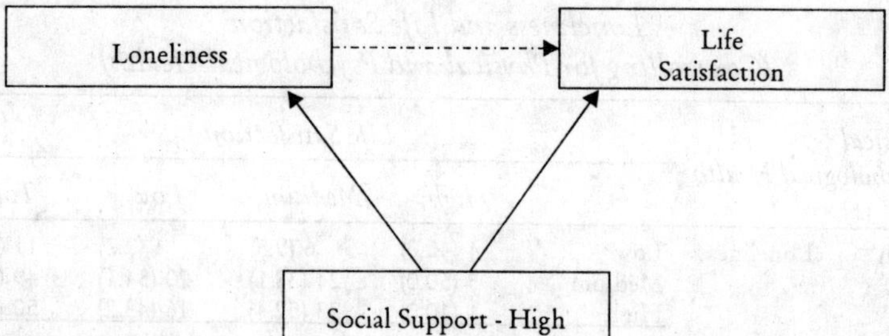

Alternatively,

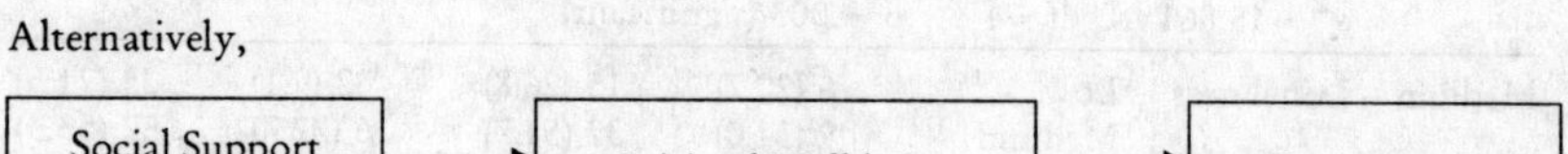

Table 5.8 displays partial results of re-examination of the bivariate association between 'loneliness' and 'life satisfaction' controlling for 'spiritual well-being' as a third variable:

Table 5.8

Loneliness and Life Satisfaction (Controlling for Spiritual Well-being)

Spiritual Well-being			*Life Satisfaction*			
			High	*Medium*	*Low*	*Total*
Low	Loneliness	Low	2 (50.0)	4 (11.8)	5 (13.9)	11 (14.9)
		Medium	2 (50.0)	14 (41.2)	13 (36.1)	29 (39.2)
		High	0 (0.0)	16 (47.1)	18 (50.0)	34 (45.9)
		Total	4 (100.0)	34 (100.0)	36 (100.0)	74 (100.0)
χ^2 =5.781		df =4	p =.216 (not significant)			
Medium	Loneliness	Low	13 (36.1)	22 (31.0)	8 (20.0)	43 (29.3)
		Medium	19 (52.8)	42 (59.2)	17 (42.5)	78 (53.1)
		High	4 (11.1)	7 (9.9)	15 (37.5)	26 (17.7)
		Total	36 (100.0)	71 (100.0)	40 (100.0)	147(100.0)
	χ^2 =15.378	df =4	p =.004 (significant)			
High	Loneliness	Low	3 (15.0)	25 (67.6)	1 (14.3)	29 (45.3)
		Medium	15 (75.0)	11 (29.7)	3 (42.9)	29 (45.3)
		High	2 (10.0)	1 (2.7)	3 (42.9)	6 (9.4)
		Total	20 (100.0)	37 (100.0)	7 (100.0)	64 (100.0)
	χ^2 =25.605	df =4	p =.000 (significant)			

Figure 5.8

Partial Effect of Spiritual Well-being as a Control Variable

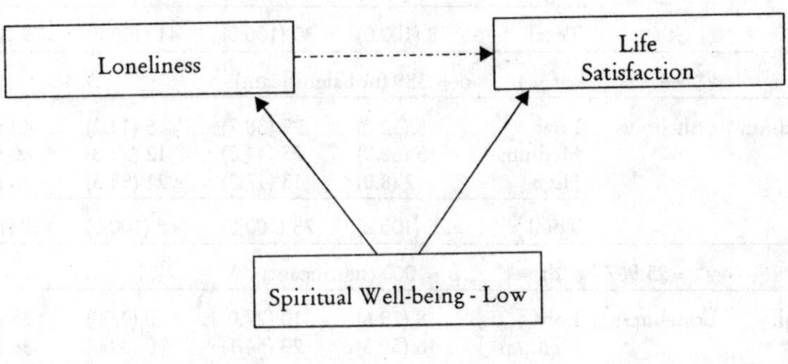

Alternatively,

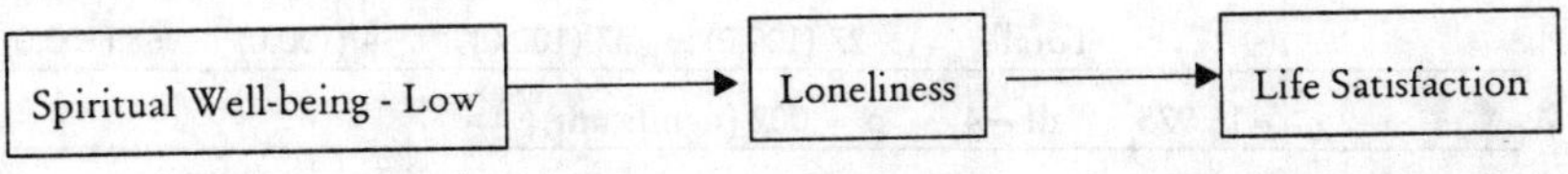

It is evident that the original bivariate association is unchanged by the third variable—'spiritual well-being'—in its first two sub-categories, that is, 'low' and 'medium'. In other words, we can say that the original bivariate association is unchanged when 'spiritual well-being' is either 'low' or 'medium'. However, it is found that the original bivariate association is affected when 'spiritual well-being' is 'high'. Therefore, it may be concluded that 'life satisfaction' is independent of 'loneliness' when 'spiritual well-being' is high. To be specific, it may be inferred that in case of high 'spiritual well-being' the 'life satisfaction' will vary, irrespective of the levels of 'loneliness'. Hence, 'spiritual well-being' appears to be a conditional variable.

Table 5.9 displays partial results of re-examination of the bivariate association between 'loneliness' and 'life satisfaction' controlling for 'social supports' as a third variable:

Table 5.9

Loneliness and Life Satisfaction (Controlling for Social Support)

Social Support			*Life Satisfaction*			
			High	*Medium*	*Low*	*Total*
Low	Loneliness	Low	2 (25.0)	12 (40.0)	9 (22.0)	23 (29.1)
		Medium	5 (62.5)	14 (46.7)	21 (51.2)	40 (50.6)
		High	1 (12.5)	4 (13.3)	11 (26.8)	16 (20.3)
		Total	8 (100.0)	30 (100.0)	41 (100.0)	79 (100.0)
	χ^2 = 4.131	df = 4	p = .389 (not significant)			
Medium	Loneliness	Low	8 (32.0)	29 (38.7)	5 (13.2)	42 (30.4)
		Medium	15 (60.0)	33 (44.0)	12 (31.6)	60 (43.5)
		High	2 (8.0)	13 (17.3)	21 (55.3)	36 (26.1)
		Total	25 (100.0)	75 (100.0)	38 (100.0)	138 (100.0)
	χ^2 = 25.967	df = 4	p = .000 (significant)			
High	Loneliness	Low	8 (29.6)	10 (27.0)	0 (0.00)	18 (26.5)
		Medium	16 (59.3)	20 (54.1)	0 (0.00)	36 (52.9)
		High	3 (11.1)	7 (18.9)	4 (100.0)	14 (20.6)
		Total	27 (100.0)	37 (100.0)	4 (100.0)	68 (100.0)
	χ^2 = 16.975	df = 4	p = .002 (significant)			

It is observed that the original bivariate association is unchanged by the third variable—'social supports'—in its two sub-categories, that is, 'medium' and 'high'. That means the original bivariate association is unaffected when 'social support' is either 'high' or 'medium'. However, it is found that the original bivariate association is affected when 'social support' is 'low'. Hence, it may be concluded that 'life satisfaction' is independent of 'loneliness' when 'social supports' is 'low'. In other words, it may be inferred that in case of low 'social supports' the 'life satisfaction' will vary, irrespective of the levels of 'loneliness'. Hence, 'social supports' appears to be a conditional variable.

Figure 5.9

Partial Effect of Social Support as a Control Variable

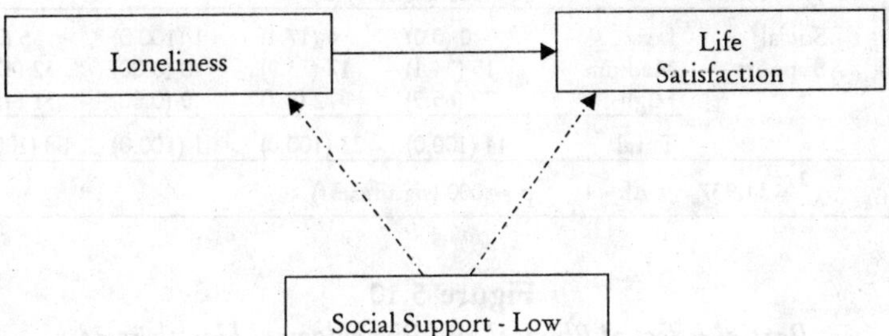

Alternatively,

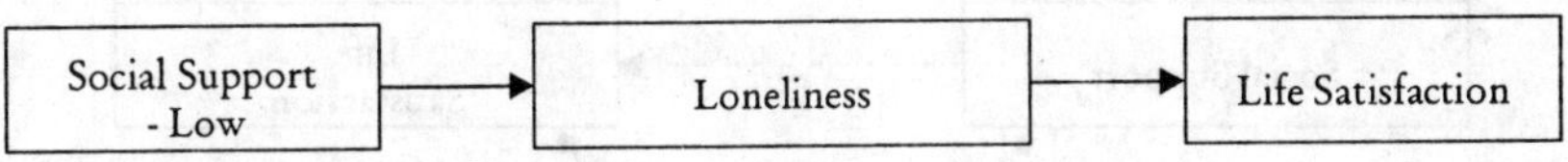

The fourth independent variable associated with 'life satisfaction' was 'social support'. To examine if the association is non-spurious, we will re-examine the original bivariate association between 'social support' and 'life satisfaction' by controlling the effect of a third variable, i.e., 'physical and psychological health'. The partial results are presented in Table 5.10.

Table 5.10
Social Support and Life Satisfaction
(Controlling for Physical & Psychological Health)

Physical & Psychological Health			*Life Satisfaction*			
			High	*Medium*	*Low*	*Total*
High	Social Support	Low	3 (30.0)	17 (20.6)	14 (37.8)	34 (30.9)
		Medium	6 (60.0)	33 (52.4)	19 (51.4)	58 (52.7)
		High	1 (10.0)	13 (27.0)	4 (10.8)	18 (16.4)
		Total	10 (100.0)	63 (100.0)	37 (100.0)	110 (100.0)
	$\chi^2 = 2.653$	df = 4	p = .617 (not significant)			
Medium	Social Support	Low	1 (3.4)	16 (28.6)	12 (54.5)	29 (27.1)
		Medium	17 (58.6)	25 (44.6)	6 (27.3)	48 (44.9)
		High	11 (37.9)	15 (26.8)	4 (18.2)	30 (28.0)
		Total	29 (100.0)	56 (100.0)	22 (100.0)	107 (100.0)
	$\chi^2 = 16.692$	df = 4	p = .002 (significant)			
Low	Social Support	Low	0 (0.0)	4 (17.4)	1 (100.0)	5 (7.4)
		Medium	15 (34.1)	17 (73.9)	0 (0.00)	32 (47.1)
		High	29 (65.9)	2 (8.7)	0 (0.00)	31 (45.6)
		Total	44 (100.0)	23 (100.0)	1 (100.0)	68 (100.0)
	$\chi^2 = 34.937$	df = 4	p = .000 (significant)			

Figure 5.10
Partial Effect of Physical and Psychological Health as a Control Variable

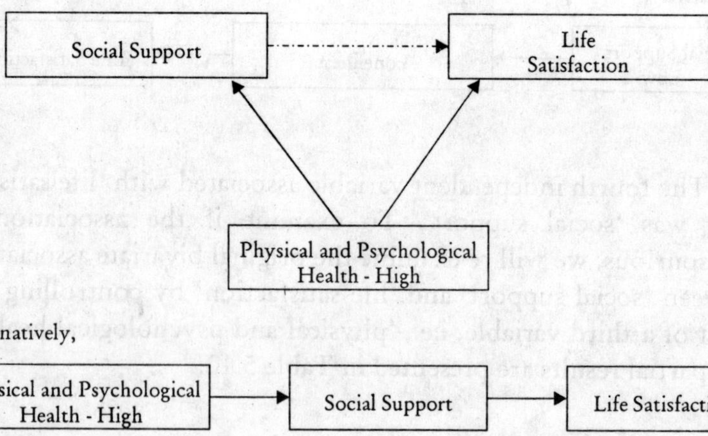

Alternatively,

The analysis of data shows that the original bivariate association is unchanged by the third variable—'physical and psychological health'—in its two sub-categories, that is, 'medium' and 'low'. In other words, we can say that the original bivariate association is unaffected when physical and psychological health is either 'low' or 'medium'. However, it is found that the original bivariate association is affected when 'physical and psychological health' is 'high'. Therefore, it may be concluded that life satisfaction is independent of 'social support' when 'physical and psychological health' is 'high'. To be specific, it may be inferred that in case of 'high' 'physical and psychological health' the 'life satisfaction' will vary irrespective of the levels of 'social support'. Therefore, the bivariate association between 'social support' and 'life satisfaction' is conditional.

Now, we will re-examine the bivariate association between 'social support' and life satisfaction controlling for 'loneliness' as a third variable. Table 5.11 displays partial results.

Table 5.11

Social Support and Life Satisfaction (Controlling for Loneliness)

Loneliness			*Life Satisfaction*			
			High	*Medium*	*Low*	*Total*
Low	Social Support	Low	2 (11.1)	12 (23.5)	9 (64.3)	23 (27.7)
		Medium	8 (44.4)	29 (56.9)	5 (35.7)	42 (50.6)
		High	8 (44.4)	10 (19.6)	0 (0.00)	18 (21.7)
		Total	18 (100.0)	51 (100.0)	14 (100.0)	83 (100.0)
	$\chi^2 = 17.450$	df = 4	p = .002 (significant)			
Medium	Social Support	Low	5 (13.9)	14 (20.9)	21 (63.6)	40 (29.4)
		Medium	15 (41.7)	33 (49.3)	12 (36.4)	60 (44.1)
		High	16 (44.4)	20 (29.9)	0 (0.00)	36 (26.5)
		Total	36 (100.0)	67 (100.0)	33 (100.0)	136 (100.0)
	$\chi^2 = 32.061$	df = 4	p = .000 (significant)			
High	Social Support	Low	1 (16.7)	4 (16.7)	11 (30.6)	16 (24.2)
		Medium	2 (33.3)	13 (54.2)	21 (58.3)	36 (54.5)
		High	3 (50.0)	7 (29.2)	4 (11.1)	14 (21.2)
		Total	6 (100.0)	24 (100.0)	36 (100.0)	66 (100.0)
	$\chi^2 = 6.684$	df = 4	p = .154 (not significant)			

Figure 5.11

Partial Effect of Loneliness as a Control Variable

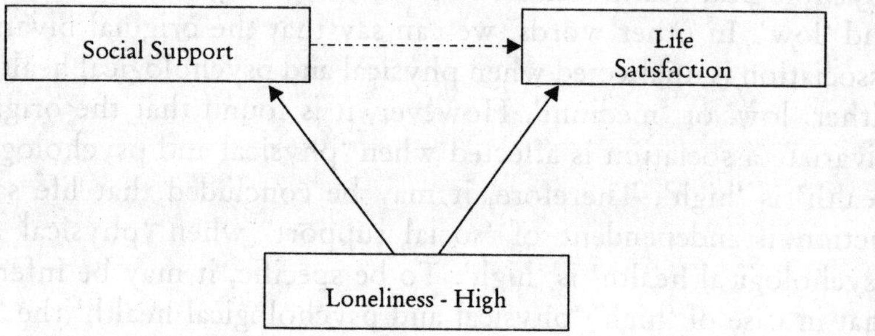

Alternatively,

It is evident from the analysis that the original bivariate association is unchanged by the third variable—'loneliness'—in its first two sub-categories, that is, 'low' and 'medium'. That means it can be inferred that the original bivariate association is unchanged when loneliness is either 'low' or 'medium'. However, it is found that the original bivariate association is changed when loneliness is 'high'. Therefore, it may be concluded that 'life satisfaction' is independent of 'social support' when 'loneliness' is 'high'. Thus, the association between 'social support' and 'life satisfaction' is conditional in case of 'high loneliness'.

Let us re-examine the bivariate associations between 'social support' (independent variable) and 'life satisfaction' (dependent variable) controlling the effect of 'spiritual well-being' (a third variable as control variable). The results of cross-tabulation of data are presented in Table 5.12.

In Table 5.12, it is observed that the original bivariate association remains unaffected by the third variable—'spiritual well-being'. In the total sample as well as in each sub-group of 'social support' the proportion of 'life satisfaction' is unchanged. The result shows that the original bivariate association between the two variables is not accounted for by the control variable—

Table 5.12

Social Support and Life Satisfaction (Controlling for Spiritual Well-Being)

Spiritual Well-being			*Life Satisfaction*			
			High	*Medium*	*Low*	*Total*
Low	Social Support	Low	0 (0.00)	7 (20.6)	18(50.0)	25 (33.8)
		Medium	1 (25.0)	13 (38.2)	17(47.2)	31 (41.9)
		High	3 (75.0)	14 (41.2)	1 (2.8)	18 (24.3)
		Total	4 (100.0)	34 (100.0)	36 (100.0)	74 (100.0)
	χ^2 = 21.595	df = 4	p = .000 (significant)			
Medium	Social Support	Low	4 (11.1)	17 (23.9)	20 (50.0)	41 (27.9)
		Medium	19 (52.8)	39 (54.9)	19 (47.5)	77 (52.4)
		High	13 (36.1)	15 (21.1)	1 (2.5)	29 (19.7)
		Total	36 (100.0)	71 (100.0)	40 (100.0)	147(100.0)
	χ^2 = 22.298	df = 4	p = .000 (significant)			
High	Social Support	Low	4 (20.0)	6 (16.2)	3 (42.9)	13 (20.3)
		Medium	5 (25.0)	23 (62.2)	2 (28.6)	30 (46.9)
		High	11 (55.0)	8 (21.6)	2 (28.6)	21 (32.8)
		Total	20(100.0)	37 (100.0)	7 (100.0)	64 (100.0)
	χ^2 = 10.896	df = 4	p = .028 (significant)			

'spiritual well-being'. Thus, it may be concluded that 'spiritual well-being' has no effect on the association between 'social support' (independent variable) and 'life satisfaction'. In other words, we can infer that the association between 'social support' and 'life satisfaction' (dependent variable) is non-spurious. The results of the analysis can be diagrammatically shown in Figure 5.12.

Review of trivariate analysis helps us to identify non-spurious and spurious relationships between the variables. It also helps the researcher to identify conditional variables, antecedent and intervening variables.

Controlling the effect of a third variable on the bivariate relationship by cross-tabulation or partial table method is quite common in the empirical research. However, the method has a serious drawback that limits its use when the number of cases is relatively small. The partial cross-tabulation involves sub-division

Figure 5.12
Non-Spurious Association between Independent and Dependent Variable

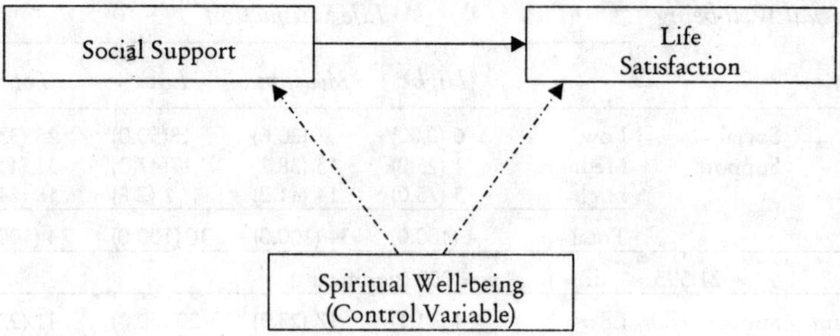

of the sample into gradually smaller sub-groups. This reduces the size of cell frequency, thus its reliability and validity is questionable.

Partial Correlation as a Method of Control

An alternative method of control is the partial correlation. This is a mathematical process of adjustment of the bivariate correlation, deemed to nullify the effect of third variable (control variable) on the independent and dependent variables. The formula for calculation of the partial correlation co-efficient is given below:

$$\Upsilon_{12.3} = \frac{\Upsilon_{12} - (\Upsilon_{1.3})(\Upsilon_{.23})}{\sqrt{(1-\Upsilon_{13})^2}\sqrt{(1-\Upsilon_{2.3})^2}}$$

Where
X_1 = independent variable
X_2 = dependent variable
X_3 = control variable

Let us suppose that we have found that there is strong correlation between 'awareness' and 'wage differential' (Υc.70). The researcher introduces third variable experience (control) as he/she has found that this variable is also correlated with wage differential (Υc.50) and 'awareness' (Υ=.40). As such he/she wants to know the correlation' with the effect of 'experience' removed.

Thus, we have:

X_1 = Awareness (independent variable)
X_2 = Wage differential (independent variable)
X_3 = Experience (control variable)

We also have:

$\Upsilon_{1.2}$ (correlation co-efficient between X_1 and X_2) = .70
$\Upsilon_{1.3}$ (correlation co-efficient between X_1 and X_3) = .40
$\Upsilon_{2.3}$ (correlation co-efficient between X_2 and X_3) = .50

The symbol on the right hand side of the decimal point indicates the variable to be controlled. Thus, $\Upsilon_{12.3}$ would mean correlation co-efficient between variable 1 and variable 2 after controlling the effects of variable 3. In the present example, it would mean the correlation between 'awareness' and 'wage differential' after, nullifying the effect of 'experience'. A partial correlation with one control is referred as a first order partial correlation to distinguish it from a bivariate correlation often known as a zero-order correlation.

The partial correlation for wage differential and awareness can now be calculated as follows:

$$\Upsilon_{12.3} = \frac{.70-(.40)\,(.50)}{\sqrt{1-(.40)^2}\,\sqrt{1-(.50)^2}}$$

$$= \frac{.70-.20}{\sqrt{1-.16}\sqrt{1-.25}}$$

$$= \frac{.50}{\sqrt{.84}\sqrt{.75}}$$

$$= \frac{.50}{.92\times.87}$$

$$= \frac{.50}{.80} = .625$$

Thus, we can see that the original relationship (Υ = . 70) has been reduced to .625 showing the effect of the third variable. Though there is decrease in strength of relationship but still enough. The square of the co-efficient of partial correlation reflects the proportion of variation left unexplained by the control variable. Thus, about 39 per cent [$\Upsilon_2 = (.625)^2 = .39$] is explained by 'awareness' after removing the effect of 'experience'.

Multivariate Analysis

So far, we have discussed the relation between two variables where one independent variable is to determine the dependent variable in question. In rarity, particularly in social sciences, however, there is hardly any situation where one independent variable determines the dependent variable. Often, we have situations where a set of independent variable is associated with dependent variable. In other words, more often, several independent variables contribute to the prediction of the dependent variable. Multiple regression is commonly used to estimate the effect of multiple independent variables. (Readers are advised to refer the book of Hubert M. Blalock, listed under *Further Readings* for procedure to compute multiple regression).

In case a bivariate association is confirmed, the researcher may proceed to a more advanced stage of analysis and elaborate the bivariate association. Elaboration usually involves the introduction of other variables to determine the links between the independent and dependent variables or the specification of the conditions under which the association takes place (Nachmias and Nachmias, 1981).

If we examine the inferences drawn above, we find that the third variables 'spiritual well-being' and 'loneliness' provide links between physical and psychological health and life satisfaction. The third variable is referred as intervening/antecedent variable. In third example when 'loneliness' was introduced as third variable between physical and psychological health and life satisfaction, it was found that the original bivariate association was partially effected. That is the bivariate association disappeared only in the case of 'high' loneliness. In this case, the original bivariate association was pronounced under certain conditions that are among elderly persons who had 'high' loneliness. The third variable, in this case, is known as conditional variable.

In order to demonstrate data analysis in general and multivariate analysis in particular, we have appended an article entitled "Some Socio-Economic Correlates of Male-Female Wage

Differential", published in a research journal towards the end of this chapter. This article also demonstrates the whole research process.

Important Terms for Review

- Introduction
- Cross-tabulation as a Method of Control
- Partial Correlation as a Method of Control
- Elaboration
- Multivariate Analysis

Further Readings

Bailey, Kenneth D., *Methods of Social Research*, London: The Free Press, 1978.

Baker, L. Therese, *Doing Social Research,* New York: McGraw Hill, 1988.

Blalock, Hubert M., *Social Statistics*, New York: McGraw Hill, 1972.

Doby, J.T. et. al., *An Introduction to Social Research,* London: Harrisburg Stackpole Co., 1953.

Kerlinger, Fred R., *Foundations of Behavioural Research,* Delhi: Surjeet Publications, 1964.

Lal Das, D.K., *Practice of Social Research: Social Work Perspective*, Jaipur: Rawat Publications, 2000.

Monete, Duane R. et. al., *Applied Social Research: Tool for the Human Services,* Chicago: Holt, 1986.

Nachmias, D. and Nachmias, C., *Research Methods in the Social Sciences*, New York: St. Martins Press, 1981.

Sellitz. G. et. al., *Research Methods in Social Relations,* New York: Holt, Rinehart and Winston (3rd edition), 1973.

Sjoberg, G. and Nett, B., *A Methodology of Social Research,* New York: Harper & Row, 1968.

Wilkinson, T.S. and Bhandarkar, P.L., *Methodology and Techniques of Social Research*, Bombay: Himalaya, 1977.

Review Questions

1. Discuss the process of examining the effect of third variable on the bivariate relationship.
2. Explain the methods of control.
3. What is trivariate analysis?
4. Discuss the need of multivariate analysis in social research.

SOME SOCIO-ECONOMIC CORRELATES OF MALE-FEMALE WAGE DIFFERENTIAL

D.K. Lal Das

The principle of "equal pay for equal work" has been accepted all over the world. The Indian Constitution categorically asserts equal pay for equal work, and the Indian Government reinforces this commitment with a legislative measure that provides for the payment of equal remuneration to men and women workers. Nonetheless, the study reveals that the wage differential on the ground of sex exists in some areas of employment. Wage differentials were found to be significantly related to the level of awareness, work experience and education of the employees.

Introduction

It has been accepted all over the world that women workers should be provided with some special protection and facilities. This opinion at the world level has crystallised in the form of Conventions of the International Labour Organisation[1] and the United Nations' Declaration on the Elimination of Discrimination against Women[2].

In India, the Constitution promises equality to all citizens and provides special protection for the realisation of equality for women. Article 39(d), specifically, envisages that the State shall see that there is equal pay for equal work, for both men and women. This principle of "equal pay for equal work" was translated into practice by the enactment of the Equal Remuneration Act, 1976 (here after referred to as 'the Act'). The Act aims to provide for the payment of equal remuneration for the same work or work of similar nature, to men and women workers and for the prevention of discrimination on the ground of sex against women, in the matter of employment.

In spite of all these legal enactments disparities still persist between the wages of male and female employees working on the same job or job of a similar nature, and discrimination on the basis of sex in the matter of employment also exists. It is rather disappointing to find that the effectiveness of this well-intentioned legislation has been extremely limited.

What causes the observed wage differentials, on the basis of sex is controversial. However, the following are a few propositions, often quoted by research scholars as causes for discrimination against women at work place:

(a) Young women are too likely to withdraw from the labour force for marriage and child bearing.
(b) Men have a greater responsibility than women do for supporting a family, and so have a greater right to a job.
(c) Women, who re-enter the labour force later in life, lack the sustained work experience that most men have.
(d) Women always earn, not to support the family, but to supplement the family income and, as such, women could be available for work even below 'the cost of living'.
(e) Women avoid confrontation for the fear of losing their jobs and suffer silently.

Thus, the areas that call for investigation are:

(a) The role of labour administration (law enforcement machinery) with regard to implementation of the Act, could be one of the important area of study, in the sense that it is the authority that can translate the provisions of the Act into actual practice.
(b) Non-compliance of the statutory provisions by the employers, which may account for much of the wage differential, requires proper investigation. There may be cases, where provisions of the Act may not be observed in their true sense. This may result in a wide gap between what the law provides for and the actual practice.
(c) Often, due to inappropriate social circumstances, state of economic development, their ignorance and the fear of losing their jobs, women accept whatever terms and conditions of employment are offered to them. As such, the existing wage disparities and discrimination could be attributed to the socio-economic characteristics of female employees (here after referred to as SECE).

This paper deals only with data relating to the third interface.

The aim of the present study was to investigate the disparities in wages/salary of male and female employees for work of similar nature, and to identify the important SECE correlates of wage differential. Specifically, the following objectives were sought to be achieved through a multivariate analysis of data:

(a) What is the relationship between the observed wage differential and SECE variables?
(b) Which SECE correlate or set of SECE correlates is most critical in explaining variation in observed wage differential?
(c) What is the individual contribution of each correlate in influencing observed wage differential?

Some Research Findings

There have been quite a few micro-studies (Gambhir, 1979; Khanna and Mathew, 1979; Patel, 1982), that show that the disparities in wages/salary of male and female employees for work of similar nature, is part of the general discrimination against women at the work place. Particularly, in unorganised sector, women are invariably paid much less than the males.

According to the studies conducted by Pais (1980), Labour Bureau (1979), Occupational Wages Surveys (1963), with respect of select industries as well as employment, the adoption of the principle of "equal pay for equal work" has discouraged employers from employing women workers profitably. Most probably, one of the reasons for employing women workers was that it was cheaper.

What is the relationship between wage differential and regional development? This aspect was studied by the Programme Evaluation Organisation of the Planning Commission (1961). The results show that inter-state variations are quite significant.

Research Methodology

Estimation of Wage Differential (Dependent Variable)

Observed wage differential is defined operationally as the difference between the total monthly incomes (before deductions) of a male and a female employee, working on the same job or job of a similar nature.

Study Area and Sampling

The study was confined to the three regions of the State of Andhra Pradesh: Coastal Andhra (developed). Telangana (developing) and Rayalseema (underdeveloped). The sampling frame included all the 52 employments specified in the list of employment under the Act.

A major portion of the 52 employments specified under the Act includes industrial establishments. Therefore, a large portion of the sample covers industrial workers. Apart from industries, the other establishments included in the sample are hospitals, educational institutions, welfare services, air transport, and sanitary services, banks, hotels, agriculture and construction work.

In order to be included in the sample, an employee had to satisfy the following conditions:

(i) Male and female employees doing the same work or work of a similar nature.

(ii) Male and female employees having same designation; and

(iii) Both working in the same organisation.

Pairs of respondents (male and female), who satisfied these conditions, were selected from the different areas of employment.

Of the 139 pairs of employees that qualified, 17 respondents (both male and female) could not be contacted. Thus, the study involves interviews with 122 pairs of respondents. The size of sample selected for the study is 244.

Tools and Methods of Data Collection

Data on wages/salary and personal characteristics were collected from payroll records and employment application forms. For other SECE variables, data were collected by using a pre-tested interview schedule.

Results and Discussion

Table I presents the inequality of income between male and female employees.

Table I

Inequality of Income Between Male and Female Employees (Observed)

Workers	*Average Monthly Income*	*S.D.*	*CV*	*T*	*Average Male-Female wage differential*	*S.D.*
Male	706.16	379.67	33.765	93.321*	118.54	455.79
Female	496.87	234.19	47.133			

* df = 242, p =.001

The mean of the total monthly income for female employees was Rs. 496.87 (SD=234.19; n=122); for the male employees this mean was Rs. 706.16 (SD=379.67; n=122). These data indicate the extent of wage differential between male and female employees. The wage differential is found to be significantly different ($t=93.32$; $p<0.001$).

The differentials are large in economic terms. For example, the Rs. 118.54 differential in monthly wages/salary, between male and female employees, implies an annual male-female wage differential of Rs. 1422.48.

Observed wage differential is defined operationally, as the difference between the total monthly income of a male and a female employee working on the same job. Ideally, the sample of female employees should have been matched with male employees for their work experience, level of education, level of skills, age, and for year of appointment (and many other variables), to determine the true wage differential. This was clearly impossible, given the occupational heterogeneity of the sample. Instead, under the assumption that sex discrimination was not operative for men, multiple regression were obtained for the male sample to determine the optimal weighing of selected variables in predicting wages. The results of these multiple regression are presented in Table 2.

Table 2

Beta Weights of Selected Variables Obtained from the Sample of Male Employees

S. No.	Variables	Beta Weights
1.	COLL	336.224
2.	DEVING	203.700
3.	TOEXP	17.651
4.	ILL	-121.574
5.	UNDEV	59.772
6.	AGE	1.494

Multiple R^2 = 0.3647

Multiple R = 0.60398

Percentage Variation Explained = 36.47914

Constant = 136.14583

On the basis of the weights provided by the multiple regression computed on the sample of male employees, expected wages/salary were computed for the sample of female employees. Ratios of wage differential to expected and observed values were then computed. The results are presented in Table 3.

Table 3

Ratios of Wage Differential to Expected and Observed Values

	Mean	*Standard Deviation*	*t-Value*	*Wage Differential (= Observed - Expected)*	*Ratio of Discrepancy to Expected Value**	*Ratio of Discrepancy to Observed Value***
Observed Value	496.86	234.1930	40.784	-89.7658	-15.30191	-18.06642
Expected Value	586.63	353.6689		(SD=503.5495)		

$$* = \frac{\text{Observed Value - Expected Value}}{\text{Expected Value}} \times 100$$

$$** = \frac{\text{Observed Value - Expected Value}}{\text{Observed Value}} \times 100$$

Negative sign affixed to the value indicates that the female worker received fewer wages than would be expected/observed.

The mean wage differential (wage differential = observed wage - expected wage) for female employees was Rs. 89.77 (SD=Rs. 503.55; n=122); for male employees this mean was Rs. 285.00 (SD=Rs. 303.85; n=122). Sex differences in wage differentials, for female and male employees, indicate the extent to which the principle of wage fixation was differentially applied to female employees and to male employees. The differentials between the wages/salary of female employees 'should' have received, based on the multiple regression equation, and the wages/salary they 'in fact' received, was significantly different from the comparable differentials for the male employees ($t=75.890$; $p<0.001$).

By dividing the mean wage differential (female) by their mean expected wages/salary, it was possible to calculate the percentage of a male employee's estimated wage/salary that an equally qualified female employee would receive. According to this estimate, an equally qualified female employee would receive 15.30 per cent less than a comparable male employee's income.

Similarly, by dividing the mean wage differential (female) by their mean observed wages/salary, it was possible to calculate the percentage of her present wages/salary that each female employee 'lost' by virtue of being a woman. The average figure that resulted was 18.07 per cent. In other words, the average female employee should have received 18.07 per cent more than her current wages/salary, to make her wages/salary equivalent to a man with the same scores on the selected variables.

In order to study the correlates of wage differentials, a set of 10 variables were considered. Table 4 presents the intercorrelation matrix for the variables.

It may be inferred from Table 4, that three independent variables are not significantly correlated to each other, which means that the effect of these independent variables on the wage differential (dependent variable) is likely to be its individual effect and is not influenced by other independent variables. However, seven independent variables (marked with asterisk) have been found to be significantly correlated with the dependent variable. The correlation is negative in nature, except in the case of 'illiterate'. Since there is only zero-order correlation, it is difficult to determine the exact contribution of each correlate in explaining variations in wage differential. To quantify the contribution of the independent variables, the technique of regression analysis was applied.

Table 4

Intercorrelation Matrix for the Selected Variables

Variable No.	X1	X2	X3	X4	X5	X6	X7	X8	X9	X10	X11
X1	1.000	0.523	0.260	-0.270	-0.033	-0.298	-0.059	-0.034	-0.317	0.024	0.025
X2	0.523	1.000	-0.031	-0.133	0.070	0.092	-0.195	0.227	-0.012	0.262	-.283**
X3	0.260	0.031	1.000	-0.666	0.196	-0.318	-0.070	0.105	-0.357	-0.040	0.320**
X4	-0.270	-0.133	-0.666	1.000	-0.162	0.212	0.027	-0.138	0.319	0.036	-0.336**
X5	-0.033	0.070	0.196	-0.162	1.000	-0.121	0.060	-0.147	-0.232	-0.036	-0.046
X6	-0.298	0.092	-0.318	0.212	-0.121	1.000	-0.134	0.324	0.848	0.148	-0.260**
X7	-0.059	-0.195	-0.070	0.027	0.060	-0.134	1.000	-0.455	-0.153	-0.473	0.187*
X8	-0.034	0.227	0.105	-0.138	-0.147	0.324	-0.455	1.000	0.198	0.530	-0.142
X9	-0.317	-0.012	-0.357	0.819	-0.232	0.848	-0.153	0.198	1.000	0.210	-0.337**
X10	0.051	0.262	-0.040	0.036	-0.036	0.148	-0.473	0.530	0.210	1.000	-0.258**
X11	0.025	-0.283	0.320	-0.330	-0.046	-0.260	0.186	-0.142	-0.337	-0.258	1.000

'R' Significant at 0.05 = 0.17613
R Significant at 0.01 – 0.22892
* Significant at 0.05 level
** Significant at 0.01 level

In all, ten variables were included in the regression analysis. One variable did not have any additional impact on the dependent variable beyond that which the first nine variables had. In other words, one variable turned out to be insignificant as far as wage differential is concerned. The regression co-efficient, given in Table 5, explains the relative importance of each variable. The negative co-efficient of the six variables indicate that increase in the value of these variables is likely to reduce the score measuring the dependent variable. Say, for example, the increase of the level of awareness of the Act by one unit, is likely to subtract 0.44 units in the score determining the wage differential.

Table 5

Regression Analysis of Independent Variables

Dependent Variable: Wage Differential (Observed)
Mean: 188.54
Standard Deviation: 455.79

Variable No.	*Explanatory Variables*	*Standardised Beta Co-efficient*	*Regression Co-efficient (b)*	*Standard Error (b)*	*t-Values*
X9	AWAR	-0.43969	-485.12908	184.85340	2.62440*
X2	TOEXP	-0.29998	-30.89918	10.53238	2.93373*
X4	COLL	-0.22218	-240.82327	117.08562	2.05681*
X5	MARR	-0.17932	-185.80535	89.29196	2.08087*
X10	OBS	-0.04076	-20.22793	51.18891	0.39516
X6	ATUNEQ	0.26494	357.73318	228.88216	1.56296
X3	ILL	0.15119	140.57127	103.37046	1.35988
X8	UNDEV	-0.16709	-154.85873	124.48085	1.24404
X1	AGE	0.01892	1.14754	6.36663	0.18024

Multiple R^2 = 0.33033
Multiple R = 0.57474
Percentage Variation Explained = 33.03299
Constant = 2143.81995
*Significant at .05 level.

The level of awareness about the Act, was found to be the most important correlate that affected the wage differential. In addition to this, work experience and level of education was also found to be important correlates. The combination of these three correlates was identified as the 'best equation' on the basis of the following criteria:

(a) The combination should explain maximum variation in the wage differential.

(b) The contribution of each correlate in the equation should be negative.
(c) The contribution of each correlate should be statistically significant at the 5 per cent level.

The 'best equation' can be expressed in the following regression form **3

$$Y = \text{Const.} + b1\ X1 + b2\ X2 + b3\ X3$$

where Y is wage differential, b1, b2 and b3 are regression co-efficients and X1, X2 and X3 are correlates.

The equation can be evaluated by using the regression co-efficients of correlates:

Wage Differential = 2143.820 – 485.129 (AWAR) – 30.899 TOEXP – 2440.823 COLL.

'Awareness', 'total experience', and 'college education', the three correlates included in the best equation, were found to be the most critical correlates of wage differentials. Together, these three correlates account for 31 per cent variations in the wage differential. The break-up of this explanatory power, in terms of individual contribution of each correlate, is shown in Table 6.

Table 6

Individual Contribution of Each Correlate

Variable No.	*Name of the Correlate*	*Zero-Order Correlation with Wage Differential Yxy*	*Ist -Order Partial Correlation with Wage Differential*	*Regression Co-efficient (b)*	*Standardised Beta Co-efficient (b)*	*Individual Contribution B.Yxy*
X13	AWAR	-0.337**	-0.242**	-485.129**	-0.440**	0.148
X2	TOEXP	-0.283**	-0.268**	-30.899**	-0.300**	0.085
X5	COLL	-0.330**	-0.192**	-240.823	-0.222**	0.073
					Total	0.306

*p<.05 **p< 01

A look at Table 7 will show that nearly 93 per cent of the respondents are not even aware of the existence of the Act. This clearly indicates that the basic *sine qua non* of a law, i.e., strong communication network, is missing in the present implementation of the scheme and, therefore, needs to be carefully articulated. Surprisingly, even till date, no suitable method has been evolved to communicate the enacted law to the people whom they concern. It is, perhaps, one of the reasons why the disparities on the ground of sex still persist, and discrimination on the basis of sex in the matter of employment exists.

Table 7

Correlates of Wage Differential

SECE	*Wage Differential*			*Total*	*X²*	*Degree of Freedom*	*Probability*
	Low	*Med.*	*High*				
1. Aware of the Act							
Yes	4 (50)	3 (37.5)	1 (12.5)	8 (100)	4.463	2	P 0.02
No	33(20.2)	47(41.2)	44(38.6)	114(100)			
Total	37	50	45	122			
2. Total Work Experience (in years)							
1-4	11(25.6)	17(39.5)	15(34.9)	43(100)			
5-6	10(19.6)	18(35.3)	23(45.1)	51(100)	3.943	4	P 0.05
10-22	6(21.4)	15(53.6)	7(25.0)	28(1000			
Total	27	50	45	122			
3. Level of Education							
Illiterate	8(9.4)	39(45.9)	38(44.7)	85(100)			
Upto Matric	5(50.0)	3(30.0)	2(20.0)	10(100)	26.793	4	P 0.001
Above Matric	14(51.8)	8(29.6)	5(18.5)	27(100)			
Total	27	50	45	122			

Table 8

Mean Values for Indicator of "Intermittency"

Sex	*Mean Value of Variable*	
	Previous jobs held	*Gap between jobs (in years)*
Male	1.35	2.15
Female	2.45	3.00

As can be seen from Table 8, the women in our sample differ from the men with respect to work experience, number of jobs held prior to the present job, and the gap between jobs. First, they are, on an average, less experienced than men. Second, women have held fewer jobs than have men, despite their greater intermittency. It could be attributed to the withdrawal of women employees from the labour force for marriage and child-bearing. This analysis, therefore, reinforces the significance of work experience as a correlate of wage differential. Though the literacy and the education of women have been of special concern to Indian planners and social reformers, the literacy among females (24.88%, according to 1981 census) lags far behind literacy among males (46.74%). These data for female and male employees (respondents), under the study, are 45.6 per cent and 71.9 per cent (Table 7), respectively. Thus, it appears that women have to go a long way, in order to achieve an equal position to men, with respect to literacy. This could be another reason, why women employees continue to be oppressed and exploited at their place of work. How will they benefit from a legislation, if they do not know how to make use of it? An examination of Table 8 reveals that wage differentials are significantly low ($X^2 = 26.793$, d.f. = 4, $p<0.001$) for respondents having a higher level of education.

Conclusion

Considering the three SECE correlates together, it may be conclusively said that strategies for reducing wage differentials, by merely enacting laws, will not work very well. Such strategies seldom involve direct efforts at making the employees aware of their rights and responsibilities. Thus, direct efforts to reduce the wage differential, would have to be focused on the education of the employees about the provisions of the Act, because education is essential for increasing their awareness of their rights and responsibilities.

Notes

1. The ILO has evolved two such conventions on the subject: (a) Equal Remuneration, 1951, (Convention-100) prescribes equal remuneration for men and women for work of equal value; and (b) Discrimination Convention (Employment and Occupation), 1958, (Convention-111), refers to any distinction, exclusion or preference made on the basis of race, colour, sex, religion or social origin which has the effect to nullifying or impairing equality of opportunity or treatment in employment or occupation.
2. In 1967, the General Assembly of the United Nations unanimously adopted a "Declaration on the Elimination of Discrimination Against Women" which guarantees a broad range of rights to equality in education, work and marriage.
3. Justification for the use of linear probability model can be found in Ladd (1966) and Maddala (1983).

References

Gambhir, G.D. 1979 "Labour in Small Scale Industries", Nagpur University: Diss.

Khanna, K.P. and Mathew, M. 1979 "Women Workers in Unorganised Sector of Coir Industries in India", I.C.S.S.R. Research Abstract.

Labour Bureau 1979 *A Study of Working and Living Condition in Industry*, New Delhi: Ministry of Labour.

Ladd, G. 1966 "Linear Probability Functions and Discriminant Functions", *Econometrics* Vol. 34: 873-85.

Maddaka, G.S. 1983 *Limited Dependent and Qualitative Variables in Econometrics*, Cambridge: Cambridge University Press.

Pais, H. 1980 "Employment of Women in India", *Indian Labour Journal*, April.

Patel, Vibhuti 1982 "Women and Work" (Mimeographed), SNDT Women's University.

II

Designs of Social Research

6

Dimensions of Research Designs

A research design is the logical and systematic planning and directing the research. The design results from translating a general scientific model into varied research problems. But, in practice, in most of the cases, it is just a plan of study, generally vague and tentative. It undergoes many changes and modifications as the study progresses and insights into it deepen. As Suchman (1954: 254) rightly puts it: "there is no such thing as a single or 'correct' design... Research design represents a compromise dictated by the many practical considerations that go into social research. As a result, every researcher ends up with a research design of his own having his own methodological strategies." A research design, as Stouffer (1962: 131) states it, "is not a highly specific plan to be followed without deviations, but rather a series of guide posts to keep one headed in the right direction". In other words, a research design is a tentative strategy of research process, which is most likely to be modified by new aspects, new conditions and new interrelations between variables, as it progresses.

Research design is a detailed plan outlining how the research will be carried out. It may be either informal if it is only for researcher's own use, or formal when it is a part of a grant proposal. Research design addresses itself to certain questions about the research project such as:

- What is the problem under study?
- What is major research question?
- What is the area of the study (the population)?
- How many people will be studied?

- How these people will be selected?
- What methods and techniques will be used to collect data from them?
- What methods and techniques will be used to analyze data?
- What statistical methods and techniques will be used to draw inferences?

Thus, the details about these issues constitute a research design. To be more specific, a research design includes the details about the problem, objectives, research questions, area of study (population), sampling plan, and method and techniques of data collection and analysis. In fact, the research design spells out in considerable detail what occur in the following steps of the research process. It also reflects the dimensions of research designs. Keeping in view the various dimensions, research designs can be organized into three groups: (1) research designs indicating the purpose of doing research, (2) research designs indicating its intended use, and (3) research designs indicating the effects of time.

Research Designs by Purpose of a Study

Research designs are closely linked with the purpose/objectives of a research study/problem (Sellitz et. al., 1959: 50). The purposes of social research may be clubbed into three groups based on what the researcher is trying to accomplish—explore a new topic, describe a social phenomenon, or explain why something occurs. Studies may have a combination of purposes, e.g., a study may aim at exploring a new topic as well as describing a social phenomenon. However, one purpose is usually dominant. It is very common that many researchers label their research design as 'exploratory research design' or 'descriptive research design'.

Exploratory Research Designs

The purpose of exploratory studies is to formulate a problem for a more precise investigation or to develop hypotheses. However, an exploratory study can also be conducted to enhance the familiarity of researcher with the phenomena, he/she wishes to study some time later in a more scientific way.

For instance, if a researcher wanted to study social interaction patterns of AIDS/HIV patients but knew little or nothing about the phenomenon, an exploratory research would be appropriate. A preliminary interview with the relatives of AIDS/HIV patients would enable the researcher to develop a specific study design. Exploratory studies, therefore, help researchers to acquaint themselves with the characteristics of their research problem.

Descriptive Research Designs

Descriptive studies, as the name suggests, describe as accurately as possible the characteristics of a group of people or a community. A researcher, who is interested in studying people of a community, their age and sex composition, caste-wise distribution, affiliation to religion, level of education, occupational status, etc., designs his study as descriptive study. Another researcher may formulate a descriptive design of study to know the proportion of people in a particular population favouring dowry or feeling that child labour should be banned. Still others may be concerned with specific prediction. For example, what percentage of population would enter voter's list in the next census operations? What will be the size of the handicapped population, which will need financial assistance in the next five-year plan? And so on.

Explanatory Research Designs

When we have a problem that is already known and has a description of it, we may like to know why things are the way they are. The purpose of explanatory research designs is to explain 'why'?. In explanatory research designs, the researcher goes beyond focusing on a topic or portraying it. He or she looks for causes and reasons. For example, a descriptive researcher may discover that 30 per cent of the elders are abused by their children, whereas the explanatory researcher is more interested in knowing why children abuse their elders.

Scott South and Kim Lloyd (1995) undertook an explanatory study to explain divorce rates. They examined a theory that says the chance of divorce increases when there is an ample supply of potential alternative partners with whom a married person comes into contact. In other words, a demographic factor (i.e., the availability of alternative spouses) has a negative impact on marriage stability. Data showed that a large number of recently divorced respondents had prior involvement with someone other than their spouses. The researchers explained a higher proportion of divorces by a greater opportunity for social interaction between married men and unmarried women.

Research Designs by its Intended Use

Research designs differ with its intended use. Some researchers focus on using research to assess the effectiveness of interventions, whereas, others use it to solve problems. Yet, another group of researchers may be interested in evaluating a programme to know if it was organized effectively. Impact analysis is yet another area of research, which needs a different research designs. These research designs may be grouped into three categories: (1) intervention research designs, (2) action research designs, and (3) evaluation research designs.

Intervention Research Designs

The process of improving social functioning of individuals, groups and communities involves study, assessment, intervention and evaluation. It requires use of a research design called intervention research design, commonly known as single-subject designs through which social work practitioners attempt to improve social functioning of individuals, groups, families and communities.

Intervention research designs or single subject designs are basically quasi-experimental research designs, which use time series analysis technique of social researches to the evaluation of the impact of interventions on individual cases, groups, family and community. Such designs involve repeated measure of the dependent variable before and after a particular intervention, to see if a sustained pattern of change in the dependent variable commences shortly after the onset of intervention (Rubin and Babbie, 1989). The intervention research designs have been discussed in detail in Chapter 9.

Action Research Designs

Action research establishes a link between knowledge and social action. The goal of action research is to improve conditions of research participants. It attracts researchers who hold specific perspectives. For example, most feminist research has a dual mission: to create social change by transforming gender relations and to contribute to the advancement of knowledge (Reinharz, 1992: 252). An action researcher worked together with union officials and management to redesign work schedule to prevent lay offs. There are several other examples where action research designs are employed, such as, working among illiterates to teach functional literacy and make them aware of their socio-economic conditions, and to attempt to improve them. The action research designs have been discussed in detail in Chapter 10.

Evaluation Research Designs

Evaluation researches assess the effectiveness of a programme, policy or a project. It is a systematic assessment of progress made by the implementing organizations. Evaluation researches also try to analyze the problems and difficulties arising in the effective implementation of a programme and suggests the corrective measures. In a very broad sense, the evaluation research is simply use of research methods to evaluate programmes or services and determine how effectively they are achieving their goals.

Most of the times it is descriptive in nature which fail to give reliable assessment of the effectiveness of a programme. Evaluation research designs using experimental techniques are usually most effective. Details about various types of evaluation research designs have been discussed in detail in Chapter 11.

Research Designs Indicating the Effects of Time

Another dimension of research, which has to be considered while designing the research, is the effect of time. Knowledge of time dimension helps researchers to design their research to assess the effect of time on the variables under consideration. Some studies are conducted at single fixed time which gives a snapshot view of the problem. Other studies provide a moving description that helps researchers to follow events, people or social relations over period of time. Research designs incorporating time dimension of research can be categorized into two groups: a single point in time (cross-sectional research) and multiple time points (longitudinal research).

Cross-Sectional Research Designs

In studies using cross-sectional research design a researcher collects data for his/her research at one point of time. This research design is most frequently used by social researchers because it is the simplest and least costly alternative. The most striking disadvantage of this research design is that it cannot cover social processes or change.

Longitudinal Research Designs

To describe the changes in the features of a social phenomenon longitudinal research designs are used. In this research design the phenomenon is studied at more than one time. It is usually more complex and costly than cross-sectional research designs. It is also more powerful, especially when researchers seek answers to questions about social change (Neuman, 2000: 30).

Components of Research Designs

Research design, as pointed out earlier, outlines how the research will be carried out. Thus, it addresses itself to certain key issues such as, sampling design, or observational design, statistical design and operational design.

Sampling design deals with the method of selecting the sample to be studied in a given research project. *Observational design* relates to methods and techniques of data collection, that is, whether the data will be collected through primary source or secondary source or whether the data will be collected through observation or interview methods. It also describes the tools of data collection to be used in collecting data. These two aspects of a research project have been discussed in detail in Chapter 11. *Statistical design* of a research project deals with methods and techniques of data analysis and the use of statistical procedures. A researcher may opt for bivariate, trivariate or multivariate analysis of data depending upon his/her objectives and hypotheses to be tested. The researcher is required to select appropriate statistical procedures to test his/her hypotheses and the level of measurement. This issue has already been discussed in Chapters 4 and 5. Finally, *operational design* of a research project spells out the sequence of activities and the time required to complete the various activities of the research project. In fact, the operational research design spells out in considerable detail what occurs in the different steps of the research process. A research design helps us in knowing successive stages of the research project. Because the stages are systematic and logical, there will be a logical, sequence and one after the other stages will follow. Thus, it helps us in identifying the importance of each step in the whole research project. It also includes the details about the personnel and financial requirements for executing the project. This aspect has already been discussed in Chapter 1.

Important Terms for Review

- Research Designs
- Dimensions of Research Designs
- Exploratory Research Designs
- Descriptive Research Designs
- Experimental Research Designs
- Pre-Experimental Research Designs
- Quasi-Experimental Research Designs
- Action Research Designs
- Evaluation Research Designs
- Intervention Research Designs
- Survey Research Designs
- Components of Research Designs
- Sampling Design
- Observational Design
- Statistical Design
- Operational Design

Further Readings

Abram, M., *Social Surveys and Social Action,* London: Heinemann, 1950.

Ackoff, R.L., *The Design of Social Research,* Chicago: University of Chicago Press, 1953.

Bailey, Kenneth D., *Methods of Social Research*, London: The Free Press, 1978.

Baker, L. Therese, *Doing Social Research,* New York: McGraw Hill, 1988.

Bennel, Carl et. al., *Evaluation Experiments,* New York: Academic Press, 1975.

Black, James A. and Champion, Dean J., *Methods and Issues in Social Research,* New York: John Wiley, 1976.

Campbell, D.T. and Stanley, J.C., *Experimental and Quasi Experimental Designs for Research,* Boston: Houghton Mifflin, 1963.

Chapin, F.S., *Experimental Design in Sociological Research,* New York: Harper, 1974.

Epstein, I. and Tripodi, T., *Research Techniques for Program Planning, Monitoring and Evaluation*, New York: Columbia University Program, 1974.

Festinger, L. and Katz. D. (eds.), *Research Methods in the Behavioral Sciences,* New York: The Dryden Press, 1953.

Goode, W.J. and Hat. P.K., *Methods in Social Research,* New York: McGraw Hill,1952.

House, E.R., *Evaluating with Validity*, Beverly Hills, California: Sage, 1980.

Kerlinger, Fred R., *Foundations of Behavioral Research,* Delhi: Surjeet Publications, 1964.

Kidder, Louise H., *Research Methods in Social Relations,* New York: Holt, 1981.

Kothari, L.R., *Research Methodology*, New Delhi: Vishwa Prakashan, 1985.

Lal Das, D.K., *Practice of Social Research: Social Work Perspective*, Jaipur: Rawat Publications, 2000.

Mill, J.S., *A System of Logic*, New York: Longmans, (8th edition), 1930.

Miller, D.C., *Handbook of Research Design and Social Measurement,* New York: David McKey Co., 1964.

Monette, Duane R. et. al., *Applied Social Research: Tool For the Human Services,* Chicago: Holt, 1986.

Moser, C.A. and Kalton, *Survey Methods in Social Investigation,* London: Heinemann Educational Books, 1975.

Nachmias, D. and Nachmias, C., *Research Methods in the Social Sciences*, New York: St. Martins Press, 1981.

Posova, E.J. and Carey R.G., *Programme Evaluation Methods and Case Studies,* NJ: Englewood Cliffs, Prentice Hall, 1985.

Ramachandran, P., "Social Work Research and Statistics" in *History & Philosophy of Social Work in India*, Bombay: Allied Publishers, 1968.

Rossi, P. and H. Freeman, *Evaluation: A Systematic Approach*, Beverly Hills, Sage, 1982.

Rubin, Allen and Babbie, E. *Research Methodology for Social Work*, Belmohf, California, Wadsworth, 1989.

Schneirer, M.A., *Programme Evaluation: The Organizational Context,* Beverly Hills, California, Sage, 1980.

Sellitz, G. et. al., *Research Methods in Social Relations,* New York: Holt, Rinehart and Winston (3rd edition), 1973.

Shah, V.F., *Research Design, Ahmedabad:* Rachna Prakashan,1977.

Stouffer, S.A., *Social Research to Test Ideas,* New York: Free Press of Glencoe, 1962.

Suchman, E.A., *Evaluative Research: Principles and Practice in Public Service and Social Action Programmes,* New York: Russel Sage Foundation, 1967.

Suchman, E.A., "The Principles of Research Design". In John T. Doby et. al., *An Introduction to Social Research*, New York: The Stackpole, 1953.

Weiss, Carol, *Evaluation Research,* Englewood Cliffs N.J. Prentice Hall, 1972.

Wilkinson, T.S. and Bhandarkar, P.L., *Methodology and Techniques of Social Research,* Bombay: Himalaya, 1977.

Yin, Robert K., *Case Study Research Design and Methods,* Applied Social Research Methods Series, Vol. 5, New Delhi: Sage, 1982.

Young, P.V., *Scientific Social Surveys and Research,* Englewood Cliff, N.J., Prentice Hall (4th edition), 1953.

Review Questions

1. What is a research design?
2. What is research objective? Discuss how research objective leads to research design.
3. Differentiate between exploratory and descriptive research designs.
4. Identify some hypothetical examples from your own experiences where exploratory and descriptive research designs would be appropriate.
5. Define experiment. Discuss the basic purpose of experimental research design.
6. What are the pre- and quasi-experimental research designs?
7. What is a survey research design?

8. What are the components of a research design?
9. What is a sampling research design?
10. What is an operational research design?
11. What is an observational research design?
12. What is a statistical research design?

7

Research Designs: Experiments

Experimental researches are designed for testing causal relationships. A causal relationship refers to relationships between two variables where one variable (characteristic or occurrence) 'X' determines another variable (characteristic or occurrence) 'Y'. For example, if a researcher wishes to test a causal relationships that punishments (X) cause low self-esteem (Y) by comparing a group of students who have been exposed to punishments (X) with one that has not been exposed, he/she has to measure the two groups with respect of 'Y', either during or after exposure to 'X'.

Before discussing about the various types of experimental studies used for testing the causal relationship, it is essential to know about the concept of causality.

In the words of J.S. Mill (1930), "a cause which is itself a phenomenon without reference to the ultimate cause of any thing". Further, he says, "causation is simply uniform antecedence". Though this explanation of the concept of 'cause' and 'causation' is more or less accepted by sciences, including social sciences there are still ambiguities about the concepts specially when one thinks of a first cause and subsequent cause and a final cause. As a result, even in 'scientific' explanation, the different measures of the term 'cause' are frequently confused.

A cause may act by impelling or by releasing or by unwinding. Let us consider an example. In the game of snooker a ball is impelled to strike another ball which may in turn strike on a number of balls. In this case, the first impulsion is the cause of movements of the second ball and the subsequent balls. The movements of second and subsequent balls are the effect of the cause induced by the impulsion. In other words, the event in question is shown to be determined by the preceding events.

In short, the investigation of preceding event (the cause) and successive events (the effects) caused by the preceding event constitutes causal relationships. Scientific research is mainly concerned with discovering of necessary and sufficient conditions for an effect. While common sense leads one to expect that one cause may provide a complete explanation for the effect, the researcher rarely expects to find a single cause or condition that is both necessary and sufficient to bring about an effect. Rather, he/she is interested in finding out multiplicity of 'effects' or 'events'.

It is rather impossible, however, to demonstrate directly that a given variable 'X' either by itself or in conjunction with other variables causes 'Y'. Hence, we prefer to infer from the data that the causal relationship (hypothesis) that 'X' is a cause for the occurrence of 'Y' is tenable only with some level of confidence.

Logic of Causal Inference

To clarify the issues raised above, we have to understand the logic of causal inference. The three conditions that have to be fulfilled to draw a causal inference are:

If

(1) the cause precedes the effect in time,
(2) there is an empirical correlation between them, and
(3) the relationship is not found to be the result of the effects of some third variable on each of the two initially observed.

The first condition in a causal relationship is that the cause precedes the effect in time. For example, in the game of snooker, the first impulsion is the cause of movements of the second ball and the subsequent balls. The movements of second and subsequent balls are the effect of the cause induced by the impulsion.

The second condition is that the two variables be empirically correlated with one another. For example, if a researcher wishes to examine if there is cause-effect relationship between gender and achievement, he/she has to use correlational technique to assess the magnitude of the relationship. It is also required that the co-efficient of correlation is substantial.

The third condition is that the observed empirical correlation between two variables cannot be explained away as being due to the influence of some third variable that causes both of them. For example, it may be observed that there is a strong correlation between 'knee joints pain' and 'amount of rainfall' but this does not mean that joints pain affects rainfall. A third variable—relative humidity—is the cause of both knee joints pain and rainfall. Any relationship satisfying all these conditions is causal, and these are the only conditions of cause-effect relationship.

In a typical experimental study two groups are chosen such that they do not differ significantly from each other except by chance. One of the groups is exposed to the independent variable (known as 'experimental group'). The two groups are then compared in terms of the effects. Research design, which involves comparison of two or more groups of, subjects who have been exposed to an experiment, there is an underlying assumption that the groups being compared were similar before the introduction of experiment. To ensure this, the techniques such as 'randomization' or 'matching' are utilized. The technique of randomization involves assignment of members of a group of subjects to experimental and control group. The procedure of assignment must give each member equal chance of being assigned to any of the groups. The technique of matching involves putting the subjects for assignment to the experimental or control group in a manner that a particular type of the experimental group is balanced by assigning his exact counterpart in the control group.

Validity of Causal Inference

While drawing causal inference, we need to consider two forms of validity: internal validity and external validity.

Internal validity refers to the confidence we have that the causal inference from a study accurately explain whether one variable is a cause of another. If the three conditions of causality are fulfilled, it is said that the causal inference has internal validity.

External validity refers to the extent to which the causal inference of a study can be generalised.

Threats to Internal Validity

Campbell and Stanley (1963) and Cook and Campbell (1971) have mentioned a number of threats to internal validity. Some of these are discussed below:

1. *History:* The threat of history refers to events that occur during the course of an experiment. It is presumed that these events might have affected the dependent variable. History is a threat to an experiment which lasts longer and allows events to affect the dependent variable.
2. *Maturation:* As time passes, a number of changes occur within experimental subjects, such as growing older, wiser, more experienced. These changes in the experimental subjects are called maturation changes. If any of these changes are found with dependent variable, it could confuse the effect of independent variable.
3. *Testing:* Repeated testing often enhances the performance without any corresponding improvement in the variable under examination. For example, people taking intelligence test for a second time tend to score higher than they did the first time. The change in performance could lead to change in the dependent variable which in fact changes due to the repeated measure rather than the impact of the independent variable.
4. *Statistical regression:* In the case of subjects scoring very high or very low, the threat of statistical regression may arise any time. When those extreme cases re-measured they will tend to score less extremely. In other words, they will tend to regress towards the average score.

Types of Experimental Research Designs

There are a large number of experimental designs. Various authors have grouped experimental designs into certain categories based on extent of control. Most common grouping comprises:

- true experimental designs
- pre-experimental designs
- quasi-experimental designs

In this chapter, we will discuss the first category of experimental designs, that is, true experimental designs. The other two categories of experimental designs will be discussed in the next chapter.

True Experimental Designs

True experimental designs have maximum control and hence highest degree of internal validity. The essential components of an experimental research design involve (a) random assignments of subjects to experimental and control groups, (b) introducing the stimulus (independent variable) to the experimental group while withholding it from the control group, and (c) comparing the amount of change in dependent variable in experimental and control groups.

Pre-test-Post-test Control Group Design

The classic experimental design, which is also known as pre-test-post-test control group design, can be shown in shorthand notation as:

$$E \longrightarrow R \longrightarrow Y_1 \longrightarrow X \longrightarrow Y_2$$
$$C \longrightarrow R \longrightarrow Y'_1 \longrightarrow \text{Non-X} \longrightarrow Y'_2$$

Where E and C represent experimental group and control groups respectively, R stands for random assignments of subjects to either experimental group or the control group. The notation X represents the introduction of a stimulus, Y_1' s represent pre-tests and the Y_2's represent post-tests. In this design, experimental group and the control group subjects are measured on a dependent variable before and after the introduction of stimulus.

Suppose, for example, a researcher wishes to test a hypothesis that punishments lead to low self-esteem using pre-test-post-test control group design. To test the hypothesis, first, he/she has to select a sample of students preferably from one particular class, say, 10th standard. Then, he/she has to randomly assign the subjects to either the experimental group (E) or the control group (C). Now, both the groups are measured for their self-esteem (Y_1, Y'_1). Punishments (X) are withheld for students who are in control group. Later, both the groups are measured and compared for self-esteem (Y_2, Y'_2). If there is a significant difference in the pre- and post-self-esteem scores, it can be concluded that suspension of punishment had an effect on self-esteem. Further, if it is observed that the average post-self-esteem scores of students in group E is comparatively lower than the students in group C, then the hypothesis that punishments lead to low self-esteem will be accepted.

The pre-test-post-test control group design, is diagrammed as shown below:

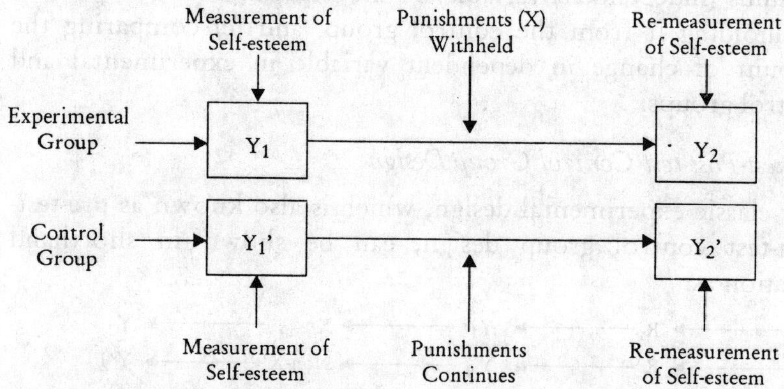

Effects on Experimental Group (D1) = Y2 – Y1

Effects on Control Group (D2) = Y'2 – Y'1

Net Effects = D2 – D1

Solomon Four-Group Design

This design has been developed to overcome the threat of testing. In shorthand notation it can be shown as:

E ⟶ R ⟶ Y_1 ⟶ X ⟶ Y_2

C ⟶ R ⟶ Y'_1 ⟶ Non-X ⟶ Y'_2

E ⟶ R ⟶ X ⟶ Y_2

C ⟶ R ⟶ Non-X ⟶ Y'_2

This design combines the classical experimental designs with the post-test-only control group design. In this design subjects are randomly assigned to four groups instead of two. Two of the groups are experimental groups and other two are control groups. One experimental group and one control group are pre-tested and post tested. The other experimental group and control group are only post tested. By comparing the two experimental groups results with each other and the two control group results with each other it can be revealed that if there is any effect caused by pre -testing.

Post-test-Only Control Group Design

Solomon four-group design is considered as one of the strongest research designs. However, it is rarely used by social researchers mainly because of the cost involved in implementing the research design. Moreover, in practice, it is really a difficult task to assign the subjects in four groups on random basis or by matching.

The post-test-only control group design is the modification of solomon four-group design by removing the pre-testing of the groups. In shorthand notation, it can be shown as under:

E ⟶ R ⟶ ⟶ X ⟶ Y
C ⟶ R ⟶ ⟶ Non-X ⟶ Y'

This design is used to nullify the effects of repeated testing, which often enhances the performance without any corresponding improvement in the variable under examination. In this design, the subjects are randomly assigned to either the experimental group or the control group and are measured during or after the introduction of the stimulus (the independent variable).

The post-test-only control group design is diagrammatically shown on the next page.

Suppose, for example, that a researcher examining the effects of punishments on the self-esteem of the students selects a sample of subjects who are randomly assigned to either of the two groups. One group is not subjected to punishments and later both groups are measured for their self-esteem and their scores are compared. A

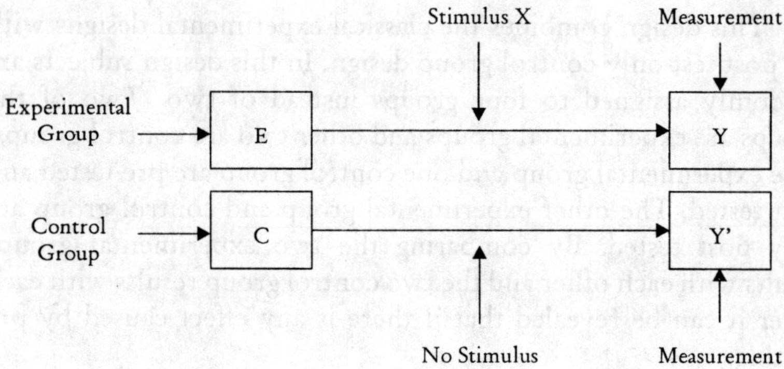

significant difference will indicate that suspension of punishment had an effect on self-esteem.

Important Terms for Review

- Experiment
- Manipulation
- Control
- Internal Validity
- External Validity
- Pre-test
- Post-test
- History
- Maturation
- Testing
- Statistical Regression
- Causality
- Cause-Effect Relationship
- Correlation
- Independent Variable
- Dependent Variable

Further Readings

Abram, M., *Social Surveys and Social Action*, London: Heinemann, 1950.

Ackoff, R.L., *The Design of Social Research*, Chicago: University of Chicago Press, 1953.

Bailey, Kenneth D., *Methods of Social Research*, London: The Free Press, 1978.

Baker, L., Therese, *Doing Social Research,* New York: McGraw Hill, 1988.

Black, James A. and Champion, Dean J., *Methods and Issues in Social Research*, New York: John Wiley, 1976.

Campbell, D.T. and Stanley, J.C., *Experimental and Quasi-Experimental Designs for Research,* Boston: Houghton Mifflin, 1963.

Chapin, F.S., *Experimental Design in Sociological Research,* New York: Harper, 1974.

Festinger, L. and Katz, D. (eds.), *Research Methods in the Behavioral Sciences,* New York: The Dryden Press, 1953.

Goode, W.J. and Hatt, P.K., *Methods in Social Research,* New York: McGraw Hill, 1952.

Kerlinger, Fred R., *Foundations of Behavioral Research,* Delhi: Surjeet Publications, 1964.

Kidder, Louise H., *Research Methods in Social Relations,* New York: Holt, 1981.

Kothari, L.R., *Research Methodology*, New Delhi: Vishwa Prakashan, 1985.

Lal Das, D.K., *Practice of Social Research: Social Work Perspective*, Jaipur: Rawat Publications, 2000.

Mill, J.S., *A System of Logic*, New York: Longmans (8th edition), 1930.

Miller, D.C., *Handbook of Research Design and Social Measurement,* New York: David McKey Co., 1964.

Monette, Duane R. et. al., *Applied Social Research: Tool for the Human Services,* Chicago: Holt, 1986.

Moser, C.A. and Kalton, *Survey Methods in Social Investigation,* London: Heinemann Educational Books, 1975.

Nachmias, D. and Nachmias, C., *Research Methods in the Social Sciences*, New York: St. Martins Press, 1981.

Rubin, Allen and Babbie, E., *Research Methodology for Social Work*, Belmohf, California, Wadsworth, 1989.

Sellitz, G. et. al., *Research Methods in Social Relations,* New York: Holt Rinehart and Winston (3rd edition), 1973.

Shah, V.F., *Research Design,* Ahmedabad: Rachna Prakashan, 1977

Stouffer, S.A., *Social Research to Test Ideas,* New York: Free Press of Glencoe, 1962.

Suchman, E.A., The Principles of Research Design, In John T. Doby et. al., *An Introduction to Social Research*, New York: The Stackpole, 1953.

Wilkinson, T.S. and Bhandarkar, P.L., *Methodology and Techniques of Social Research*, Bombay: Himalaya, 1977.

Young, P.V., *Scientific Social Surveys and Research*, Englewood Cliff N.J. Prentice Hall (4th edition), 1953.

Review Questions

1. What is causality?
2. Differentiate causality from correlation.
3. What is an experimental research design?
4. What is control in an experiment?
5. What is internal validity?
6. What are the threats to the internal validity?
7. What is external validity?

8

Research Designs: Pre-Experimental and Quasi-Experimental

Pre-experimental Research Designs

Research designs, in which most of the sources of internal and external validity are not controlled, are termed as pre-experimental research designs. These designs are the weakest kind of research designs. In fact, the risk of drawing causal inference from these designs is extremely high. Still, they are used quite often in social research. These designs help to illustrate the advantages of experimental research designs.

Types of Pre-experimental Research Designs

The three very commonly used pre-experimental research designs are:

1. One Shot Case Study
2. One Group Pre-test-Post-test Design
3. Post-test Comparison Group Design

One Shot Case Study

The shorthand notation for one shot case study design is:

$$X \longrightarrow Y$$

where 'X' represents the introduction of stimulus and 'Y' represents the measurement of dependent variable. In this research design, a group of subject is measured on a dependent variable after the introduction of stimulus. In this design, it is not possible to ascertain if the change in the dependent variable is higher (or lower) than it was before the introduction of stimulus. It also does not tell that there is no change among the comparable subjects where stimulus was not introduced. Thus, this design fulfils only two of three conditions of causal inference, that is, time order and correlation. Hence, we cannot rule out the possibility that the extraneous variables caused the observed change.

For instance, to solve the problem of absenteeism, an incentive scheme is launched for the employees who are found to be chronic absentees. After a month or so, the attendance is checked. In case there is decrease in rate of absenteeism, it can be inferred that the decrease in the rate of absenteeism is because of new incentive scheme. This example may be shown diagrammatically as under:

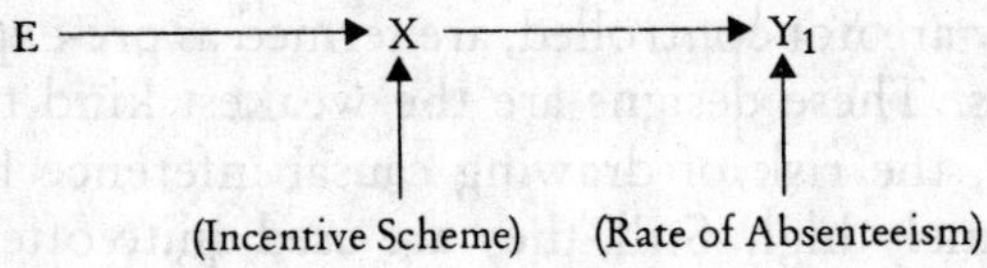

One Group Pre-test-Post-test Design

The shorthand notation for this design is:

$$Y \longrightarrow X \longrightarrow Y_1$$

The notations Y an Y_1 refer to the measurement before and the measurement after the introduction of stimulus. In this design, the dependent variable is measured before and after the introduction of stimulus is introduced. Although this research design measures time-order, correlation and control for internal factors, it does not take into account factors other than the independent variable that might have caused the change between pre-test and post-test results. The factors that might have caused the change may be associated with the various threats to the internal validity, such as, history, maturation, testing and statistical regression.

Suppose, we wish to assess the effect of cognitive behaviour intervention on abusive parents and we decide to undertake the study using one group pre-test-post-test design. The shorthand notation for this design may be diagrammed as shown below:

$$E \longrightarrow Y_1 \longrightarrow X \longrightarrow Y_2$$

where:

X = independent variable (intervention)
Y_1 = dependent variable before introduction of X (pre-test)
Y_2 = dependent variable after introduction of X (post-test)
E = Experimental group

To conduct the study, first, we select a group of abusive parents and measure their parenting skills and cognition about childhood behaviours. The test is followed by introduction of cognitive behavioural intervention with the abusive parents. After a specified period of intervention, its effects on parental skills are assessed. If it is found that there is significant increase in the parental skills scores of the abusive parents, we may infer that the change in the score is due to the intervention.

Post-test Comparison Group Design

The third commonly used pre-experimental research design involves post-test measurement only but does employ a comparison group. The term 'comparison group' denotes a group which is not formed by random selection of subjects and whom experimental manipulation is not performed. This research design can be symbolized as follows:

$$\begin{array}{lcl} E \longrightarrow X \longrightarrow Y_1 \\ C \qquad \longrightarrow \qquad Y'_1 \end{array}$$

In example mentioned above, if we compare the parenting skills and cognition about childhood behaviours of the group of abusive parents who participated in experiment with the parenting skills and cognition about childhood behaviours of a group of abusive parents who did not, it exactly demonstrates the post-test comparison group design of research. The comparison group is usually chosen to be as similar as possible to the group that was introduced to the intervention. The example may be shown diagrammatically as follows:

E ⟶ X ⟶ Y_1

C ⟶ Non-X ⟶ Y'_1

where:

X = independent variable (cognitive behaviour intervention)
Y'_1 = dependent variable (parental skills) before
= introduction of X (pre-test)
E = experimental group
C = comparison group

One serious disadvantage of this design is that the groups were not equivalent before introduction of the stimulus (intervention). In other words, it is possible that the subjects in the two groups might have differed initially with respect to the dependent variable measured (parenting skills and cognition about childhood behaviours).

The internal validity of the three pre-experimental research designs discussed above is a week. Hence, causal inferences drawn from pre-experimental research designs are inconclusive.

Quasi-experimental Research Designs

Many a time, it is not possible to achieve random assignments of subjects to experimental and control groups and withhold stimulus (intervention) to one group (control group). In such cases, instead of foregoing the study altogether, it is sometimes possible to create and execute alternative research designs that have less internal validity than experimental research designs but still provide reasonably good amount of evidences for causal inferences. These designs are called quasi-experimental research designs and are distinguished from experimental research designs due to lack of random assignments of subjects to experimental and control groups. In this section, we will discuss some quasi-experimental research designs that are applicable to social research.

Pre-test Post-test Non-equivalent Control Group Design

When it is not possible to divide subjects into experimental and control groups by random assignments, we try to get an existing control group (comparison group) that appears to be similar to experimental group. This research design is commonly called as pre-test post-test non-equivalent control group design and can be symbolized as follows:

$$\begin{array}{l} E \longrightarrow Y_1 \longrightarrow X \longrightarrow Y_2 \\ C \longrightarrow Y_1 \longrightarrow \text{Non-X} \longrightarrow Y_2 \end{array}$$

where:

X = independent variable (intervention)
Y_1 = dependent variable before introduction of X (pre-test)
Y_2 = dependent variable after introduction of X (post-test)
E = experimental group
C = comparison group

Suppose, we wish to evaluate the effects of an intervention (say, counselling) on level of loneliness of inmates of an Old Age Home. It is unlikely that we would be permitted to select randomly in any Old Age Home those inmates who will be given counselling and those who will not be given. As an alternative, we may find two Old Age Homes that agree to participate in our research study and which appear to be very similar in all respects. That is, we make sure that the inmates in two homes are very similar in terms of age, socio-economic status, mental and physical disabilities, psychological functioning, and so on. We can introduce the intervention in one home, and use the other as a comparison group. The two homes could be compared by a pre-test measurement to make sure that they really are equivalent on the dependent variable before introducing the intervention (independent variable). If their average loneliness scores are approximately same, then it would be reasonable to infer that differences in post-test scores are due to the effects of intervention. The example may be shown diagrammatically as follows:

$$\begin{array}{l} E \longrightarrow Y_1 \longrightarrow X \longrightarrow Y_2 \\ C \longrightarrow Y'_1 \longrightarrow \text{Non-X} \longrightarrow Y'_2 \end{array}$$

where:
X = independent variable (intervention: counselling)
Y_1 = dependent variable before introduction of X (pre-test)
Y_2 = dependent variable after introduction of X (post-test)
E = experimental group
C = comparison group

Time-Series Designs

Simple Time-Series Designs

When comparison group is not available for assessing cause-effect relationship, time-series designs can be used. In time-series designs pre-test and post-test measures are taken a number of times before and after the introduction of stimulus. Usually, the researcher attempts to obtain at least five sets of measures before and after the introduction of independent variable. A typical time-series design can be represented as follows:

$$Y_1 \quad Y_2 \quad Y_3 \quad Y_4 \quad Y_5 \quad X \quad Y_6 \quad Y_7 \quad Y_8 \quad Y_9 \quad Y_{10}$$

where:

Y1 to Y5 = measurements of dependent variable before introduction of X (pre-test)

X = independent variable (intervention: counselling)

Y6 to Y10 = measurements of dependent variable after introduction of X (post-test)

The above diagram indicates that the dependent variable was measured at five points in time before the intervention (X) was introduced and at another five points after that.

To illustrate the time-series design we will take a group of students whose morale has been observed as very low. First, we will measure the morale of students by using a standardized scale. The measurement will be repeated another four times with an interval of a week. After recording the fifth observation, the intervention (a play which has been tested for boosting morale of students) is introduced. After completion of the intervention the dependent variable (morale in this case) is measured five times with an interval of a week. These measurements can be compared with the measurements recorded before the intervention to infer if there is significant change in the dependent variable. In case there is significant increase in the morale of students after witnessing/participating in the play, it can be inferred that it is has been caused by the intervention (the play). The simple set of data is presented graphically in Figure 8.1.

Figure 8.1

Effect of Intervention on Morale

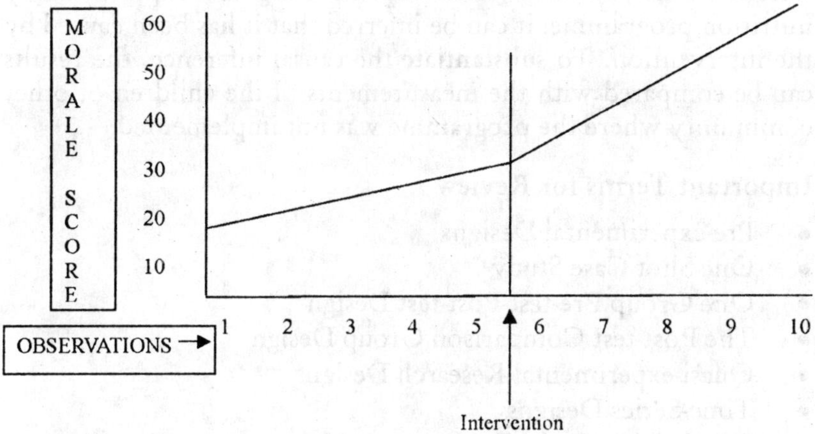

Multiple Time-Series Design

Multiple time-series design is another form of time-series designs with greater internal validity. The shorthand notation for this design is as under:

In this design, both an experimental group and a non-equivalent comparison group are measured at multiple points in time before and after intervention is introduced to the experimental group.

E ⟶ Y_1 Y_2 Y_3 Y_4 Y_5 X Y_6 Y_7 Y_8 Y_9 Y_{10}

C ⟶ Y_1 Y_2 Y_3 Y_4 Y_5 Non-X Y_6 Y_7 Y_8 Y_9 Y_{10}

We will consider a hypothetical study of children at risk (severely underweight) to illustrate the multiple time-series design. In this study, first, age and weight of children in two communities are measured and children at risk are identified The measurements are repeated for five times with an interval of a week or so. After recording the fifth observation, the intervention (a supplementary nutrition programme) is introduced in one of the communities. On completion of the intervention the dependent variable (weight) is measured five times with an interval of a week. These measurements can be compared with the measurements recorded before the intervention to infer if there is significant change in the dependent variable. In case there is significant increase in the weight of the children after implementing the supplementary nutrition programme, it can be inferred that it has been caused by the intervention. To substantiate the causal inference, the results can be compared with the measurements of the children of other community where the programme was not implemented.

Important Terms for Review

- Pre-experimental Designs
- One Shot Case Study
- One Group Pre-test-Post-test Design
- The Post-test Comparison Group Design
- Quasi-experimental Research Designs
- Time-Series Designs
- Simple Time-Series Designs
- Multiple Time-Series Design

Further Readings

Ackoff, R.L., *The Design of Social Research,* Chicago: University of Chicago Press, 1953.

Bailey, Kenneth D., *Methods of Social Research*, London: The Free Press, 1978.

Baker, L. Therese, *Doing Social Research,* New York: McGraw Hill, 1988.

Bennel, Carl et. al., *Evaluation Experiments*, New York: Academic Press, 1975.

Campbell, D.T. and Stanley, J.C., *Experimental and Quasi-Experimental Designs for Research,* Boston: Houghton Mifflin, 1963.

Chapin, F.S., *Experimental Design in Sociological Research,* New York: Harper, 1974.

Epstein, I. and Tripodi, T., *Research Techniques for Program Planning, Monitoring and Evaluation*, New York: Columbia University Program, 1974.

Festinger, L. and Katz, D. (eds.), *Research Methods in the Behavioral Sciences,* New York: The Dryden Press, 1953.

Goode, W.J. and Hat, P.K., *Methods in Social Research,* New York: McGraw Hill, 1952.

Kerlinger, Fred R., *Foundations of Behavioral Research,* Delhi: Surjeet Publications, 1964.

Kidder, Louise H., *Research Methods in Social Relations,* New York: Holt, 1981.

Kothari, L.R., *Research Methodology*, New Delhi: Vishwa Prakashan, 1985.

Lal Das, D.K., *Practice of Social Research: Social Work Perspective*, Jaipur: Rawat Publications, 2000.

Miller, D.C., *Handbook of Research Design and Social Measurement* New York: David McKey Co., 1964.

Monette, Duane R. et. al., *Applied Social Research: Tool for the Human Services* Chicago: Holt, 1986.

Moser, C.A. and Kalton, *Survey Methods in Social Investigation* London: Heinemann Educational Books, 1975.

Nachmias, D. and Nachmias, C., *Research Methods in the Social Sciences*, New York: St. Martins Press. 1981.

Rubin, Allen and Babbie E., *Research Methodology for Social Work*, Belmohf, California, Wadsworth, 1989.

Sellitz, G. et. al., *Research Methods in Social Relations,* New York: Holt. Rinehart and Winston (3rd edition), 1973.

Stouffer, S.A., *Social Research to Test Ideas,* New York: Free Press of Glencoe, 1962.

Suchman, E.A., *Evaluative Research: Principles and Practice in Public Service and Social Action Programmes,* New York: Russel Sage Foundation, 1967.

Suchman, E.A., 'The Principles of Research Design'. In John T. Doby et. al., *An Introduction to Social Research*, New York: The Stackpole, 1953.

Weiss, Carol, *Evaluation Research,* Englewood Cliffs N.J., Prentice Hall, 1972.

Wilkinson, T.S. and Bhandarkar, P.L., *Methodology and Techniques of Social Research*, Bombay: Himalaya, 1977.

Yin, Robert K., *Case Study Research Design and Methods,* Applied Social Research Methods Series Vol. 5, New Delhi: Sage, 1982.

Review Questions

1. What is a quasi-experimental research?
2. What are the major weaknesses of pre-experimental designs?
3. What are the strengths of quasi-experimental research?
4. What is a time-series design?
5. Differentiate simple time-series design from multiple time-series design.

9

Intervention Research Designs

The ultimate goal of practice of social research is to improve the social functioning of individuals, groups and communities. In brief, the process of improving social functioning of individuals, groups and communities involves study, assessment, intervention and evaluation. In most cases these steps require use of research techniques in general, and measurement techniques in particular, such as rating scales, score analysis, statistical significance etc. The purpose of this chapter is to describe some special intervention research designs, commonly known as single-subject designs, through which social researchers attempt to improve social functioning of individuals, groups, families and communities.

Single-Subject Designs

Intervention research designs or single-subject designs are basically quasi-experimental research designs, which use time-series analysis technique of social research to the evaluation of the impact of interventions on individual cases, groups, family and community. Such designs involve repeated measure of the dependent variable before and after a particular intervention, to see if a sustained pattern of change in the dependent variable commences shortly after the onset of intervention (Rubin and Babbie, 1989).

The unit of analysis in this design of research is one, irrespective of whether the unit of analysis is one individual, one family, one community, or one organisation. As such, one of the major limitations of these designs is their dubious external validity. But we should not forget that single-subject experiments can identify with a high degree of internal validity in those interventions that seem to work in one, perhaps idiosyncratic, context and can be tested for generalizability in subsequent studies. These subsequent studies might include larger-scale experiments utilizing control groups, or they might be additional single-subject experiments that attempt to approximate replications of the original single-subject experiment in other contexts (Rubin and Babbie, 1989).

Such research designs are also termed as 'single-case designs' or 'single-system designs'. These two terms are used to indicate that subjects need not be individual only, but can include a family, a community, and so on. But, the term 'single-subject designs' is more commonly used and hence will be used in this text with the understanding that it would also apply to cases or systems that may involve groups, family members and a community.

Background

Prior to single-subject designs, social researchers had no alternative other than to use conventional experimental research designs such as comparison of experimental group with control group. Such experimental researches, however, were often inappropriate or impossible to conduct in practice settings. It was often too time-consuming and expensive to identify clients with similar problems and randomly assign some to treatment and others to control groups.

In such experiments the results were an average of the whole group's response, obscuring individual reactions which are significant to practitioners. For example, knowing that a given intervention was effective on majority in an experimental group may be interesting, but it does not help at all in inferring about a particular client (Monette et. al., 1986).

Conventional experimental researches essentially require complying with probability theory of sampling and assumptions of the statistical procedures, which certainly rule out the possibility of conducting research on an individual (N=1) or a small group (say N=5).

Finally, the use of control groups, to whom intervention is withheld, has been a source of ethical concern to professionals. Thus, although conventional experimental researches are appropriate for some purposes, the drawbacks associated with the method have led social researchers to find an alternative approach for evaluating the effects of social interventions and modify and update intervention techniques.

As with advances in other areas of social research, interest in single-subject designs based on time-series research design grew out of problems faced by social work researchers with existing techniques of social research.

Gradually, the single-subject designs became as instrument to merge research and practice, and today it includes much more than single-subject designs. It involves a stance toward practice that includes the following basic points (Bloom and Fischer, 1982):

1. The human service professional views service delivery as a problem-solving experiment in which a major responsibility of the researcher/practitioner is to hypothesize and test relationships between client problems and intervention effects.
2. The professional incorporates single-subject designs as a routine strategy in the monitoring and evaluation of all clients.
3. In the selection of practice strategies, the clinician-researcher gives preference to knowledge that has been substantiated by empirical testing in contrast with knowledge that is primarily of a traditional, intuitive, or experimental nature.
4. The researcher/practitioner places high value on the professional responsibility to continue learning and evaluating practice techniques in order to improve intervention.

In a nutshell, single-subject designs aim at the systematic evaluation of practice through the use of scientific research techniques. It must be kept in mind, however, that this research design does not reject conventional large-group experimental researches. Such researches are necessary for evaluating complete programmes and for confirming the generalizability of programme effectiveness. In the following sections, we will discuss the stages in the single-subject design research.

Use of Single-Subject Designs

Single-subject designs can be used in social work practice/clinical/ child psychology in different situations in different ways. A few psycho-social situations where this research technique will be appropriate are illustrated in the following sections. Clinicians/practitioners as part of their own practice can use single-subject designs in studying their clients, diagnosing the target problem and selecting the appropriate treatment. They also need to monitor the client's progress. By single-subject designs research they can measure changes in the target problem and monitor client progress (or lack thereof) and acquire systematic understanding of events or circumstances that may deteriorate or ameliorate the target problem. For example, suppose, a child in a special school is being treated for aggressive behaviour, and further that the problematic behaviour occurs shortly before the child is about to enter the classroom. Repeated measures of the target behaviour might help the social worker/psychologist chronologically identify this coincidence during the initial stages of service delivery, which in turn would help better understand the causes of the target problem and develop an appropriate strategy to deal with it. Social researchers, who spend considerable amounts of time unsystematically attempting to record and evaluate their practices, may find conducting single-subject designs research to be one way to make that effort more systematic and valid. The very use of such research techniques helps social workers/psychologists to become scientific practitioners. As another example, let us consider an illustration. Suppose, a school social worker seeking to enhance the self-esteem and social functioning of a group of school students who are at high risk of dropping out of school and monitors the student's disciplinary referrals and administers a standardised self-esteem scale on a weekly basis. Suppose, further, that the social worker requests the school authorities to suspend disciplinary actions for a specified period to see whether self-esteem improves. If the student's self-esteem scores improves, then the social worker would have reasonable grounds for inferring that it was probably the intervention, and not history, that accounted for the student's improved functioning.

There are, however, some practical problems in using single-subject research design in practice. Many a time, the situation needs immediate intervention and hence does not allow researchers enough time to take repeated measures to identify baseline trends prior to implementing the intervention. In some situations social workers are heavily loaded with cases which reduce the amount of time they have to plan or conduct single-subject design studies. Despite these problems, researchers should make efforts to use single-subject designs whenever they can. Social services have not yet received adequate scientific testing concerning their effects on clients. In the light of this, the question may not be whether cases need immediate intervention or whether we can afford the time needed to use single-subject design research as part of our practices, but whether we can afford to use untested interventions to see whether they help the clients or harm them.

By using single-subject designs as part of our practice, we can get immediate feedback that would help us to modify the service or chose other alternative interventions for our client.

Apparently, it looks simple and easy to implement single-subject research designs. It also gives an impression that single-subject researches would clear all the doubts about the effectiveness of social work interventions. In practice, however, conducting repeated measures of target problems to provide reliable and valid data is not always a simple task. It is easy to introduce intervention only when the baseline is established, but it is rather difficult in situations where cases are in dire need of treatment. Nevertheless, barring a few situations, the technique of single-subject designs are very useful for social researchers.

Baseline Phase

The single-subject design researches are based on the principle of time-series data analysis. As such, it requires measurements of dependent variable at successive intervals of time. The measurement points before the intervention are called baseline phase. These measurements serve as control, that is, they serve the same function as control groups do in conventional group experiments. The data collected during the baseline phase or compared to the data collected during the intervention (experimental) phase. In order to infer that an intervention is effective, that is, change in the dependent variable can be attributed to the intervention and not to history or maturation, we look for shifts in the trend or pattern of data that coincide with the intervention.

To assess the shift in data pattern, it is necessary that the data trend in the baseline phase is clear and stable. A trend is one that shows the target problem to be occurring in a predictable and orderly fashion.

The stability of observed trend is identified by plotting the data on a graph, and then observing whether the trend is clearly increasing (Figure 9.1), decreasing (Figure 9.2), cyclical (Figure 9.3) or stable (Figure 9.4).

Figure 9.1
Baseline - Increasing

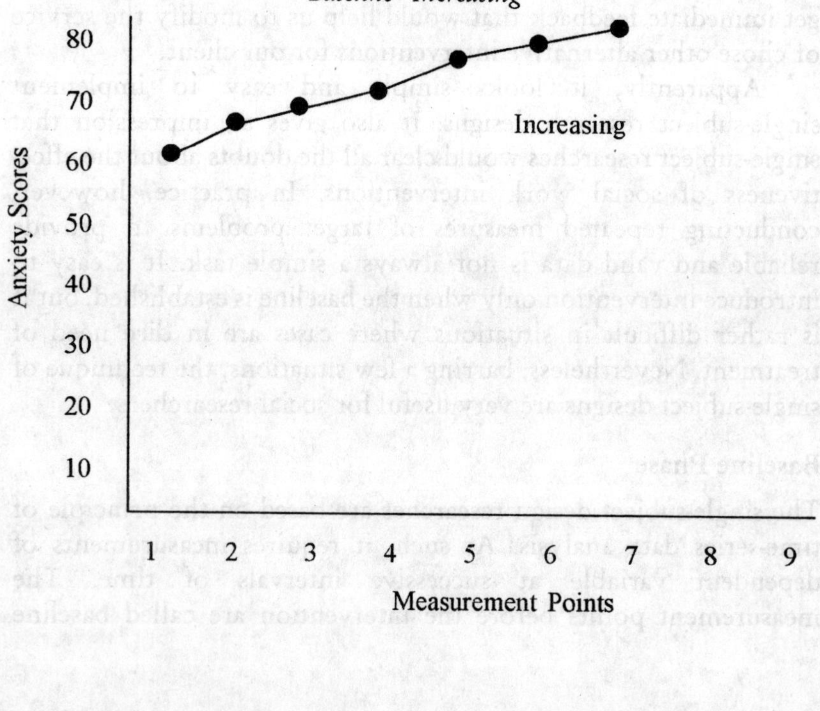

Figure 9.2
Baseline - Decreasing

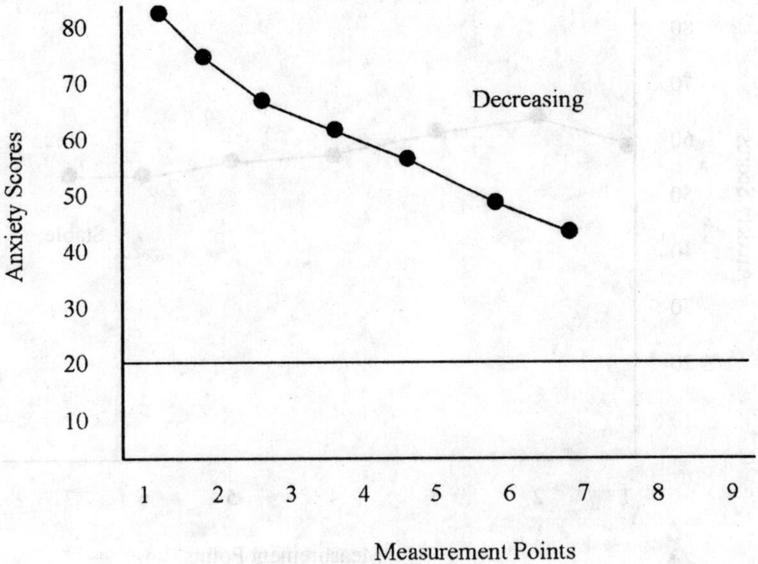

Figure 9.3
Baseline - Cyclical

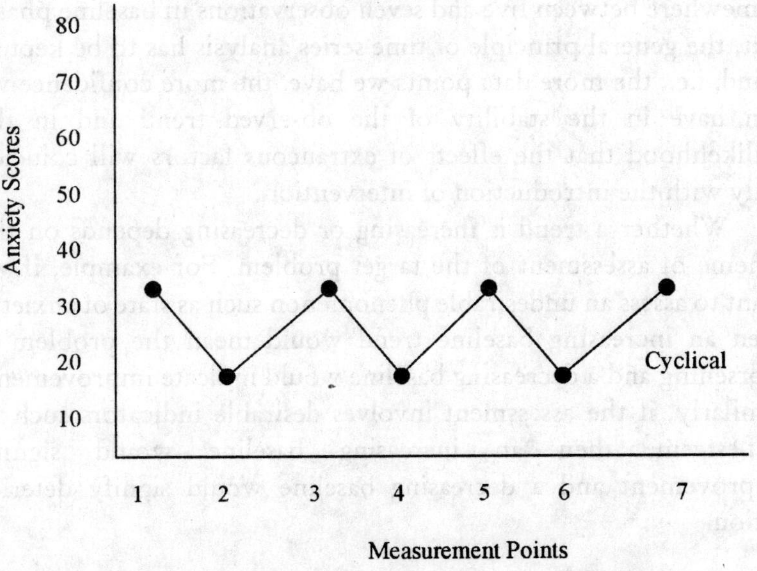

Figure 9.4
Baseline - Stable

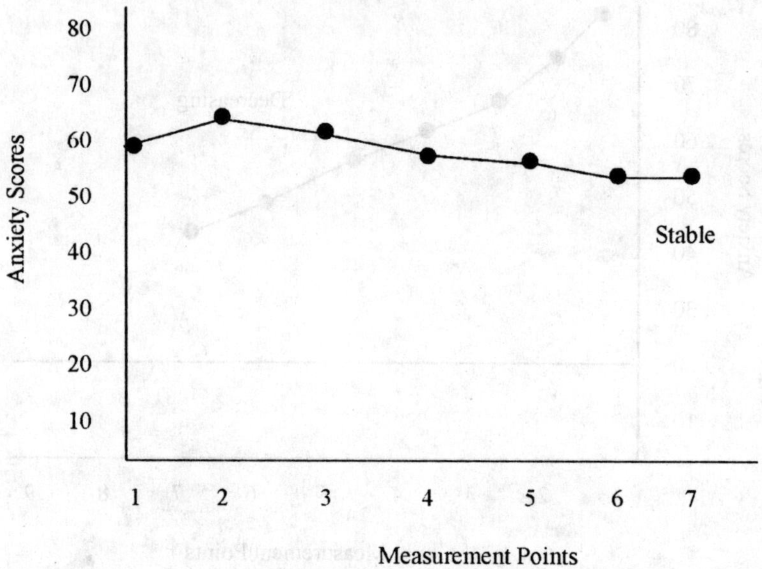

Although the number of observation points in baseline phase varies depending on individual cases, it is reasonable to plan for somewhere between five and seven observations in baseline phase. But, the general principle of time-series analysis has to be kept in mind, i.e., the more data points we have, the more confidence we can have in the stability of the observed trend and in the unlikelihood that the effects of extraneous factors will coincide only with the introduction of intervention.

Whether a trend is increasing or decreasing depends on the scheme of assessment of the target problem. For example, if we want to assess an undesirable phenomenon such as state of anxiety, then an increasing baseline trend would mean the problem is worsening and a decreasing baseline would indicate improvement. Similarly, if the assessment involves desirable indicators such as self-esteem, then an increasing baseline would signify improvement and a decreasing baseline would signify deterioration.

Single-Subject Designs: Research Process

Single-subject designs have many similarities with scientific practice. Single-subject designs, however, bring in objectivity and empiricism into the practice. By following these research designs, social researchers are in a position to know precisely what intervention was applied and how much effect was produced and to have supporting data for proof. These designs link research and practice by putting the practitioner in the enviable position of not only bringing about change but also having valid evidence as to why the change occurred (Monette, et. al., 1986: 255). The process of single-subject design research is presented below:

Figure 9.5

Steps in Single Subject-Design Research Process

STEP I: Problem Formulation

STEP II: Identification of Objectives

STEP III: Selection of Single-Subject Design

STEP IV: Pre-Intervention Assessment

STEP V: Intervention Strategies

STEP IV: Assessment of Intervention Effects

STEP VII: Drawing of Conclusions

Problem Formulation

In the first stage, the researcher strives to obtain as clear and specific an understanding of the problem as possible, using various assessment methods and techniques, such as interviewing the individual, his peer group and family members, case history etc.

Identification of Objectives

After the problem is identified, the next step is to determine what objectives are to be achieved through intervention. At this point, the first real difference between the research-based practice and traditional practice is encountered. In research-based practice, it is to be ensured, firstly, that the objectives are measurable in some way and secondly that they are more specific and precisely defined than is often done in conventional practice.

Selection of Single-Subject Design

Once a problem and corresponding objectives for intervention have been identified, the next phase of the research process is to select an appropriate single-subject design that will suit the objectives and constraints of a particular subject.

Pre-Intervention Assessment (Baseline Phase)

Pre-intervention assessment or needs assessment is a systematic appraisal in evaluating the client's problems, needs and potential solutions. For this, the researcher generally uses one of the standardized rating scales designed to measure the degree or level of target behaviours or problems.

Single-subject designs call for repeated measures of the subject's behaviour or condition so that trends and changes can be noted. Thus, the fourth step in the research process is to establish a baseline, or a series of measurements of the subject's behaviour or condition prior to intervention. These baseline measurements are used as a basis from which to compare the subject's behaviour or condition after the intervention is introduced. Typically, three

Figure 9.6

Hypothetical Baseline followed by Successful Intervention

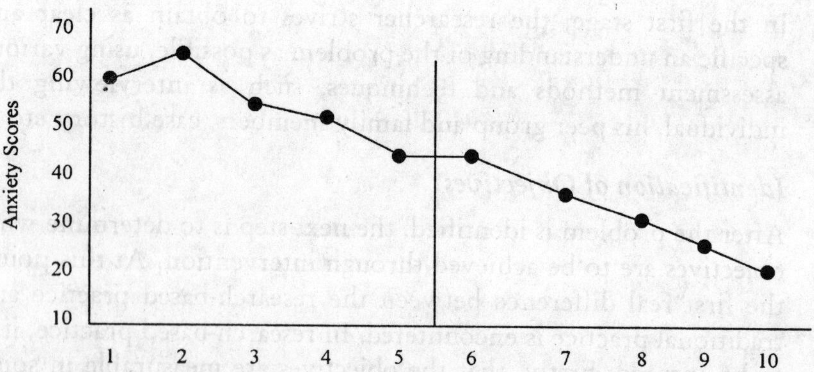

measurements are needed, as an absolute minimum, to establish a baseline (Barlow and Hersen, 1973).

Figure 9.6 illustrates how pre-intervention measurement can serve as a basis for assessing intervention effects. The hypothetical data show a high level of undesirable client behaviour prior to treatment. After treatment is initiated, this drops sharply. Results are not always as dramatic as these are, so making interpretations can be more difficult. We will deal with the issue of assessing treatment effects in more detail later.

Intervention Strategies

In this phase of research, the researcher develops an intervention strategy which aims at modification of behaviour or conditions of the subject. The strategies may include a single intervention or a set of interventions at a time or in succession depending upon the degree of severity of the subject's condition. For example, a researcher may decide to use counselling technique to modify the behaviour of an adolescent student who is at high risk of dropping out along with other supportive intervention such as facilitation, ventilation of feelings and universalization.

Once the intervention strategy is decided, the next is the introduction of intervention. When the intervention is introduced, it is important that only a single, coherent intervention be introduced during any intervention phase (Barlow and Hersen, 1973).

During the intervention phase, the measurement of the subject's condition, started during the baseline phase, is continued. This, of course, is done to track what changes (if any) the intervention is producing in the subject's condition. It is crucial that the conditions under which measurements are made during the intervention phase remain consistent with those under which the baseline measurements were obtained (Jayaratne and Levy, 1979).

Assessment of Intervention Effects

Assessment of intervention effects ascertains whether the intervention strategy has achieved the desired result in the subjects. It reviews all the other components of the process to make an appraisal of the result. It also gives answers to whether the intensity of the problem has reduced or otherwise.

The sixth stage of the research process addresses itself to assessing the effects of intervention. Let us assume that higher scores represent improvement, as in the case of 'self-esteem'. If the goal of intervention was to increase self-esteem, higher scores would indicate improvement. A stable baseline is ideal since post-intervention comparisons will then readily reveal intervention effects. If the intervention is helpful, there should be a pronounced upward move in measurement levels. An ineffective intervention would be revealed by little changes from baseline levels. The value of a stable baseline is that it allows all three possible intervention outcomes to be readily noted.

In the last stage of the research process, conclusions are drawn.

Types of Single-Subject Designs

Although there are numerous types of single-subject designs, all involve repeated measurements during baseline and intervention phases and a comparison across phases as it provides better evidence of intervention effects. The designs differ in the number of phases involved, the number of interventions applied, and the number of baselines employed. Perhaps, the most important differences are in the internal validity of the designs. Some are more capable of providing evidence for the effect of an intervention when such an effect actually exists. Ideally, of course, researchers should select the most valid design that fits their particular case. There are three alternative single-subject designs:

(1) AB: Basic Single-Subject Design
(2) ABAB: Withdrawal/Reversal Design
(3) ABCD: Multiple Component Design

AB: Basic Single-Subject Design

The basic single-subject design, as the name suggests, is the simplest single-subject design and most popular design among researchers

Figure 9.7
Hypothetical Baseline followed by Successful Intervention

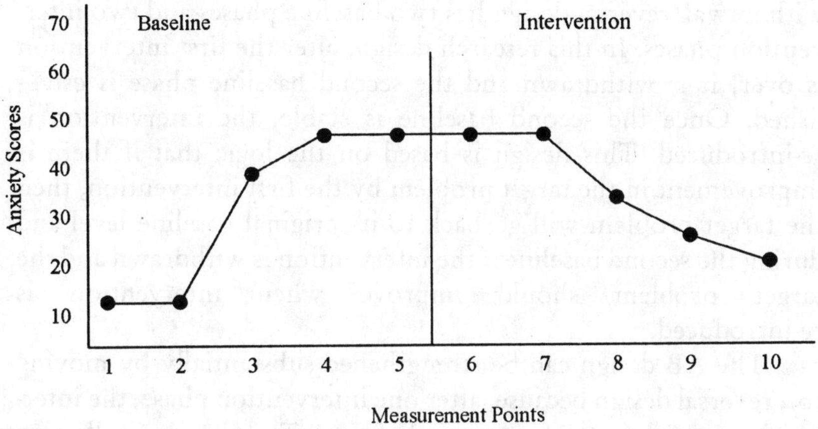

mainly because it involves only one baseline phase (A) and one intervention phase (B) as illustrated in Figure 9.7.

This design is more commonly known as AB design. The letter 'A' signifies baseline phase and a period when intervention is withdrawn in some of the more complex designs. The letter 'B' indicates an intervention phase when some specific intervention is introduced.

In this research design the effects of intervention are ascertained by comparing the client's condition during intervention phase with that of the baseline phase.

Since this design involves one baseline assessment and one intervention phase, its validity is threatened by history: events other than the intervention could be responsible for the change in the client's behaviour.

Despite the limitations of the AB design, it provides better evidence of intervention effects than non-experimental case histories. It also has the advantage of being applicable to most clinical situations, especially in cases where more rigorous designs might be precluded.

Besides, with enough repeated observations this design can provide valid and reliable evidence concerning the effectiveness of interventions.

ABAB: Withdrawal/Reversal Design

In order to have better control over extraneous factors withdrawal/reversal design has two baseline phases and two intervention phases. In this research design, after the first intervention is over, it is withdrawn and the second baseline phase is established. Once the second baseline is stable, the intervention is re-introduced. This design is based on the logic that if there is improvement in the target problem by the first intervention, then the target problem will go back to its original baseline level and during the second baseline if the intervention is withdrawn and the target problem should improve when intervention is re-introduced.

The AB design can be strengthened substantially by moving to a reversal design because, after one intervention phase, the intervention is withdrawn for a period of time. There are basically two versions of the reversal design: ABA and ABAB. The two versions differ only in that the ABA design ends in a no intervention phase whereas, in the ABAB design, the intervention is re-introduced a second time (see Figure 9.8).

Figure 9.8

Hypothetical Examples of ABAB Design

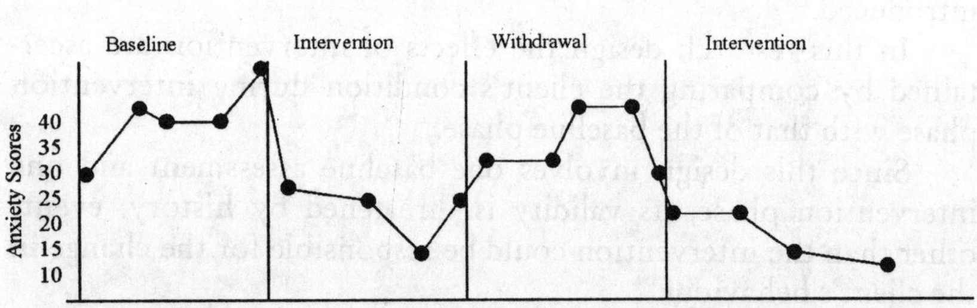

The value of the reversal designs stems from their ability to demonstrate more conclusively that it is the intervention and not some extraneous factor that is producing change in the client's condition. If the client's condition deteriorates when the intervention is withdrawn, we have evidence that the intervention is the controlling factor. Even more evidence is provided with the

ABAB design if the re-introduction of the intervention coincides with renewed improvement of the client. Although it is possible for a set of extraneous factors to produce the first client improvement, it is likely that the same set of factors would recur at precisely the right time to produce improvement on re-introduction of the intervention. As Figure 9.8 illustrates, especially with the ABAB design, we would have great confidence in the efficacy of an intervention that produced similar real-life results.

This research design has higher strengths on internal validity when compared with the AB design. However, there are practical problems that restrict the use of ABAB designs. First, the changes in clients due to first interventions, which more or less permanent in nature cannot be put in reverse order. Second, putting clients to their baseline is not only unwise but also unethical.

Multiple-Baseline Designs: The multiple-baseline designs attempt to control for extraneous variables by having more than one baseline and intervention phase. But, instead of withdrawing the intervention in order to establish more than one baseline, multiple-baseline designs begin with two or more baselines simultaneously. This is done by measuring different target behaviours in each baseline or by measuring the same target behaviours in two different target behaviour in two different settings or across two different individuals. Although each baseline starts simultaneously, the intervention is introduced at a different point for each one. Thus, as the intervention is introduced for the first behaviour/setting/individual, the others are still in their baseline phases. Likewise, when the intervention is introduced for the second behaviour/setting/individual, the third (if there are more than two) is still in its baseline phase.

A multiple-baseline design involves establishing more than one baseline for different clients who suffer from a similar problem. Let us consider an example. A social worker, who is working with a group of three alcoholics, establishes initial baselines for all the three alcoholics and introduces intervention only to one alcoholic. He establishes second baseline for the

Figure 9.9
Hypothetical Example of the Multiple-Baseline Design

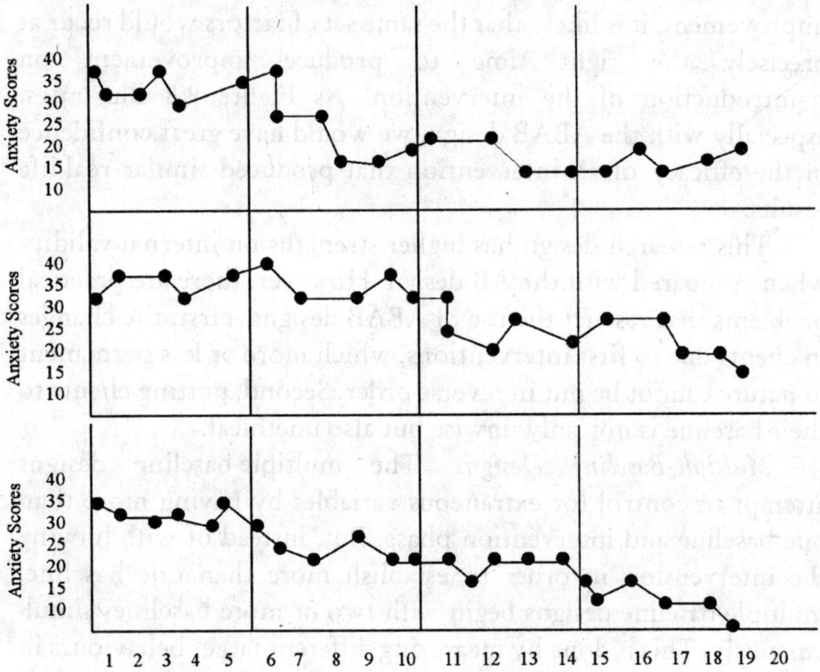

remaining two alcoholics and introduces the same intervention now to second alcoholic. Finally, the social worker establishes baseline for the third alcoholic, who then is exposed to the same intervention. Thus, as the intervention is introduced to the first alcoholic, the other two alcoholics are still in their baseline phase. When intervention is introduced to the second, the third alcoholic is still in the baseline.

The efficacy of the intervention is assessed across three individuals. Furthermore, the sequential introduction of three interventions after first, second and third baselines helps researcher to rule out the possibility that the effects of interventions across the three individuals were due to extraneous variables. This makes multiple-baseline designs fairly strong on internal validity. So far as internal validity is concerned, the multiple-baseline designs are superior to AB designs. However, it is not as strong internal validity as are ABAB designs.

The main logic here is that if the intervention effects improvement, then that improvement will occur on individuals graphs at a different point that corresponds to the introduction of the intervention. On the other hand, if some extraneous variables coincide with the introduction of intervention and causes the client's improved functioning, then that improvement will show up in the graph of each individual at the same time, even though some might still be in baseline.

ABCD: Multiple Component Design

The multiple component designs are prepared to handle special problems in different situations. These are commonly known as specialized designs and symolized as ABCD designs where B, C, D stand for alternative interventions. These designs are basically used to evaluate the impact of changes in the intervention and modify the intervention that does not appear to be effective. Conversely, the researcher seeks to determine which intervention package is really responsible for the improvement in the target problem. Let us consider the problem of a client who is an alcoholic. Say, for example, first, we introduce problem experiencing in relation to drinking behaviour as a treatment (B) and find that it is not effective. Then, we try the costs and benefits of drinking behaviour as a technique (C) in its place. Suppose, there still is no improvement, then method for resolving drinking problems is used. The process describes a typical ABCD designs:

A = Baseline

Interventions

B = Problems experienced in relation to drinking behaviours
C = Costs and benefits of drinking behaviours
D = Methods for resolving drinking problems

Data Analysis

The results of single-subject experiments are presented in graphic form from Figure 9.10 to Figure 9.12. In analyzing data from the

Figure 9.10
Hypothetical Example of the Multiple Component Design

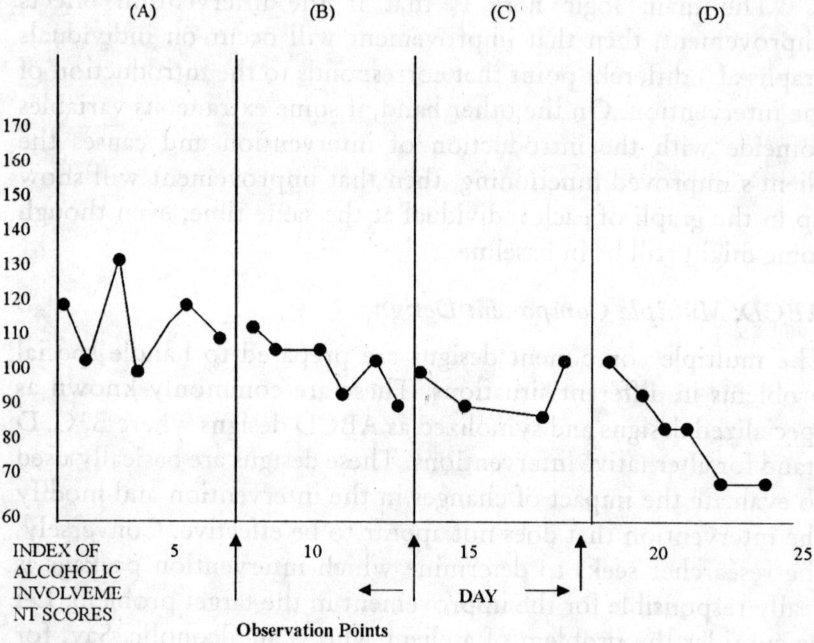

graph, generally, we look for pattern or trend of data and the slope of the line graph. When we analyze the meaning of a graph, we look for the data pattern and its trend so that we can see the shifts in the target problem when intervention is introduced. That is, we try to get evidence for supporting that the intervention is affecting the target problem.

The single-subject design experiment data are depicted by way of graph. Its purpose is to show at a glance what the facts are about data. Rather than displaying information in the form of tables, data are converted into graph for an easy understanding of information. Thus, a graph depicting single-subject design data provides reader with a great deal of information while using only a few words.

While analyzing data through graph, generally, we look for pattern or trend of data and the slope of the average. Let us consider Figures 9.11, 9.12 and 9.13 which depict three patterns of data. Pattern 1 suggest that problem is on increase before the intervention and continues to be unaffected even after the intervention.

Figure 9.11

Pattern of Chronological Graph

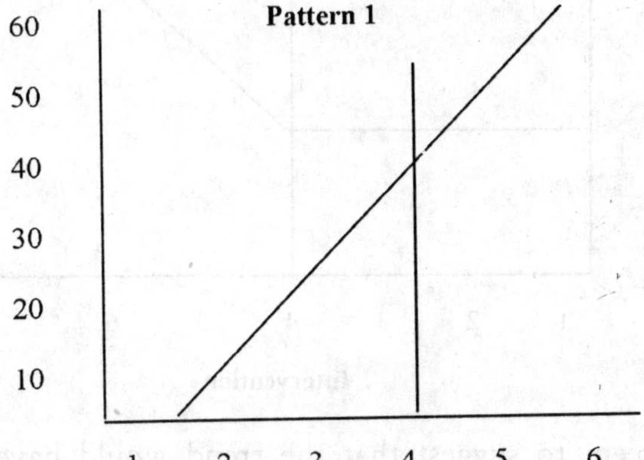

Figure 9.12

Pattern of Chronological Graph

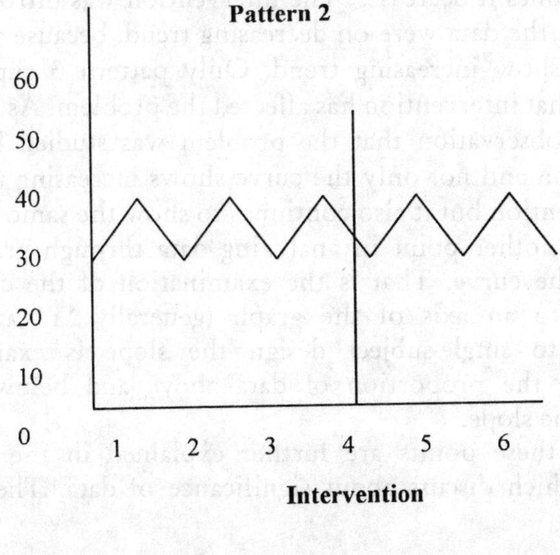

Figure 9.13
Pattern of Chronological Graph

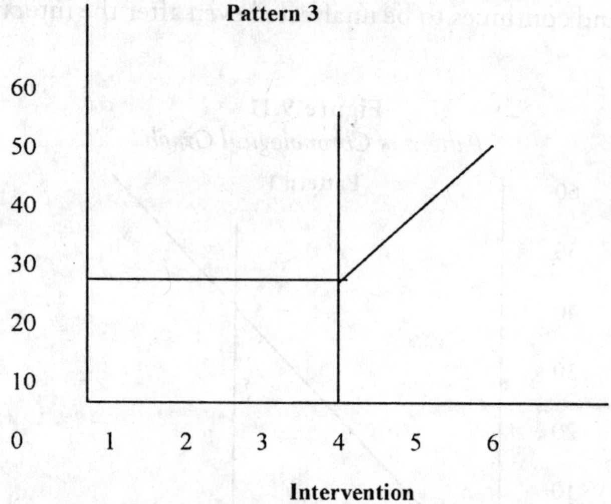

The data seem to suggest that the trend would have occurred without the intervention also.

Pattern 2 contradicts the researcher's assertion. It indicates that the problem has been cyclical throughout the process. Sometimes, it increases from one point of observation to the other and sometimes it decreases. The intervention was introduced at a time when the data were on decreasing trend, because we can see that data show increasing trend. Only pattern 3 supports the assertion that intervention has affected the problem. As we can see from the observation that the problem was studied before the intervention and not only the curve shows increasing trend after the intervention but it also continues to show the same trend.

The another point in analyzing data through graph is the slope of the curve. That is the examination of the curve with reference to an axis of the graph (generally 'Y' axis). With reference to single-subject design the slope is examined by comparing the proportion of data above and below the line showing the slope.

Both these points are further explained in the following section, which discuss about significance of data. The trend or slope analysis of observed data tells us whether a particular intervention has caused the change or whether the change is caused by chance variation.

Tests of Significance for Single-Subject Research Designs

There are a number of statistical procedures for testing the significance of change caused by interventions. Two procedures, namely, two-standard deviation method and celeration line approach method, which will be discussed in this section, are most popular among researchers mainly because they involve simple mathematical operations.

Two-Standard Deviation Method

The two-standard deviation procedure is based on the presumption that if the difference between the average baseline value and the average intervention value are larger than twice, the value of the standard deviation then the changes in the target problem are not due to chance. This procedure is used if the data points are not dichotomous and the baseline trend is relatively flat or cyclical; it should not be used when there is a pronounced trend in the baseline.

The steps for computing two-standard deviation is given below:

1. Compute arithmetic mean of the baseline score.
2. Find standard deviation (SD) of the scores by using the formula $SD = \sqrt{\frac{\Sigma d^2}{n-1}}$
3. Multiply the SD by 2
4. Find out $\overline{X} \pm 2$ SD
5. Calculate the difference between the baseline mean and intervention mean.

Let us take an example of scores obtained by a social worker in a single-subject design research. In a study mean baseline scores and standard deviation were found to be:

$\overline{X}$ (Mean Baseline Score) = 57.2 and SD = 2.29

Therefore,

$$\begin{aligned} 2SD &= 2 \times 2.29 \\ &= 4.516 \\ &= 4.6 \\ &= \overline{X} \pm 2SD = 57.2 \pm 4.6 = 61.8 \text{ or } 52.6 \end{aligned}$$

Method of Celeration Line Approach

Test of significance through celeration line approach is based on the assumption that the data would continue increasing or decreasing at the same rate as was in the baseline phase. As such, this test of significance is used when the slope of baseline is clearly showing the increasing or decreasing trend of the data.

This test of significance is carried out in two stages. In the first stage the slope of the baseline is determined and is extended into the intervention period. Then, in the second stage, the proportion of data points above or below the line showing the slope of baseline to the proportion during the intervention phase.

The procedure involves the following computation steps suggested by Gingerich and Feyerherm (1979) and illustrated in Figure 9.14:

1. Construct a chronological graph of the baseline scores.
2. Divide the baseline in half chronologically. (If there is an odd number of baseline data points, do not include the middle point in either half).
3. Calculate the mean score of each half.
4 Plot the mean of each half at the chronological halfway point of each half (the one-quarter and three-quarter points of the overall baseline).
5. Draw a straight line connecting the two points plotted in step 4.
6. Extend the above line from the beginning of the baseline to the end of the intervention period. This is the celeration line.
7. Calculate the percentage of baseline observations that fall in the desired zone. The desired zone is above the celeration line if we are looking for an increase in he data points and below the celeration line if we are looking for a decrease.
8. Count the total number of data points in the intervention period.

Figure 9.14

Chronological Graph Showing Celeration Line

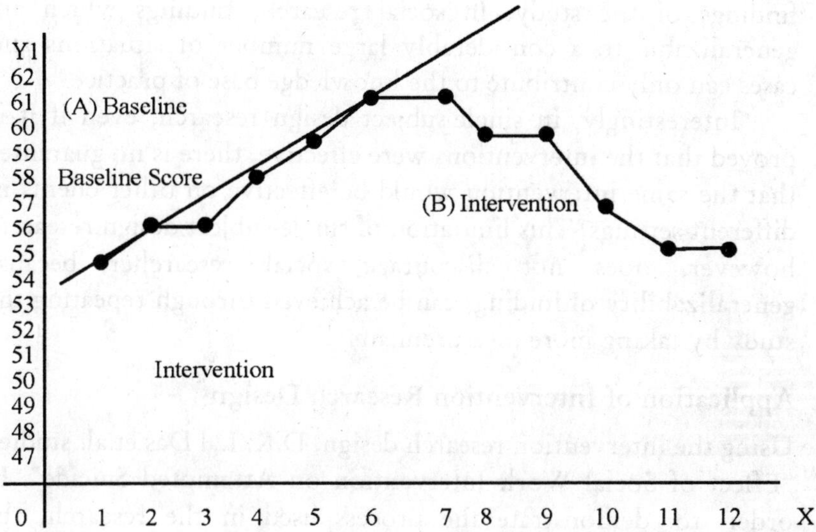

9. Count the number of data points that fall in the desired zone during the intervention period (see number 7 for definition of desired zone).
10. Examine the cell entries in Appendix A to see if the proportion of data points in the desired zone is significantly greater during intervention than during baseline.

To rule out the possibility of change variation, a number of statistical procedures have been evolved. However, some statistical procedures require a large number of measurements of observation points, which makes it impossible for researchers to use. Yet, some another statistical procedures are highly controversial.

Before we draw our conclusions, we have to ascertain that the change in the target problem is not due to chance variation. In other words, we have to ascertain that the difference between baseline and intervention levels is too great to be due to chance variation. The procedure to rule out the chance factor is known as the *test of statistical significance.*

Generalizability of Single-Subject Designs

The ultimate goal of a scientific research is generalizability of the findings of the study. In social research, findings which are generalizable to a considerably large number of situations and cases can only contribute to the knowledge base of practice.

Interestingly, in single-subject design research, even if it is proved that the interventions were effective, there is no guarantee that the same intervention would be effective on other clients in different settings. This limitation of single-subject design research, however, does not discourage social researcher because generalizability of findings can be achieved through repeating the study by taking more measurements.

Application of Intervention Research Design

Using the intervention research design, D.K. Lal Das et.al. studied "Effect of Social Work Intervention on Attempted Suicide". In order to demonstrate the process used in the research, the research report is reproduced at the end of this chapter in an abridged form.

Important Terms for Review

- Single-Subject Designs
- The Logic of Single-Subject Designs
- Use of Single-Subject Designs in Social Work Practice
- Baseline Phase
- Single-Subject Designs Research Process
- Pre-Intervention Assessment
- Intervention Strategies
- Post-Intervention Assessment
- Basic AB Design
- ABCD: Withdrawal/Reversal Design
- Multiple Baseline Designs
- Specialized Designs
- Multiple Intervention Designs
- Changing Criterion Designs
- Data Analysis

- Visual Significance
- Statistical Significance
- Two-Standard Deviation Procedures
- Celeration Line Approach
- Practical Significance
- Generalizability of Single-Subject Designs
- Assessment of the Single-Subject Design
- Limited Generalizability of Results
- Per-Intervention Assessment
- Intervention Assessment
- Individual Counselling
- Supportive Treatment
- Facilitation/Ventilation of Feelings
- Universalization
- Post-Intervention Assessment

Further Readings

Barlow, D.H., and M. Hersen, "Single-Case Experimental Designs: Uses in Applied Clinical Research", *Archives of General Psychiatry*, 29 (1973), 319-325.

Bennel, Carl et. al., *Evaluation Experiments*, New York: Academic Press. 1975.

Bloom, M., "Challenges to Helping Profession and the Responses of Scientific Practice", *Social Service Review,* 52, 584-595, 1978.

Bloom, M. and J. Fischer, *Evaluating Practice: Guidelines for the Accountable Profession*, Englewood Cliffs, N.J.: Prentice-Hall, 1982.

Epstein, I. and Tripodi, T., *Research Techniques for Programme Planning, Monitoring and Evaluation*, New York: Columbia University Programme, 1973.

Fansel, David, "Services to and by the real people", *Social Work,* 34, 195-196, 1980.

Gingerich, W. and Feyerherm, W., "The Celeration Line Technique for Assessing Client Change", *Journal of Social Service Research*, 3,1, 99-113, 1979.

House, E.R. *Evaluating with Validity,* Beverly Hills, California: Sage, 1980.

Jayaratne, Srinika, Tripodi, Tony, and Talsama, Engene, "The Comparative Analysis and Aggregration of Single Case Data", *Journal of Applied Behavioural Sciences*, 1,24, 119-28, 1988.

Jayaratne, Srinika and Levy, Rona L., *Empirical Clinical Practice*, New York: Columbia University Press, 1979.

Lal Das, D.K., *Practice of Social Research: Social Work Perspective*, Jaipur: Rawat Publications, 2000.

Monette, Duane R. et. al., *Applied Social Research: Tool For the Human Services*, Chicago: Holt, 1986.

Reid, W. "The Social Agency as a Research Machine", *Journal of Service Research*, 2, 11-23, 1978.

Rossi, H.P. and Williams. W. (eds.), *Evaluating Social Programs: Theory, Practice and Politics*, New York: Seminar Press, 1972.

Rossi, P. and H. Freeman, *Evaluation: A Systematic Approach*, Beverly Hills, California: Sage, 1982.

Rubin, Allen and Babbie E., *Research Methodology for Social Work*, Belmont, California, Wadsworth, 1989.

Schneirer, M.A., *Programme Evaluation: The Organizational Context*, Beverly Hills, California: Sage, 1979.

Thomas, E.J. "The BBESDAS Model for Effective Practice", *Social Work Research and Abstract*, 13, 12-16, 1977.

Review Questions

1. What is an intervention research design? Why is it called as a modified form of time-series designs? Discuss.
2. What is a single-subject research design?
3. Discuss why, pre-intervention measurement is called 'baseline phase'.
4. What do you understand by the term 'establishment of baseline'? Discuss.
5. Select a behaviour problem from one of the following and prepare a research proposal based on single-subject research design:
   (a) Truancy
   (b) Low self-esteem among children
   (c) Cigarette smoking among school children
   (d) School drop-outs
   (e) Child abuse
   (f) Feeling depressed
6. What are the various single-subject designs? Discuss its advantages and disadvantages.
7. Discuss how a multiple baseline study is designed?

Single Subject Design: A Case Study

EFFECT OF SOCIAL WORK INTERVENTION ON ATTEMPTED SUICIDE

D.K. Lal Das, Anna Mathew and K. Mrudula*

Abstract

The article reports the results of a study evaluating the effectiveness of an intervention package on a male young adult who attempted suicide. Data indicate that cognitive therapy was found to be the most effective in the intervention package consisting of crisis intervention, cognitive therapy and developing problem-solving skills.

Introduction

Amongst the young adults today, there has been an increased sense of hopelessness and despair creating suicidal ideation and eventually leading to suicidal attempts. Unrealistic expectations and aspirations, family pressures, high life ambitions, cut-throat competitive spirit in examinations, insufficient financial resources and fast paced life are some of the reasons that can lead a young adult to this condition.

Besides, young suicide attempters also often manifest special deficiencies in problem-solving. This finding has been shown to extend to children, adolescents as well as adults. It has been speculated that the reduced problem-solving skills in suicidal young adults are more lethal than would be the case for adults (Stillion, McDowell and May, 1989:102).

Problem Identification and Assessment

Suicide is a term applied to all cases of death resulting directly or indirectly from a positive or negative act of the victim himself, which he knows will produce this result (Durkheim, 1951:44). Suicide has been viewed as an individual phenomenon in terms of processes occurring within the psyche

* Dr. D.K. Lal Das is Principal at R.M. College of Social Work, Panmaktha, Hyderabad.
Dr. Anna Mathew is Reader in Social Work at R.M. College of Social Work, Panmaktha, Hyderabad.
Ms. K. Mrudula is Faculty Member at R.M. College of Social Work, Panmaktha, Hyderabad.

of the person. It also indicates that man is against himself in the society of his own making. Suicide indicates a disorganization of the ties that binds the members of the organized group together. It is the final and irreversible culmination of personal disorganization (Elliot and Merrill, 1961:315).

This study evaluates the effectiveness of social work intervention on a case of attempted suicide expressing chronic depression with low self-esteem and impaired general functioning. Effectiveness of interventions such as crisis intervention, cognitive therapy and developing problem-solving skills were evaluated.

Objectives

The objective of the study is to assess the effectiveness of an intervention package consisting of the following therapies:

a. Crisis intervention strategy,
b. Cognitive therapy, and
c. Developing problem solving skills.

Further, the interest of the researchers has been to assess the effectiveness of an intervention package in dealing with suicidal tendencies, accompanied by the prevalence of suicidal ideation amongst young adults studying in educational institutions.

Major Research Studies

Several studies have found depressive symptoms amongst young adult suicide attempters and completers (Berman and Carroll, 1984:97; Beck, 1967: 50-51). Beck (1967: 50) describes depression as disturbance in thinking leading to disturbance in mood. Depressive youth tend to have a general pessimistic attitude towards the world, tend to engage in awfulizing, focussing on negative and de-emphasizing what is positive in his/her life (Stillion McDowell and May, 1989:51). Symptoms of depression include depressed mood along with poor appetite or over eating, insomnia, low energy or fatigue, low self-esteem, poor concentration or difficult decision-making, hopelessness, recurring thoughts of death or suicidal ideation (American Psychiatric Association, 1987).

Theoretical Framework

The theoretical foundation for the causes and factors of suicide consists of sociological, psychological, behavioural and cognitive orientations. Durkhiem (1951:46) contended that the social suicide rate can be explained only sociologically which he classified into egoistic, altruistic and anomie, which was later challenged by Henry and Short (1954).

Compared to the sociological explanation, the psychological explanation appears to be more relevant to the suicidal phenomenon. It tends to focus on factors deep in the unconscious which according to Freud (1949), the exponent of the psychoanalytical theory, cause the individual to take his own life.

Several prominent followers of Freud like Menninger (1938), Fenichel (1945) and Fisch (1954) followed the same line of thinking. Fromm (1955) attributes the causes of suicide to the feeling that life has been a failure and that it is not worthwhile living any more.

Profile of the Subject

The subject in this study is a male student, 22 years of age, enrolled for a postgraduate course in Social Sciences. He stays with his relatives in Hyderabad, capital of Andhra Pradesh, while his parents live in their village. His father is a businessman and his mother a housewife.

He expressed that his goal was to secure a seat in the M.Sc. course for which he did not get a call in the first counselling. He was awaiting the call for the second counselling, which was scheduled a month later. In the meantime, he sought admission for a course in Social Sciences; a subject, which his parents felt, was less prestigious.

He is of medium stature, big-built, with drooping shoulders. He appeared extremely shy and withdrawn. He was quite willing to talk and seemed to answer all the questions with sincere and well-formulated responses. He said that his parents expressed dissatisfaction with the course he was attending and that they were anxious and impatient about his obtaining the M.Sc. seat. He felt that his parents were expecting too much from him. He seemed a little worried about what his parents would say.

Method

Measurement of the Dependent Variables

While the problem was being identified and assessed using assessment strategies such as interviewing and paper-pencil assessment tools, the negative and positive indicators were selected. The client's expressed difficulties; dissatisfaction and complaints of the specific problem were relied upon. As a general rule of thumb, two to three operational indicators are considered appropriate to meet the criterion of triangulation (Rubin and Babbie, 1993:302-303). The indicators that signified the presence of the problem of attempted suicide were found to be:

- Signs of depression and low self-esteem,
- Feelings of hopelessness and uselessness,
- Engaging in 'awfulizing' and de-emphasizing what is positive, and
- Impaired problem solving techniques.

Beck's Depression Inventory (BD!), Global Assessment of Functioning (GAF) Scale of the DSM-III-R and Hudson's Self-Esteem Scale (SES) were used to measure the indicators of the target problem. These instruments were used in conjunction with converging information from interviews, direct observations and collateral others.

Study Design

The study has been carried out using Single-Subject Design. The design applies the logic of time-series research designs to the evaluation of the effect of intervention on client. Such designs involve obtaining repeated measures of the client with regard to particular outcome indicators of the target problem before and after the intervention is introduced to see if there is improvement in the target problem. The repeated measure before intervention is called the base line, which serves same function as control groups do in experiments. The data collected during the base line are compared to the data collected after the intervention in order to infer that an intervention is effective. Among the several single-subject designs, Multiple Component Design was found to be most appropriate for the study.

Establishment of the Baseline

The instruments (BDI, GAF and SES) were administered to the subject and the total scores obtained by the client were recorded. To establish the baseline the measurement of each instrument was repeated seven times with one-week interval between the readings and one-day interval between the administration of each instrument to assess the stable pattern of no constant change in the target problem.

Table 1

Pre- and Post-Intervention Scores of BDI, GAF and SES

No. of Observations	*BDI*		*GAF*		*SES*	
	Pre-	*Post-*	*Pre-*	*Post-*	*Pre-*	*Post-*
First	30.00	35.00	41.00	40.00	80.00	87.00
Second	37.00	25.00	30.00	51.00	85.00	76.00
Third	30.00	20.00	25.00	62.00	89.00	69.00
Fourth	34.00	17.00	25.00	75.00	92.00	63.00
Fifth	44.00	16.00	25.00	80.00	92.00	57.00
Sixth	44.00	12.00	25.00	80.00	92.00	50.00
Seventh	44.00	10.00	20.00	82.00	98.00	35.00

Table I shows the obtained score range of the baseline for BDI: 30 to 44, GAF: 41 to 20 and SES: 80 to 98.

Description of Intervention

An intervention package consisting of crisis intervention, cognitive therapy, and problem-solving skills was designed to bring improvement in the target problem.

Post-Intervention Measurement

After the completion of the intervention, the instruments (BDI, GAF and SES) were administered again to the subject and the total scores of the post-intervention measurement were obtained and were recorded. To establish the post-intervention measurement, each instrument was administered seven times with one-week interval between the readings and one-day interval between the administrations of each instrument to assess the improvement in the target problem (Table I). The range of the post-intervention scores for BDI obtained were 35 to 10, GAF 40 to 82 and for SES 87 to 35.

Findings

Data (Table I) show an overall difference in the pre- and post-intervention scores of each instrument. These findings reflect the efficacy of intervention in reducing depression, enhancing the general functioning and the self-esteem of the client.

Analyzing the pattern during the pre-intervention level separately for depression reveals that the scores had steadily increased till they remained stable in the last three measures (Table I). This indicates the intensity of the problem of depression that existed in the client before the intervention was introduced. Such was the trend found in GAF and SES also.

Table 2

Analysis of Pre- and Post-Intervention Scores of BDI, GAF and SES

Intervention	*N*	*Mean*	*Std. Deviation*	*Minimum*	*Maximum*
BDI-PRE	7	37.57	6.47	30.00	44.00
GAF-PRE	7	27.28	6.70	20.00	41.00
SES-PRE	7	89.71	5.79	80.00	98.00
BDI-POST	7	19.28	8.51	10.00	35.00
GAF-POST	7	67.14	16.51	40.00	82.00
SES-POST	7	62.42	17.16	35.00	87.00

Data in Table 2 also show that with the introduction of the intervention, the mean and standard deviations of scores of the BDI and SES instruments had decreased while the scores of GAF, as expected had increased.

To know whether there is significant difference in the means and standard deviations of scores in the pre- and post-intervention of the GAF, BDI and SES, the Wilcoxon Sign Test was used. The results show that the differences between the pre- and post-scores were statistically significant. (BDI: 2.197, P<. 05; GAF: 2.201, p<. 05; SES: 2 197, p<. 05).

Further, to assess whether the intervention was statistically significant Celeration Line Approach method was used. Celeration Line (Figure 1) was drawn to take into account the specific direction in which the baseline data were moving, that is the slope or trend of the baseline in the determination of statistical significance (Rubin and Babbie, 1993:516).

To test whether effectiveness of interventions was statistically significant, we refer to the statistical table showing the number of observations during the intervention period that are necessary to represent a significant increase at the 0.05 level over the proportion of observation during the baseline period. (Rubin and Babbie 1993: 520). Data show that the numbers of observations during the intervention period are 8, 6 and 5 for SES, BDI and GAF respectively. All the three numbers are more than the critical numbers. Hence, it can be inferred that the effectiveness of interventions was statistically significant.

Discussion and Implication for Social Work Practice

The statistically significant results of the intervention suggest that the client showed considerable amount of improvement in his condition. The results showed that a focussed cognitive approach coupled with a counselling was an intervention package of effectively addressing and alleviating the problems of suicide attempters.

The study used both quantitative and qualitative measures to analyse the outcome of a combined intervention approach. Multiple Component Design had a significant role to play. It is basically used to evaluate the impact of changes in the intervention. It was sought to determine which intervention was really responsible for the improvement of the target problem. From the graph, it can be inferred that cognitive therapy appeared to be most effective in reducing the suicidal ideation and depression in the client.

The Multiple Component Design typically resembled the way intervention would naturally be implemented. The client could not be helped with numerous problems simultaneously but repeated measures of the relevant behaviours could be seen and observed when they changed. The predictable and orderly changes related to where and when the intervention was used were seen and concluded that the intervention was causing the change.

There were extraneous variables that were not controlled that could have had an effect on the attempt on suicide. The suicide committed by the client's relative had increased the feelings of depression and deprivation and precipitated the attempt of the client to suicide. The counselling sessions held for M.Sc. admissions further aggravated the situation.

Figure 1

Graph Showing Effects of Interventions

A ⟶ Baseline

Interventions

B ⟶ Crisis intervention strategy

C ⟶ Developing problem solving skills

D ⟶ Cognitive therapy

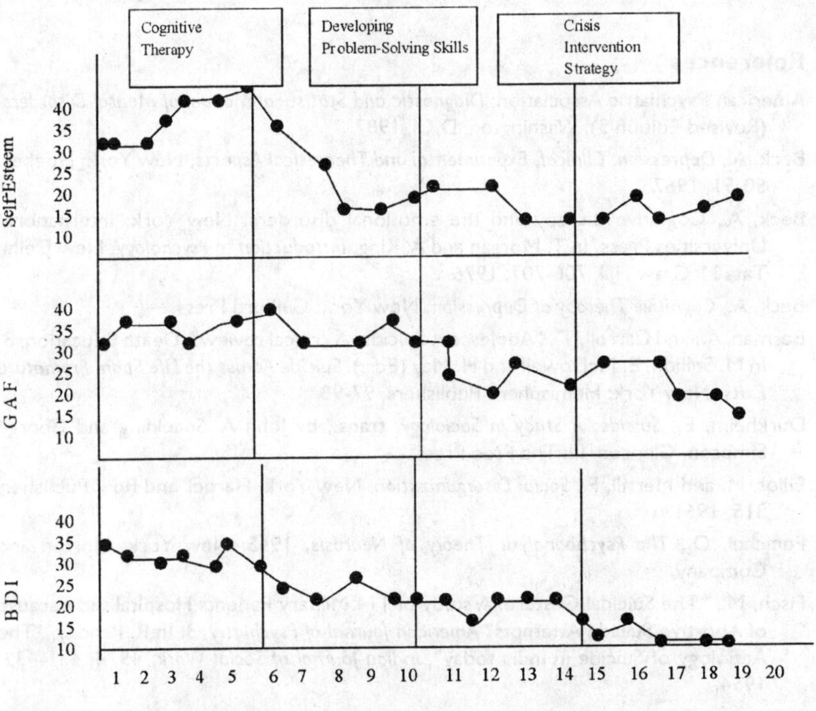

Visual significance was ascertained by eye balling the data pattern the extent that we could see the shifts in the level or trend of the target problem coinciding with the introduction of the intervention (Rubin and Babbie, 1993: 323-324).

The results of the study need to be considered in context of several methodological limitations. This study being a single-subject design study, has limited generalisations. As such, the generalizability of these findings to other populations may be limited.

However, the study can be replicated using the same design and intervention package for a similar condition. It may help social work practitioners understand the importance of maintaining outcome data on an ongoing basis to evaluate practice with each client. The intervention described in the study may also be an efficient mechanism for social workers working in crisis management centres.

Above all, the study also indicates that it is essentially important to understand that social work research and practice are complementary and social work research, basically intervention research is complete only when it is integrated into practice.

References

American Psychiatric Association: *Diagnostic and Statistical Manual of Mental Disorders*, (Revised Edition 3), Washington, D.C., 1987.

Beck, A., *Depression: Clinical, Experimental and Theoretical Aspects*, New York: Hoeber, 50-51, 1967.

Beck, A., Cognitive therapy and the emotional disorders. New York: International Universities Press. In T. Morgan and A. King, *Introduction to Psychology*, New Delhi: Tata McGraw Hill, 706-707, 1976.

Beck, A., *Cognitive Therapy of Depression*. New York: Guilford Press.

Berman, A., and Carroll, T., "Adolescent Suicide: A critical review". Death Education, 8. In M. Stillion, E. McDowell and H. May (Eds.). *Suicide Across the Life Span, Premature Exits*, New York: Hemisphere Publishers, 97-98.

Durkheim, E., *Suicide: A Study in Sociology*, trans., by John A. Spaulding and George Simpson, Glencoe, Ill: The Free Press.

Elliot, M. and Merrill, F., *Social Disorganization*, New York: Harper and Row Publisher, 315, 1961.

Fenichel, O., *The Psychoanalytic Theory of Neurosis*, 1945, New York: Norton and Company.

Fisch, M., "The Suicidal Gesture: A study of 114 Military Patients Hospitalised because of Abortive Suicide Attempts" *American Journal of Psychiatry*, 3. In R. Pandey, "The Aetiology of Suicide in India today", *Indian Journal of Social Work*, 45, 4, 431-432, 1954.

Freud, S., *An Outline of Psychoanalysis*, New York: Norton, 1949.

Fromm, E., *The Sane Society*, Greenwich, Conn: Fawcett Publications, 1955.

Henry, A. and Short, F. Jr., *Suicide and Homicide*, Glencoe, Ill. The Free Press, 1954.

Menninger, K., *Man against Himself*, New York: Harcourt, Brace and Company, 24-25, 1938.

Resnik,H. and Lettieri, D., *Encyclopedia of Social Work*, (18th edition) Vol. 2, National Association of Social Workers, Silver Spring, Maryland, 741-742, 1974.

Rubin, A. and Babbie E., *Research Methodology for Social Work*, Brooks/Cole Publishing Company: California, 1993.

Stillion, M., McDowell, E. and May, H. (eds.), *Suicide Across the Life Span, Premature Exits*, Hemisphere Publishers: New York, 1989.

10

Action Research Designs

Action researches are primarily for problem-solving researches. The main objective of this type of research is to diagnose the causes of a problem, assess the magnitude and provide an action plan to solve the problem.

Different types of research have been undertaken for this purpose. Most distinguishing feature of this type of research is its action plan, which is designed, tried out and evaluated to assess exactly the extent of alleviation of the problem. Action research is commonly termed as *applied research.*

The methodological rigour of this kind of research is as important as we have mentioned in the previous section. Action research deals with the application of research methods and skills in solving the social problems. In other words, action research is combination of research and practice. Therefore, when we undertake action research, we have to keep in mind the action plan to resolve the problem under study.

What is Action Research?

Action research is one of the recent developments in the field of research. Understanding of the process of action research is the fundamental for the community workers. Unlike other forms of social researches, action research deliberately sets out to create change. It is a series of cycles that begin and end with research and incorporate planned action to bring change.

Action research has its roots in community development programmes. Modern action research brings together social research methodology and community organisation/development programmes together. McTaggart (1997) argues that this convergence has occurred because it has been demonstrated over and over again that research findings from one context do not necessarily work when applied to new contexts. Instead, "people must conduct substantive research themselves on the practices that affects their lives".

Thus, involvement of people, for whom the action research is conducted, is the key to action research. For this reason, perhaps, some authors prefer to call action research as 'participatory action research'. This type of action research always contains the following:

1. the researcher,
2. involvement of individuals who are fundamental to the issue being researched, and
3. focus on action to bring social change.

Approaches to Action Research

McNiff and Whitehead (2000: 201) identify three approaches to action research as described below:

Interpretive Approach

In this approach, practitioners undertake researches on the issues related with their practice problems. The main objective of this approach of the action research is to diagnose the causes of a problem related with practice. In this research, they assess the magnitude and develop an action plan to solve the problem.

Participatory Action Research

The focus of this approach of action research is on emancipatory issues and collective action, and on reflection and ownership of the action research process in the struggle against oppression.

Living Educational Theories

This approach encourages individuals to clarify the value base in their work.

Why Action Research?

We undertake action research when we wish to work together to bring change in our lives, community, organizations or social structure. The change is of course based on rigorous research. For action research following points may be looked into:

1. relevance and magnitude of the problem,
2. the quality of the solution identified,
3. replicability of the approach,
4. sustainability of the solution, and
5. transferability of the experience.

As stated above, action research intends to solve practical problems through research and planned actions. In this research, the emphasis is on solving problems through adoption of alternative practices suggested by a research study. The two distinct purposes of action research are: (a) to find out the causes of the problem, and (b) to suggest actions to resolve the problem.

Action research is applied research that treats knowledge as a form of power and abolishes the line between research and social action. There are several types of action research, but most share common characteristics: those who are being studied participate in the research process; research incorporates ordinary or popular knowledge; research focuses on power with a goal of empowerment; research seeks to raise consciousness or increase awareness; and research leading to political action.

Nature of Action Research

The ultimate object of action research is to solve the practical problems with the help of research techniques. Action research, then, like social research, seeks to identify the exact nature and magnitude of the problem, analyze the causes in all their variety and intensity. Action research, however, assumes a distinct character of its own in a significant measure when it comes to the action to solve social problem. Action research emerges out of situational needs and a solution is also designed with respect to the situation.

Unlike other social researches, action research is increasingly becoming a team work where researchers collaborate with practitioners and subjects/beneficiaries participate in the research process. Although the researcher takes the initiative and leads the team, action research is a team work wherein other partners, viz., beneficiaries and other stakeholders, have to put in conscious effort in the research process.

Action research is a self-evaluative process where the research team evaluates the outcome of the exercise. It is initiated by practising individual or group. Hence, it becomes necessary for the researchers to understand the problem as it exists and develop the action research design.

Action research concerns with social data, which are much more complex than that of the physical data. The basis of all social interactions, whether it is a large complex group or a small cohesive group, is expectations of behaviour, which in turn is result of many factors. The complex nature of social data reduces the power of exact solution of the problem. Most of the subject matter of action research is qualitative and does not admit quantitative measurement. In action research, it is difficult to segregate the cause and effect. It is because many a time the cause is also the effect. This makes it very clear that the social data typically pose certain problems when it is analyzed for taking action to solve social problems.

Objective of Action Research

The major objective of action research is to search for answers to questions raised while trying to resolve social problems. In other words, action research attempts to provide knowledge about what interventions or treatments really help in resolving social problems. In addition, it also helps in searching for answers to problems or difficulties faced by practitioners in the practice of their profession.

Areas of Action Research

In a very broad sense, action research concerns itself with the problems faced by social activists/practitioners. It encompasses those questions, which are encountered in working with people or in planning or administering social services, which are capable of being solved through research and which are appropriate for social investigation.

Action research utilizes the same scientific methods and techniques, as does social research. No doubt, when some research designs/procedures of social research are not suitable to action research, it would be necessary to develop the tools which would be appropriate to action research.

Action research can cover almost every area of activity of socio-psychological context. The areas of action research may be broadly categorized as follows:

(i) Community Health
(ii) Child Abuse
(iii) Youth Unrest
(iv) Substance Abuse
(v) Poverty Alleviation
(vi) Indiscipline at Workplace
(vii) Low Productivity
(viii) Communal Harmony
(ix) Social Inequalities
(x) Democratic Processes
(ix) Crime and Corrections

The list is not exhaustive, it is only an exemplary one, which enlists broad areas that is very frequently studied by action researchers. Again, within one or more problem areas, research might focus on individuals, families, groups, community organizations or broad social systems. It might deal with characteristics of a larger population, and the services available to them.

Process of Action Research

It must be borne in mind that the process of action research is not that of social research. In fact, there are many similarities between this process and the traditional research process. The process of action research, however, has some additional steps designed to suit its objectives. By following the process researchers are in a position to know precisely what actions are applied and what effect is produced. The process also links research and practice. There are six major stages of action research. These are clearly demarcated. It can be linear or cyclical process.

Action research starts with problem identification. Often, the perceived problem is only symptomatic and not the real one. It becomes necessary to go deep into the problem through the symptoms to diagnose it clearly. After the problem is identified and diagnosed, the next step is to set up goals to be achieved. The goals are required to be specific, precisely defined and measurable in some way. This is followed by the process of assessment of the nature and magnitude of the problem. During these initial stages, the researcher strives to obtain a clear and specific understanding of the problem, using assessment tools such as interviewing, observation, case studies etc.

Once the problem is identified, diagnosed and assessed, the researcher is required to develop an action research design. Most of the social research designs with little modifications are suitable for action research. This is followed by actions/interventions. In the last stage, we assess the outcome/effects of intervention.

The process of action research can be diagrammatically presented as shown below:

Figure 10.1
Action Research Process

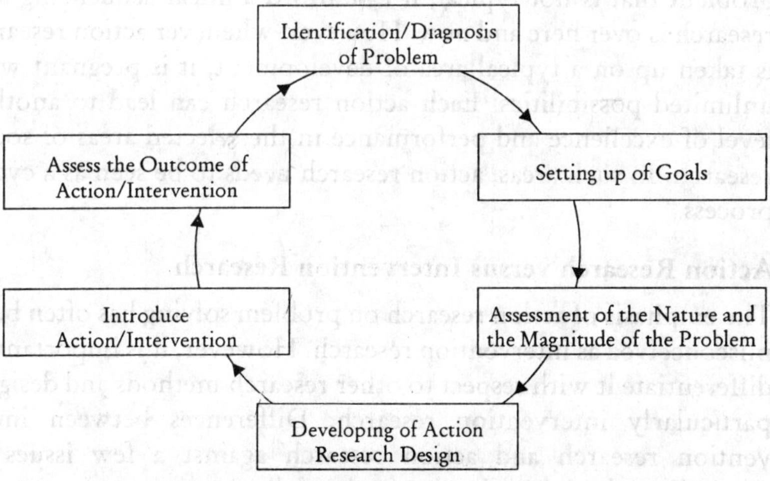

These stages can be broken down into ten steps as discussed below:

1. Identification, and formulation of problems.
2. Preliminary discussions and negotiations among the various stakeholders.
3. Review of literature: Though it is not necessary in all action research, certain types of problem may call for reviewing research literature.
4. Modification and redefinition of the statement of the problem based on review of literature.
5. Setting up the goals.
6. Assessment of the nature and magnitude of the problem.
7. Selection of action research design survey/experimental research design, sampling, method and tools of data collection etc.
8. Implementation of actions/interventions.
9. Analysis and interpretation of data to assess the impact of the actions/interventions.
10. Discussions on the findings and future actions.

Although these steps are clearly demarcated, it is possible to analyze them in a linear sequence as well as in cyclic process. Whenever the purpose of an action research is limited to solving a problem that is not typical, it can afford a linear sequencing and research is over here and now. However, whenever action research is taken up on a typical area of development, it is pregnant with unlimited possibilities. Each action research can lead to another level of excellence and performance in the selected areas of social research. In such areas, action research needs to be seen as a cyclic process.

Action Research versus Intervention Research

The emphasis of action research on problem solving has often been misconceived as intervention research. However, it is important to differentiate it with respect to other research methods and designs, particularly intervention research. Differences between intervention research and action research against a few issues of research methodology is presented as follows:

Comparison of Intervention Research and Action Research on Methodological Issues

Research Methods	*Intervention Research*	*Action Research*
Goals	Assessment of effectiveness of intervention	Local specific problem solving
Hypothesis	Not necessary	Not necessary
Research design	Single-subject designs	Survey/experimental
Treatment	Specified-Intervention like methods and techniques of Social Work	Not specified; it depends on the problem assessment; it can be income generation, functional literacy, health education etc.
Sample	Individual (N = 1), a family, a group or a community	Sample is not an issue. Whole community or a village may participate in an action research.
Tools of data collection	Only standardized research instruments are used for data collection	Generally interview schedules are developed by the researcher. Standardized research Instruments are also used in some situations.
Statistical analysis of data	Special statistical procedures like Two Standard Deviation, Celeration Line Approach etc are used	Only simple descriptive statistics are used

Partners in Action Research

Action research is basically a collaborative research. As such, to accomplish the goals of action research, the collaboration of its partners is essential. There are at least three possible partners in action research. First, an individual as a researcher may take action research to solve the problem of a village (say, for example). The second important partner in action research is the villagers. The third partner is the group of people who frequently interact with the villagers, such as governmental and non-governmental officials.

This collaborative action research brings the strength of the two or more types of professionals to bear upon the quality of research and also on the quality of the solution arrived at. In this case, research may take a more sophisticated form than normally it does in action research.

Important Terms for Review

- Action Research
- Action Research Process
- Local Specific Problem
- Problem-Solving Goal
- Self-Evaluative Process

Further Readings

Alston M. and Boweles W., 2003, *Research for Social Workers: An Introduction to Methods*, 2nd Ed., Rawat Publications, Jaipur.

Hart, E. and Bond, M., 1995, *Action Research for Health and Social Care: Guide to Practice*, Open University Press, Buckingham.

McNiff, J. and Jack Whitehead, 2000, *Action Research in Organisation*, Routledge, London.

McTaggart, R. (ed.), 1997, *Partcipatory Action Research. International Context and Consequences*, State University of New York Press, New York.

Reason, P. and Bradbury, H., 2001, *Handbook of Action Research: Participative Inquiry and Practice*, Sage, London.

Schmuck, R.A., 1998, *Practical Action Research for Change*, Hawker and Brownlow, Australia.

Wadsworth, Y., 1997, *Do it Yourself Social Research*, 2nd Ed., Allen and Unwin, Sydney.

Review Questions

1. What is action research?
2. What are the goals of action research?
3. What is the nature of action research?
4. What is participatory action research?
5. How does it differ from other researches?
6. What stages do action researchers pass through during the process of action research?
7. What is interpretive approach in action research?

11

Evaluation Research Designs

Concept of Evaluation

Voluntary organizations undertake many welfare programmes and provide services to individuals, groups and communities. While providing the services, they are constantly concerned about the outcome of their services. In other words, do they achieve their goals while providing services? A set of questions in this regard is raised: Are the services effective? Are these programmes leading to undesirable consequences? Are the services relevant? Will these services achieve their pre-determined goals? As many such questions puzzle agency administrators, they need some reliable and valid data that can give answers to these questions. These services are funded by various sources: it could be a government agency or non-governmental, national or international funding organizations. Whoever may be the funding organization, they insist on some reliable and evident assessment whether the funds are being effectively utilized in general and whether the intended goals are being achieved.

The term used for the process of getting these reliable data in assessment using some scientific technique is known as *evaluation*. Broadly speaking, evaluation is a systematic assessment of progress made by the implementing machinery; an analysis of problems and difficulties arising in the effective implementation of a programme; and an indication of the corrective measures necessary.

The attempt to conceptualize evaluation indicates a concern both with information on the outcomes of programmes and judgements regarding the desirability or value of programmes. Different definitions emphasize different aspects—information seeking, effectiveness of procedures, achievement of goals and efficiency. In this chapter, we will discuss about the concept of evaluation and evaluation research designs.

In a very broad sense, the concept of evaluation research simply connotes use of research methods to evaluate programmes or services and determine how effectively they are achieving their goals. The terms like evaluation research, evaluative research, programme evaluation and evaluation are synonymous, interrelated and hence used interchangeably.

All the programmes undertaken are to be evaluated for the results they have achieved or failed to achieve. Evaluation provides objective assessment of the performance. It is indispensable as it provides the programme administrator with effective use of resources and of accountability for their use.

Evaluation is now considered as an integral part of voluntary welfare organizations. Today, it is recognized as an important process to improve the working of voluntary welfare organizations. Its chief function is to determine as systematically and objectively as possible the relevant effectiveness and impact of their objectives.

Evaluation is an indispensable action-oriented tool in the organizational process for improving both activities still in progress and future planning, programming and decision-making.

Evaluation is a process, which covers aspects relating to the accessibility, availability and quality of the services and their utilization, relevance or appropriateness to local needs and expectations, and viability of the consequences or impact of the programme.

The American Public Health Association defines evaluation as the process of determining the value or amount of success in achieving a pre-determining objective. It includes at least the following steps: formulation of the objective, identification of proper criteria to be used in measuring success, determining and explaining the degree of success and recommendations for further programme activity.

These terms have different connotations. The term 'evaluation' is a generic term, which includes the process of assessment or judgement. It may not use methods and techniques of research. For example, a report of a study team or review committee is considered as evaluation of programme.

Evaluative research is an area of social research and implies the use of research designs with a view to measure the contribution of the programmes towards the changes brought in relation to the social conditions. Evaluative research uses different social research designs to study the contribution of the programmes.

Evaluation is a systematic assessment of the role and progress of the implementing machinery and analysis of problems and difficulties arising in the effective implementation of programmes, and an indication of the corrective measures necessary for an independent agency.

Evaluation of administration means appraisal or judgement of the worth and effectiveness of all the processes designed to ensure achievement of the agency's objectives. Evaluation is essentially the study and review of post-operating experience. It implies critical analysis of the quality of the relationships which have been developed between all groups. It implies a willingness to measure results and to make changes in both goals and methods as a result of considered evidence. Evaluation becomes a resource for the continuous strengthening of all the individuals and groups in the agency setting.

For example, when a programme director of a voluntary, welfare organization, after completing an income-generation skill training programme for women in a slum, evaluates whether the programme was effective, this is called as evaluation. However, one may raise a question here: How was effectiveness evaluated? If the programme director has evaluated the effectiveness by discussing with the trainees or by his impressions (without applying any scientific method), we call it informal evaluation. Such evaluation may be objective and accurate but the chances are only fair that they will be.

On the other hand, when an agency administrator tries to know to what extent a film on birth control devices is more or less effective than group discussions in increasing knowledge of birth control by dividing his beneficiaries into two groups and studying them through a questionnaire, it can be called as *evaluation research*.

Purpose of Evaluation Research

The evaluation research refers to the purpose of research rather than to any specific research methods (Rubin and Babbie, 1989: 481). Its purpose is to assess the utility of social interventions and human service programmes (Rossi and Freeman, 1982). Towards that end, evaluation research uses research designs, methods and techniques to plan social intervention programmes, monitor the implementation of programmes and determine how effectively programmes achieve their goals.

As evaluation research has more to do with the purpose of research than with specific research methods, as such, we will focus more on the implications of those purposes for carrying out research than on particular methodologies or designs.

People who are engaged in social service are constantly evaluating effectiveness. For example, a social case worker evaluates the extent to which changes in the anxiety of a particular client are associated with her/his treatment activities; a group worker wishes to assess the extent to which a film on birth control devices is more or less effective than group discussion in increasing knowledge of birth control; a programme director of an organization having substance-abuse clinic wants to know whether group therapy is as effective as individual therapy in reducing drug intake among clients; and an administrator is concerned about whether a new service is in fact effective. But we do not claim all such evaluations as 'evaluation research' just because, most of the time we do not think of applying scientific method. We use a term called 'informal evaluation' for all such evaluations. Informal evaluation is necessary, otherwise one would not be in a position even to decide the next phase of practice. Hence, evaluation research applies the scientific method.

Need of Programme Evaluation

Although non-governmental organizations (NGOs) have increased in number and financial clout, there have been very few systematic evaluation reports of their effectiveness (UNDP, 1993). To contribute effectively to sustainable human development, NGOs as well as donor/funding agencies have to recognize the significance and activities in the area of human development.

In this chapter, an attempt has been made to propose various evaluation research designs to be used at different stages of project/programme planning, implementation and outcome.

Thus, evaluation research can play multifarious roles to make services more effective (Monette, 1986). The various roles of evaluation research at different stages of programme planning, implementation and outcome can be classified into three categories: (a) evaluation research for programme formulation, (b) evaluation research for monitoring of programmes, and (c) evaluation research for programme outcome evaluation.

Evaluation Research for Programme Planning: Needs Assessment

In order to enhance programme effectiveness evaluators may assess problems and needs of a programme/target population. They assess the extent and location of the problems, the programme as well as the target population's characteristics, problems, expressed needs and desires (Monette, 1986). This information is then used to guide programme planning and implementation concerning such issues as the type of services to offer, how to maximize service utilization by targeted sub-groups, where to locate services, and so on (Jain, 1992).

In the first stage of project/programme evaluation research is undertaken to facilitate administrators to select right programme to be implemented, the services likely to be rendered, the scope in which the programme will operate etc.

The evaluation research in this stage is commonly known as need assessment/baseline study or feasibility study. Data generated through the research help administrators to justify programme and its feasibility and potential (Mullen et. al., 1972). It also provides baseline data, which are compared with evaluation/impact data at the end of the programme, and outcome/impact of the programme is assessed.

Evaluation Research for Programme Implementation

Some programmes have unsuccessful outcomes simply because they are not implemented properly. In that case no matter how well an outcome evaluation is designed, if it is not supplemented by an evaluation of programme implementation, it risks not being able to identify or misinterpreting the meaning of negative results (Reid, 1978). In turn, no matter how highly we value outcome studies; there is a clear need for the evaluation of programme implementation (Service, Mantal and Reismen, 1972).

Though appropriate methodology depends on the nature of research question, survey research utilizing questionnaires or scales may be used to assess staff, client or community attitudes that affect programme implementation decisions. Participant observation might be used to assess how staff relates to clients or to one another. Available records might be analyzed to assess whether the attributes of clients beings served match programme priorities.

Single-system designs of evaluation research can be used to assess the effect of interventions. These designs are basically quasi-experimental (time-series) designs. Such designs include repeated measure of a client system with regard to particular outcome indicators of a target problem (Rubin and Babbie, 1989). Repeated measures of the dependent variable are obtained before and after a particular intervention is introduced to see if a sustained pattern of improvement in the target problem commences shortly after the onset of intervention (Rubin and Babbie, 1989).

Evaluation Research for Impact, Outcome and Efficiency

Evaluation of programme outcome and efficiency may assess whether the programme has effectively attained its goals, whether it has any unintended harmful effects, whether its success (if any) has been achieved at reasonable cost and how the ratio of its benefits to its costs compares with other programmes having similar objectives (Bhatt and Subramaniam, 1984). This approach to evaluation, sometimes called the goal attainment model of evaluation, refers to the formal goals and mission of programme, whether it has achieved what the planners wanted to achieve.

A development programme is designed to produce significant outputs/results of social change and social transformation. Based on these facts, it is believed that experimental designs are best suited for a precise assessment of the results. In other words, the experimental designs should therefore be used wherever the essential conditions for organizing it are available. These are basically measurements at two or more points in time (before, during and after the project period) in regard to both experimental groups (those who participated in the programme) and control groups (those outside the influence of the programme). In evaluation studies that used experimental designs a few used a substitute approach of experimental design. A very common characteristic of the studies is that the scope of most of the conclusions of the evaluations is usually emphasized at the expense of depth (Engstne, 1970). The reports, one observes, are extensive rather than intensive and by and large, very informative regarding efforts in the area of social development.

Goal of Evaluation Research

The goal of evaluation research is to contribute to a body of verifiable knowledge. At a minimum, evaluative research should offer an objective assessment of programmes. Ideally, it should contribute to knowledge for the field at large, that is, it should contribute to practice theory.

Differences between Evaluation Research and Basic Research

Evaluation research differs from conventional social research already discussed in preceding chapters. In a very broad sense evaluation research is applied social research. By and large, conventional social research is concerned to add to our knowledge, test hypotheses, construction of theories and sometimes find some practical application in the future. Social research, in general, and basic research, in particular, is carried on for its own sake. There may not be a practical purpose—to produce results that are practical and useful. Evaluation research is a special branch of applied research, designed to evaluate social programmes and projects, such as adult/non-formal education, welfare schemes, innovative intervention methods, health care delivery systems, job training programmes etc. The findings of evaluation research are not meant merely to add to our knowledge or construct theories. They are used to decide whether the programme should continue as it is or with some modifications or be abandoned, whether budgets should be enhanced or reduced, whether staff should be hired or fired—all based on whether the programme achieved its intended goals.

As evaluation research is carried out to evaluate ongoing programmes, is designed with a shorter time span than basic research. The social problems are not solved immediately, but decisions about programmes are made immediately because budget allocations and personnel decisions are frequently based on demonstrable 'results'. Lynn Jr. (1978: 72) points out that "social problems are seldom solved by a single decisive act or policy declaration; rather, policies to deal with them are fashioned incrementally over time in a series of measures which are partial and not necessarily reversible". However, policy makers often have 'short time horizons' and wish to see research results to justify continuing or terminating a programme. The need for quick and definite answers makes most evaluation research different from basic research.

Although evaluation research is intended to produce immediate results that have an immediate impact, two circumstances often prevent this from happening. The first arises when results are equivocal or contradictory, so that it is not clear what the policy decision should be. There have been many evaluations of adult education, for instance, and they do not all agree about the programme' success or failure. Community Development Programmes have been evaluated many times in many places, and the results are contradictory. If the planners and policy makers are to use these evaluation results, which should they use, is very difficult to decide?

The second situation that prohibits the use of the results of programme evaluation arises when the effects of social welfare programmes are not immediately visible. For instance, education was originally introduced to educate three to four-year-old children so that they would become self-sufficient adults. However, educational planners are not prepared to wait for 15 or 20 years for an evaluation before they decide whether to continue with the early childhood education programmes. Instead, they use immediate outcomes; the children's subsequent academic achievement in primary school and assume that adult educational achievement will follow from childhood scholastic performance. There is positive but weak connection between the two.

Weiss (1972: 38) calls these immediate or short-run effects 'proximate' goals and the long-term desired effects 'ultimate' goals. She says short-run effects suffice when previous research shows a direct and strong connection between proximate and ultimate goals. For instance, in evaluation of a smokers clinic, it is probably enough to discover that the programme led participants to stop smoking. It is not essential to investigate the ultimate incidence of lung cancer. Many of our more ambitious social programmes, however, are designed to have long-range effects. Proximate outcomes in such cases are unsatisfactory, but they are all that we have.

Evaluation Research Models

Evaluation research has been undertaken on the following two models:

(i) Goal Attainment Model, and
(ii) The System Model.

The first model starts with taking into account the goals. This is followed by determination of measures of goals, collection of data and appraisal of the effect of the goals. Finally, the initial goals are modified in the light of the appraisal.

The second model, on the other hand, is concerned not only with goals and sub-goals but also the coordination of organization's sub-units, the execution and maintenance of necessary resources.

Types of Evaluation Research

Similarly, evaluation research can be classified into two types:
(1) Formative Evaluation Research, and
(2) Summative Evaluation Research.

Formative Evaluation Research

Formative evaluation research focuses on providing information to guide the planning, development and implementation of a specific programme. For initiating a programme, certain basic data are essential. First, it is necessary to have data on the personal and socio-economic characteristics of the target population. Second, it is important to be aware of existing services. Third, the programme planners should have knowledge about intervention strategies. Finally, it is necessary that it should be measurable.

Formative evaluation research is usually qualitative research and uses case histories rather than statistics to make a judgement. As such, it uses participatory research techniques like observation.

Summative Evaluation Research

Summative evaluation research involves assessing the impact of a programme. The results of these researches are basically used for policy making or decision-making, such as whether to continue, expand or cancel a programme. Summative evaluation research also examines the effects of a programme. It uses experimental, quasi-experimental and survey research designs. Besides, it usually uses statistical analysis of quantitative data.

Formative evaluation seems more desirable because it is used to help the agency administrators formulate their programme, review them, and improve them. Formative evaluator provides feedback to the programme director about how the participants react to the programme, how the implementors are carrying out the programme, and whether the actual programme is in line with the intended programme. They analyze the programme as it appears in action and describe how it works. This feedback is received during the initial stages of a programme, when it is still possible to change and improve, hence, the name formative evaluation. By contrast, summative evaluations are most often carried out during the terminal phase of the programme.

It is difficult to make precise categorization of numerous types of evaluations used by researchers. Some researchers prefer to classify evaluation researches according to evaluators, i.e., the persons responsible for evaluation of the programme. Based on this classification, evaluation researches can be of three types:

(a) *Internal evaluation*: In internal evaluation the personnel and the executive of the agency and the group participate. It is a continuous process, which is done at various points and in respect of various aspects of the programme/project activities. This is an approach to programme/project administration that involves fairly continuous self-evaluation by principal actors and participants, according to pre-established criteria related to the purpose and goal. Usually, this type of evaluation is included in the project plan during the design stage and given funding as part of the project.

(b) *External evaluation*: Persons outside the agency do external evaluation. Funding organizations retain evaluators from outside the agency to evaluate the programme/project activities for the purpose of finding out how the money given is utilized by the agency. External evaluators are chosen basically for two reasons. The first arises from the fact that the 'outsiders' are assumed to be more objective or at least neutral. The second is to obtain specialists and experts in certain areas. They add fresh perspectives and thinking; they may possess expert technical knowledge and skills that are absolutely necessary for a thorough evaluation; and their presence in an evaluation team helps give evidence of impartiality and thus enhances the credibility of the results.

(c) *Joint evaluation*: This type of evaluation involves external evaluators and one or more representatives of the agency. While joint evaluations are difficult, they can be very useful for training agency personnel and gaining their ownership of results.

Another categorization of types of evaluation is based on the timing of the evaluation. These types of evaluations comprise a continuous process of evaluation through different points in the life of a project or programme. Three such evaluations are very common:

(a) *Appraisal ex ante*: This is a critical examination of the identification report (feasibility report), which selects and ranks the various solutions from the standpoints of relevance, technical, financial and institutional feasibility and socio-economic profitability.

(b) *Mid-term evaluation*: This is an evaluation carried out during implementation. Its aim is to draw conclusions for administering the project/programme.

(c) *Ex-post-evaluation*: This is an evaluation of a completed programme/project. Its purpose is to study whether the programme/project objectives have been achieved. It also includes the lessons to be drawn for future improvement in a later phase or in a similar programme elsewhere.

Planning for Evaluation Research

The planning for an evaluation study involves making decisions about the choice of evaluation design, the techniques to be employed for collection of relevant data, validity, reliability and precision of the instruments of data collection, the sampling design and the size of the sample that would serve as a basis for drawing acceptable inferences, organizing, analyzing and interpretation of data. The evaluator engaged thus has to anticipate the general and specific difficulties that may arise from time to time and threaten the chances of getting reliable results. Through the planning of evaluation, the evaluator ensures that he will most probably achieve his objective within the optimum limit of time, money and energy.

Planning of evaluation research involves three operations, namely, evaluability assessment, specification of variables and measurement of variables.

Evaluability assessment is conducted to know whether a programme has the necessary pre-conditions to be evaluated. Once evaluability is assessed, immediately after that the researcher tries to specify the variables. He also decides how to measure those specified variables. Usually, the inputs to a social programme constitute the independent variables. The goals of a programme are generally the dependent variables. Measurement of the variables is the next stage in the planning of evaluation research. Some inputs or outcomes can be readily measured because they are quantifiable. Other effects or outcomes will require more inventiveness on the part of the evaluator to measure.

Evaluation Research Designs

In general, any of the basic research designs can be used for the purpose of evaluation research with some modifications. However, evaluation research often calls for testing of cause-effect relationship. As such, experimental designs are more appropriate for the purpose of evaluation research.

Further, true experimental designs use the process of randomnization to control the validity threats that can lead to false causal inferences. Therefore, ideal approach to determine the effects of a programme is randomized experiments. Though it sounds as the most appropriate research design for evaluation research, there are many practical difficulties in using randomized experimental research designs, which compare experimental group with control group. As a result, such experimental researches are considered inappropriate or impossible to conduct in practice settings. It was often too time-consuming and expensive to identify clients with similar problems and randomly assign some to treatment and others to control groups.

Another problem about conventional experimental researches was that of the complicated pre-conditions and assumptions of statistical analysis of data, which essentially require complying with probability theory of sampling, which is certainly a difficult, if not absurd, proposition for social researchers.

Finally, the use of control groups, to whom intervention is withheld, has been a source of ethical concern to social scientists. Thus, although conventional experimental researches are appropriate for some purposes, the drawbacks associated with the method have led social researchers to find an alternative approach for evaluating the effects of interventions and modify and update intervention techniques.

The evaluation designs consist of organization of measures to demonstrate achievement or non-achievement of intended effects of the programme/project. Designing evaluation studies also give credible objective measurement of development, change and impact. The choice of the evaluation design determines the degree of confidence that can be placed in the results of the evaluation. Various evaluation designs need to be examined and considered according to their ability to distinguish the affects of the programme/project from other possible effects not related to the programme/project. These evaluation designs may be set out as follows:

The After-Only Evaluation Design without a Control (Comparison) Group

In this study design, the measurements are limited to the target group and taken only once at some point of time after completion of the programme/project activities. This is by far the weakest evaluation design. It is difficult to know whether any change has occurred or to assess the degree to which the changes, if any, can be attributed to the programme/project implementation.

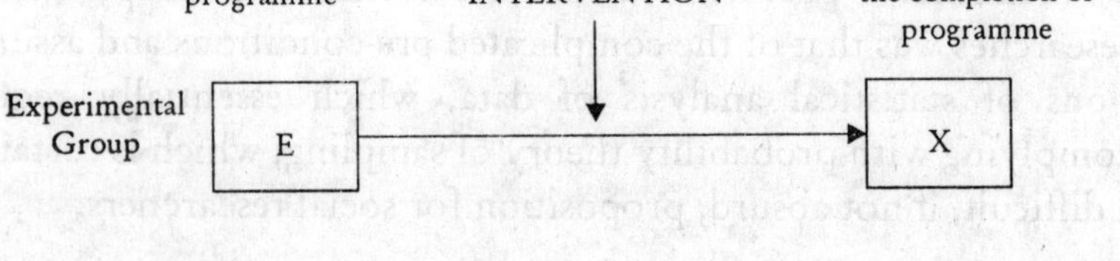

The After-Only Evaluation Design with a Control (Comparison) Group

In this design a control (comparison) group, similar to the experimental group for which programme/project activities have been implemented, is selected. Both the groups are measured with respect to the dependent variable only after completion of the programme/project activities.

The major weakness of this design is that the 'before' measurements are not taken. Both the groups are assumed to be similar in respect of the 'before' measures on the dependent variable. Hence, it is quite likely that the change in the dependent variable may really be due to the initial differences between the two groups.

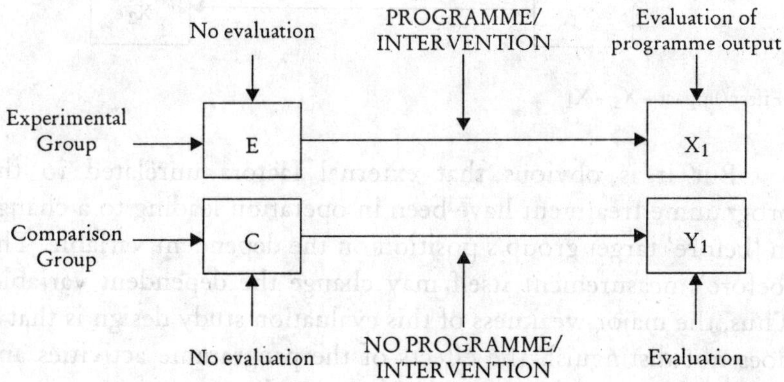

Effects $= X_1 - Y_1$

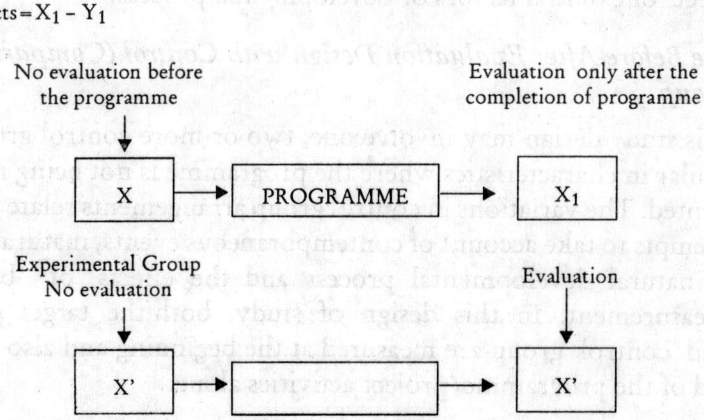

The Before-After Evaluation Design without Control (Comparison) Group

This design involves two measurements on the target/treatment group: one before the implementation of the programme/project and another after the completion of the programme/project. The difference between the target group's positions on the dependent variable (the effect of the programme) is taken as a measure of the effect of the programme (dependent variable).

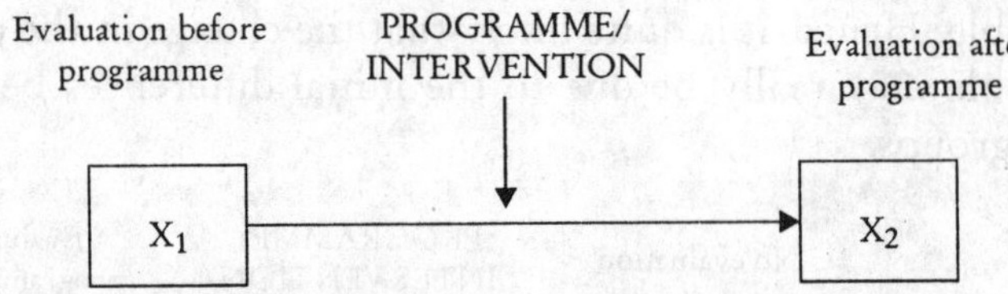

Effect/Impact – X_2 – X_1

But it is obvious that external factors unrelated to the programme treatment have been in operation leading to a change in 'before' target group's position on the dependent variable. The 'before' measurement itself may change the dependent variable. Thus, the major weakness of this evaluation study design is that it does not distinguish the effects of the programme activities and effects of external factors or developmental process.

The Before-After Evaluation Design with Control (Comparison) Group

This study design may involve one, two or more control group(s) similar in characteristics where the programme is not being implemented. The variations in control group arrangements relate to the attempts to take account of contemporaneous events, maturational or natural developmental process and the effects of 'before' measurement. In this design of study, both the target group and control group are measured at the beginning and also at the end of the programme/project activities alone.

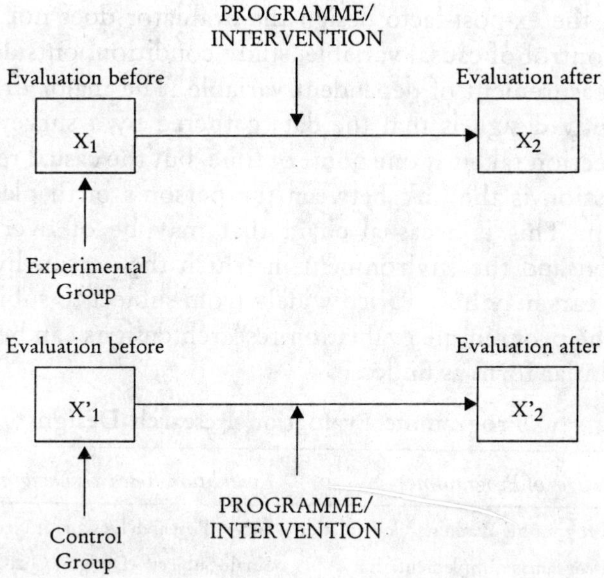

D_1 (Difference in Target Group) = $X_2 - X_1$

D_2 (Difference in Control (Comparison) Group) = $X'_2 - X'_1$

Effect/Impact = $D_1 - D_2$

The Ex-Post-Facto Evaluation Study Design

The ex-post-facto study design is an attempt to detect causal relationships with data gathered by survey. Here, the evaluator controls the crucial variables only by selecting one, which has already been recorded. For example, an agency has conducted an opinion survey of adult beneficiaries aged 25 or more, taking their age, gender, place of birth and so on. The agency authorities are interested in the causal effect of place of birth (the independent variable) on respondent's opinion on the effectiveness of the programme of non-formal education (dependent variable). Through manipulation of data the evaluator achieves some control over the other dependent variable (opinion) and the independent variable (birth place).

In the ex-post-facto design the evaluator does not have very good control of causal variable, study condition, outside variables and measurement of dependent variable. The major drawback of this study design is that the data gathered by a survey is only a cross section taken at one point of time, but the casual relationship in question is the link between the person's birth place and his opinion. This is a casual chain that may be of over 25 years' duration and the environment in which the person lived during these years may have varied widely from subject to subject.

The programme evaluation research designs can be presented in a tabular form as under:

Programme Evaluation Research Designs

Step	*Stages of Programmes*	*Evaluation Research Designs*
I	Programme Planning/Formulation	Survey Research Design for Need Assessment
II	Programme Implementation	Single-Subject Designs/Quasi-experimental Research Designs
III	Programme Impact/Outcome	Impact Study Design/Before-After Research Design (with control groups)

Alternative Evaluation Research Designs

Because of the problems encountered in setting up control groups, several alternative impact study designs have also been evolved. One of them is differentiation of samples according to degree of exposure and comparison amongst groups characterized by different degrees of exposure. To understand the alternative impact study design, we will take up the following example.

In a study of mid-day meals programme, where neither there was benchmark data nor was it possible to study a control group, comparing the children who had more exposure to the programme with those who had less exposure helped assess the programme impact. The children with less exposure were treated as a control group. The relationship between the level of programme efficiency and magnitude of impact on the children was tested, the magnitude of impact on the beneficiaries was found to be greater with higher programme efficiency.

Multiple Study Designs

Sometimes, multiple research designs are also used to assess the impact of a programme instead of a single design. For example, while using quasi-experimental design, some evaluators suggest supplementing the outcome with the case studies. By doing so, evaluators are able to capitalise on the merits of both the methods and impact assessment becomes more objective and reliable.

Impact Study based on 'Opinions' or 'Views'

An overview of some of the important impact studies would reveal serious lapses by the evaluators. For instance, in a study of impact of Applied Nutrition Programme, opinions/views about the impact were used to study the impact itself. Basing on impact study almost entirely on 'views' and 'opinions' would be a very superficial assessment and there is likelihood of varied opinions and views on which inferring something specific would be absolutely impossible.

Cost-Benefit Analysis

One special type of evaluation research is cost-benefit analysis. In this type of evaluation, all one has to do is to add up the costs of a programme, subtract them from the value of benefits, and we get the results. Either benefit exceeds costs or vice versa. On the surface, it appears simple. But, in practice, it is one of the most difficult evaluation designs, as quantifying benefits, in particular, is really a difficult task.

This is more popular among policy makers and programme planners concerned about the cost involved and benefit accrued out of a programme. In the present context, when everyone asks about accountability, programme evaluation is probably here to stay.

Cost-benefit analysis is not as simple as it appears. Converting programme benefits into a monetary value is extremely difficult, particularly when a programme is intended to accrue long-term benefits.

Estimating Costs

The costs are calculated in two parts. The first part involves the estimation. This part of analysis is comparatively simpler than the second part. In the first part one has to just refer to the records of actual expenditures. Considerably, it is more difficult to estimate the cost of programme benefits. That is, it becomes not only difficult but sometimes unreliable when a researcher determines the cost of programme benefits and tries to attach a monetary value to it. In general, if the benefits of a programme are related to some economic activity, such as income generation programme, it becomes easy to convert the benefits into a monetary value. However, it is difficult to express the level of awareness or self-esteem or mental health in monetary terms. Cost-benefit analysis may be tried in such case making some assumptions and value judgements which requires complicated procedures. Because of this, cost-benefit analysis is useful when the quantification of benefits is simple and measurement tools are available.

Another problem in cost-benefit analysis is when the benefits do not accrue simultaneously with the programme implementation. That is, cost is incurred immediately upon the implementation of the programme whereas the benefits may accrue after lapse of considerable time. For example, the benefits of programme of early childhood education can be assessed only after a few years of schooling. The gap is a problem because the value of both costs and benefits changes with time. To make useful analysis over time, one has to adjust costs and benefits so that the analysis is in the current monetary value.

In cost-benefit analysis, the costs and benefits are calculated from three angles, namely, the funding organization, the beneficiaries and the society. A comparative cost-benefits analysis takes into consideration all the three.

Cost-Effective Analysis

Cost-effective analysis is an alternative to cost-benefit analysis because it is difficult to quantify the benefits. Instead, cost-effective analysis compares programme costs with programme effects measured in achievement test scores, skill performance level, coping abilities etc.

In the first stage of cost-effective analysis the cost of the programme is determined. Going through the records of expenditures could do this. In the second stage, the programme effects are required to be quantified. The cost per beneficiary is calculated by dividing the total costs by number of beneficiaries. The cost thus obtained for each programme is calculated and compared to find out which programme is more effective.

Let us suppose, for example, two groups of disadvantaged children in a residential school are provided with remedial programmes. For one group conventional coaching by teachers and for other group the special coaching (supplemented with a number of extra-curricular activities) was arranged. At the end of the programme an achievement test was conducted. The average per student costs of conventional coaching programme and special coaching were found to be Rs. 600 and Rs. 800 respectively. The average achievement scores for the groups were found to be 40 and 80 respectively. It may be concluded that the special coaching programme was more effective because on an average it involved an extra cost of Rs. 200 per student. The change in achievement test score is double which certainly is a significant change. Such cost-effective analysis of competing programmes makes it possible to select the most efficient approach.

Problem of Quantification

On the surface, cost-effective analysis appears to be simple. All we need to do is add up the costs of a programme, divide it by number of beneficiaries and then compare the effectiveness of the programmes and we have the result. Such an approach is very appealing as it seems to simplify complex issues and programmes through quantification. The programme, which is more effective, can be logically expanded and the less effective programme can be curtailed or completely stopped.

The really difficult and often unreliable part of cost-effective analysis comes in quantifying effectiveness of programmes which are related to some economic activity, is easier. But, it is really difficult when the programme does not lead to economic gain, such as programmes resulting in improved quality of life, improved mental health, social awareness or other non-economic outcomes.

Impact Study Designs

The focus of social impact analysis is to explain whether the programme has achieved its goal and if yes, then, whether the analysis has to use experimental or quasi-experimental designs of research involving serious quantitative measures. In an impact study programme participants/beneficiaries will make up the experimental group, and their counterparts who do not receive benefits/participate in the programme, will make up the control group. In a social impact study a programme is assessed to see what effect, if any, is produced. Typically, the goals of the programme are identified and measured in terms of how well it achieves the goals (Monette et al., 1986).

Social Impact Analysis

A social development project is designed to produce significant effect in order to affect social structure and lead to social change and social transformation. This effect is commonly known as social impact.

Impact and Output

Many a time, the outputs of a programme are misconceived as impact of the programme. The impact of a programme is different from output. To understand the difference between 'output' and 'impact' let us take an example. The 'output' of a family planning project/population control programme may be measured by the number of people availing of the services offered. However, a decline of the population growth rate or more specifically reduction of birth and/or fertility rates in the target population is 'impact' of the family planning/population control project. The major problem in analysis of social impact is identification of social indicators to measure the impact.

A programme of health education for mother may result in higher intake of nutritive food by the children like number of eggs or quantity of milk. But, the desired impact would be the improvement in the health status to be measured in terms of weight and height of children.

The discussion clearly suggests that to start with social impact analysis one has to have very specific statement of the problem so that the impact can be visualized in measurable terms. Next step in social impact analysis is to identify social research techniques.

Social impact analysis explains whether the programme has achieved its goal and if yes, then, whether the impact was really caused by the programme. By and large, quasi-experimental research designs are used for social impact analysis.

One of the most important developments in recent years has been the initiation and growth of a large number of new programmes in the field of social welfare in developed and developing countries. The chief objective of all these programmes has been to bring about overall change in the existing socio-economic structure in the country, providing thereby a dignified way of life to a citizen as a unit and socio-economic upliftment of the society.

Evaluation Techniques and Methods

(a) *Tools of data collection*: The plan of evaluation is followed by the implementation part of evaluation study. This involves the task of formulation of instruments or tools of data collection, such as questionnaire, interview schedule, etc. This needs a considerable preparation in order to achieve a deep understanding of the programme/project activities, discussions with agency personnel and target groups, systematic study of pertinent literature and so on. The tentatively formulated instruments have to be 'pre-tested' with a view to detect their shortcomings before their final administration in the field. The choice of techniques to be utilized for data collection depends on the level of education of the respondents, the objectives of the programme, area of study and many other considerations. Certain studies require more than one technique to be used for data collection.

PROCESS OF EVALUATION RESEARCH

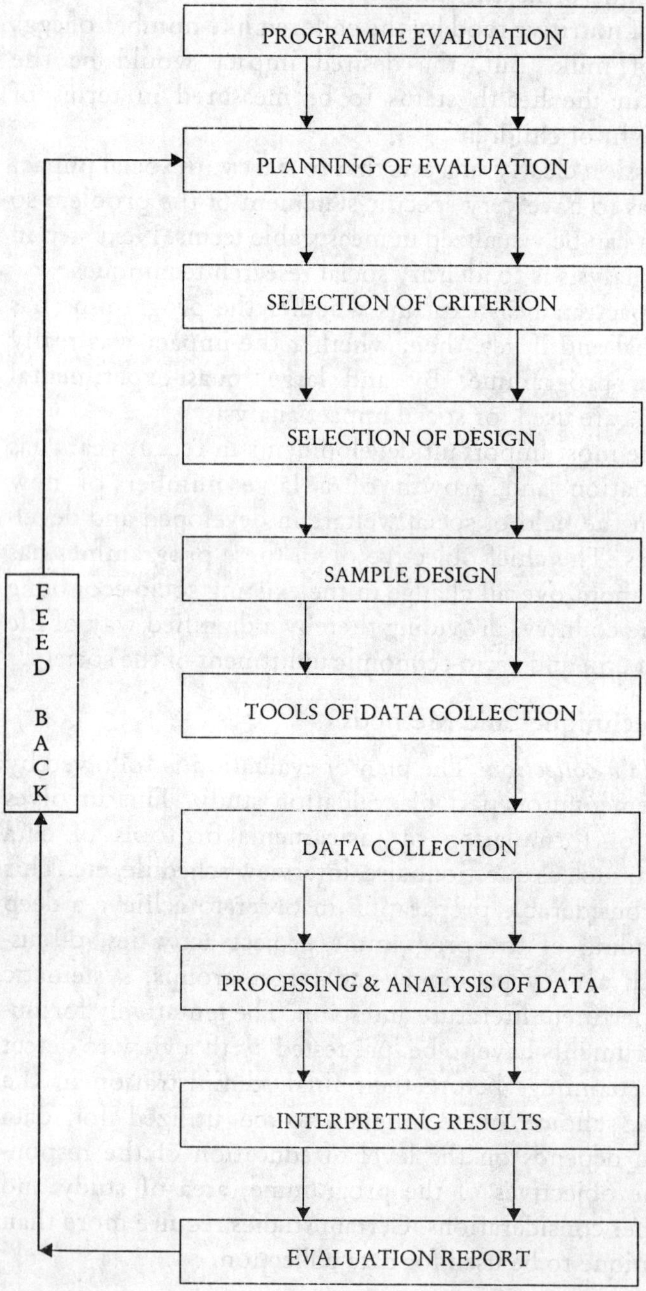

(b) *Choice of sample design*: It is seldom necessary and feasible to study the total number of people related. One sample of the programme is enough to afford a basis for making estimates about the variation within the population, required confidence, number of sub-groups considered, etc.

(c) *Selection of the criterion*: One of the most important issues in evaluation study is the selection of the criterion: the standard by which success or failure is to be judged. It is desirable that the variables be chosen to meet the requirements of reliability, especially inter-observer reliability. Another important consideration is the economy. If it costs more to measure the effectiveness of a service than to offer it, questions will be raised.

(d) *Techniques to determine results*: Funding organizations have an interest in 'objective' determination of results. Usually, this is done through an evaluation design that allows them to make comparative statements by incorporating methodology of 'before and after' research designs.

Important Terms for Review

- Evaluation
- Evaluation Research
- Programme Evaluation
- Evaluation for Programme Planning: Needs Assessments
- Evaluation Research for Programme Implementation
- Evaluation Research for Impact, Outcome and Efficiency
- Evaluation Research Models
- Formative Evaluation Research
- Summative Evaluation Research
- Planning of Evaluation Research
- The After-Only Evaluation Design
- The Before-After Evaluation Design
- The Ex-Post-Facto Evaluation Study Design
- Alternative Evaluation Research Designs
- Multiple Study Designs
- Impact Study
- Cost-Benefit Analysis

- Cost-Effective Analysis
- Quantification
- Estimating Costs
- Impact Study Designs
- Social Impact Analysis
- Impact and Output
- Evaluation Techniques and Methods
- Evaluation Report
- Programme Effects

Further Readings

Bennel, Carl et. al., *Evaluation Experiments*, New York: Academic Press, 1975.

Bhatt, Anil and Subramaniam, A., "Directing Program, Evaluation towards the Field Worker: An Experiment", *Management in Government*, Vol. XVI, No. 3, 1984.

Bloom, M., "Challenges to Helping Profession and the Response of Scientific Practice", *Social Service Review*, 52, 584-595, 1978.

Campbell, D.T. and Stanley, J.C., *Experimental and Quasi-Experimental Designs for Research,* Boston: Houghton Mifflin, 1963.

Chapin, F.S., *Experimental Design in Sociological Research,* New York: Harper, 1947.

Cook, Thomas D. and Charles S. Reichardt (eds.), *Qualitative and Quantitative Methods in Evaluation Research,* Hills: Sages, 1979.

De Geyndt, W., "Five Approaches for Assessing Care", *Hospital Administration*, Vol. 15, No. 21, 1970.

Epstein, I. and Tripodi, T., *Research Techniques for Programme Planning, Monitoring and Evaluation*, New York: Columbia University Programme, 1973.

Freeman, H. and Sherwood, C., "Research in Large-Scale Intervention Programme", *Journal of Social Issues*, Vol. 21, No. 11, 1965.

Glaser, E.M. and Taylor, S.H., *Factors Influencing the Success of Applied Research: A Study of Ten NIHM-Funded Projects,* Los Angeles: Human Interaction Research Interaction Research Institute, 1969.

Goel, S.L. and Jain, R.K., *Social Welfare Administration,* New Delhi: Deep and Deep.

Gopalan, V., *Evaluation of Social Welfare Program, Evaluation of Social Welfare in India V-I Ministry of Welfare*, Government of India. 1987.

House, E.R., *Evaluating with Validity,* Beverly Hills, California: Sage, 1980.

Jain, S.C., *Application of Social Research in Developmental Projects*, Baroda: Baroda Citizens Council, 1982.

Kidder, Louise H., *Research Methods in Social Relations*, New York: Holt, 1981.

Levin, M.H., *Costeffectiveness: A Primer*, New Delhi: Sage, 1985.

Lynn, L.E. (Jr.), *Programme Evaluation*, London: Sage, 1978.

Micheal, J. and associates, *Evaluating Your Agency's Programme*, London: Sage, 1982.

Mishan, E.J., *Cost-Benefit Analysis: An Informal Introduction*, London: George Allen and Unwin Ltd., 1971.

Monette, Duane R. et. al., *Applied Social Research: Tool for the Human Services*, Chicago: Holt, 1986.

Mullen, E.J. et. al. (eds.), *Evaluation of Social Intervention*, San Francisco: Jossey Bass, 1972.

Panadikar, A. Pai (ed.), *Program Planning and Management in Development Administration in India*, Delhi: The Macmillan, 69-70, 1974.

Paul Choudhary, D., *Social Welfare Administration*, Delhi: Everest Press, 1962.

Posova, E.J. and Carey R.G., *Programme Evaluation Methods and Case Studies*, NJ: Englewood Cliffs: Prentice Hall, 1985.

Reid, W., "The Social Agency as a Research Machine", *Journal of Service Research*, 2, 11-23, 1987.

Report of the Working Group on Evaluation, New Delhi: Planning Commission, Government of India, 1964.

Report of the Working Group on Evaluation in the State Planning Commission Government of India, 1964, New Delhi.

Rossi, H.P. and Williams, W. (eds.), *Evaluating Social Programs: Theory, Practice and Politics*, New York: Seminar Press, 1972.

Rossi, P. and H. Freeman, *Evaluation: A Systematic Approach*, Beverly Hills: Sage, 1982.

Rubin, Allen and Babbie E., *Research Methodology for Social Work*, Belmont California: Wadsworth, 1989.

Schneirer, M.A., *Programme Evaluation: The Organizational Context*, Beverly Hills, California: Sage, 1979.

Service, A.l., Mantal, S.J., and Reismen, A., "System Evaluation of Social Agencies" in *System Approach and the City* by M.D. Mesorovic and A. Reisman (eds.), Amsterdam: North Holland Publishing, 1972.

Suchman, E.A., *Evaluative Research: Principles and Practice in Public Service and Social Action Programmes*, New York: Russel Sage Foundation, 1967.

UNDP, *Human Development Report*, Oxford, New York, Press, 1993.

Weiss, Carol, *Evaluation Research,* Englewood Cliffs, N.J.: Prentice Hall, 1972.

Review Questions

1. What is the difference between 'impact' and 'output'?
2. Why is clear statement of objectives of a programme an important prerequisite for social impact analysis?
3. Why is it necessary to use experimental or quasi-experimental research designs for social impact and analysis?
4. Why a social impact analysis should not be based on 'opinion' and 'view'?
5. Discuss the purpose of cost-benefit analysis.
6. List out the problems of estimating the costs.
7. Identify the problems, which an evaluator faces while doing cost-effective analysis.
8. Discuss the important elements of cost-benefit/effective analyses of social work services.

EVALUATION OF SCHEME OF ASSISTANCE TO ORGANISATIONS FOR THE DISABLED A REPORT

Introduction

Though disability is a universal phenomenon existing in developing as well as in under-developed countries it is much more acute in the later because of ignorance, poverty, lack of basic medical facilities and pseudo-religious beliefs. A large number of voluntary organisations have come into being to provide the necessary rehabilitation for the disabled. The government felt that the organisations working in this field have financial problems, which hamper the growth of services. With a view to remove this handicap and encourage development of essential services for the disabled, the government came up with the scheme of assistance to organisations for the disabled persons. The object of this scheme is to extend financial resources to the voluntary organisations which are working for the rehabilitation of the disabled.

Objectives of the Study

This study deals with the evaluation of the scheme of assistance of Government of India to the voluntary organisations rendering help for the disabled in the state of Andhra Pradesh. The chief objectives of this study were:

(a) To evaluate availability and standard of services,
(b) To assess and review the grants-in-aid procedure, and
(c) To find out the effectiveness of services rendered by the voluntary organisations.

Area of Study and Sampling

This study deals with the evaluation of the scheme of assistance to voluntary organisations for the disabled in the state of Andhra Pradesh during the period of 1980-85. During the period from 1980 to 1985 eight organisations received grants-in-aid. Initially it was decided to include all the organisations in the state that have received grants during the period. As such, effort was made to contact all the eight organisations in the state. However, we could get information from seven organisations only.

Research Design

This is mainly a descriptive evaluation study based primarily on assessment of (a) functioning of the organisations, and (b) views of the beneficiaries and non-beneficiaries.

Methods and Tools of Data Collection

Data were collected from the various sources, such as, the chief functionary of the organisations, beneficiaries, non-beneficiaries, local people, authorities and records of the organisations.

The data from the various sources were collected through questionnaire, interview schedule, interview guide, observation schedules, and documentary schedules.

Through these tools data were collected on various aspects of the problems such as physical setting of the organisations, services available, administration and organisation, staffing pattern, financial position of the organisations, socio-economic background of the beneficiaries and non-beneficiaries, opinions of the beneficiaries and non-beneficiaries, local community people and authorities on functioning and effectiveness of the scheme.

Evaluation of the Institutional Services

Opinion of Beneficiaries on Services

Under the scheme of assistance voluntary organisations are required to supply various aids and appliances, such as, sticks, tricycles, crutches etc. free of cost to the disabled. The study was intended to find out whether these aids and appliances were made available to the disabled free of cost. The study revealed that most of the beneficiaries had to pay for the aids/appliances. Only a few of them said that they got the aids/appliances free of cost. They also reported that the repairing services for aids and appliances were not available at the organisations from which they received it. The scheme has a provision of allowance to maintain the aids/appliances. With regard to the maintenance allowance, an overwhelming majority of the beneficiaries stated that they did not receive any maintenance allowance for the aids and appliances.

Another important service rendered by the organisation receiving grants-in-aid was to provide board and lodging facilities to the disabled. The beneficiaries were asked to give their opinion on these facilities. A large number of beneficiaries who participated in the evaluation study were of the view that the board and lodging facilities provided by the organisations were satisfactory.

The beneficiaries were of the opinion that the scheme would be more effective and useful if suitable measures are taken to ensure that the durable aids and appliances are supplied to them. Another important suggestion, which could be taken into consideration, was continuity of the grants-in-aid. The beneficiaries were of the view that the scheme would work more effectively, if the organisations were given grants-in-aid for a longer period without any gap.

Opinion of Non-Beneficiaries on Services

The organisations for the disabled could cover only a section of the disabled in the state. A large number of them though eligible to avail the benefits under the scheme of assistance, could not do so because of limited grants-in-aid. Those disabled who were not availing the benefits were termed as non-beneficiaries. They were also contacted to know their views on the scheme. Majority of the non-beneficiary respondents were not able to decide whether the services were satisfactory or unsatisfactory. This is obvious because until and unless one avails of a facility he or she will not be able to say whether the facility is satisfactory or unsatisfactory. A small number of them were of the opinion that whatever services were provided by the organisations were inadequate in relation to the needs of the disabled.

An organisation, which renders services for the disabled, should adhere to certain minimum standards for the provision of physical facilities. The Ministry of Welfare should lay down the criteria. The organisation for disabled must be asked to adhere to those criteria while implementing the scheme of assistance.

As disabled persons are from all over the state, more residential facilities must necessarily be provided. All voluntary organisations working for the disabled should be encouraged to provide residential facilities. Minimum standards for physical facilities should be laid down. Adequate ventilation, sanitary facilities minimum furniture and other amenities should be provided.

Administration

Instead of secretary/chairman being in-charge of the scheme as found in almost all the organisations chief functionary should be appointed to supervise the implementation of the scheme. It is strongly suggested that a trained social worker should be appointed in each organisation implementing the scheme to deal with the problems of the disabled persons.

Salary scales for the staff should be more objectively structured and should be related to the qualifications and the experience of the candidates. Insecurity of job tenure, poor remuneration and benefits lead to a high job turnover. Unless the terms and conditions of work are improved, it will be difficult to attract and retain qualified and suitable staff.

Finance

The shape of a social welfare programme is often determined by the finance at its disposal. The problems of accommodation, staff and adequate facilities and services are dependent, to a large extent, on the budget allocations available to the organisations. On the basis of analysis of the budgets of different organisations, a few general suggestions are made.

On examining the items in the expenditure statement it was seen that the amount spent on travelling and maintenance was very low. It is suggested that while sanctioning conveyance or maintenance allowance it should be recognised that the costs have been multiplied in the last few years and it is unrealistic to expect the beneficiaries to manage the costs of conveyance and maintenance in the amounts sanctioned. It is suggested that actual expenditure on travelling and maintenance of aids and equipment be granted.

For residential organisations an allocation for building maintenance and required staff should be provided. Five to 10 per cent of the budget should be added *ad valorum* every year to absorb the cost of inflation on foodstuffs and other contingency expenditure.

A social welfare programme which must develop and change according to the changing needs of the disabled cannot be run without establishing continuity in time, staff and finances. It is, therefore, suggested that organisations once selected for the grants-in-aid must be sanctioned the grants for at least five consecutive years.

Financial records should be maintained more systematically. Detailed budget heads and items must be included so that a comparison of the expenditure patterns and problems therein, and an evaluation of the benefit-cost may be possible.

The organisations should maintain all other records properly and systematically. This would provide adequate statistical information. Certain valuable data were not available for the study, as they were not included in the application forms of the disabled. The Ministry should design appropriate forms so that yearly feedback of essential data is made possible for the regular monitoring of the scheme.

Conclusions and Suggestions

It was felt that the purpose of the scheme was not clear to the disabled, most of whom come with the intention of staying at the organisations. This could be most detrimental for the future of this type of social welfare programmes, and more particularly the need and objectives for which this scheme has been designed, namely, the welfare of the disabled.

Special efforts should be made to give counselling to the disabled. A trained social worker should be assigned this task of giving individual counselling. Three major factors need to be given special consideration.

1. In Andhra Pradesh there were about 1,00,552 disabled persons (1981). Out of which, 89 per cent live in rural areas. And if one examines the location of organisations that were sanctioned grants-in-aid during 1980-85, it can be seen that seven out of eight organisations were located in urban areas. This shows a clear imbalance is location of organisations. Therefore, it is suggested that more organisations from rural area should be encouraged to take up the scheme.
2. Supply of aids and appliances is one of the most important activities of the organisations implementing this scheme. It is suggested that the organisations must give more attention on durability of aids and appliances, while supplying it to the disabled. Supply of durable aids/appliances will reduce lot of burden of the disabled.
3. Finally, to make the scheme more effective, it is essential that organisations must be able to render effective repairing services. Alternatively, the organisations must take the responsibility of making arrangements with other organisations/institutions for repair of the aids and appliances.

12

Survey Research Designs

Survey method is used to collect detailed descriptions of existing phenomena and with the aim of examining the data to justify current conditions or practices or to make plans to improving them. The objective may not only be to ascertain status, but also to determine the adequacy of status by comparing it with selected or established norms. Survey is probably the most widely used method for obtaining descriptive and evaluative information.

Surveys are appropriate for research questions about self-reported beliefs or behaviours. Surveys are considered as most appropriate method in case of measuring variables through answers of questions. A wide range of subjects are covered by survey method of research. Broadly, it can be categorized as under:

1. Attitudes/beliefs/opinions
2. Behaviour
3. Reactions/comments
4. Characteristics
5. Expectations/aspirations
6. Knowledge/awareness
7. Suggestions
8. Need assessment
9. Interpersonal relations

The list is not exhaustive; it is an exemplary one, which includes only broad areas that are very frequently studied by using survey research.

Survey Research Designs

The two main sources of data in social research are 'people' and 'paper'. The responses of questions put to people constitute the major sources of data in social research. This source is labelled as primary source of data. A large amount of data is already available in the form of 'paper' sources. These includes document, historical records, diaries, biographies, statistical records etc. The 'paper' sources are commonly known as 'secondary sources of data' or 'available data source'.

Based on the two sources of data the major survey research designs can be organized into two categories: (1) correlational studies, and (2) analysis of available data.

Correlational Studies

The methodology of social research is based on its basic presumption that in human relations as well as in natural phenomena, a large degree of measurable and even predictable sets of associations occur. Hence, social research seeks to establish, measure, analyze and predict these associations in all their variety and intensity. Data collected through survey method are analyzed keeping this presumption in mind. This design of survey research is commonly known as *correlational studies.*

Much of the social researches establish interrelationships among variables as its first step. Correlational studies are concerned with determining the extent of relationship existing between variables. They enable us to measure the extent to which variations in one variable are associated with variations in another. We may wish to know, for example, how delinquency is related to social background or whether a relationship exists between the number of years spent in full-time education and subsequent annual income, or whether there is a relation between gender and achievement.

By and large, correlational studies intend to answer the following questions:

1. Is there a relationship between two variables?
2. What is the direction of the relationship?

3. What is the magnitude of the relationship?

For example, if a researcher wishes to test a hypothesis that there is a relationship between gender and achievement, he or she has to use correlational technique to test his/her hypothesis about the relationship between the two variables by assessing the magnitude and direction of the relationship. Karl Pearson's Co-efficient of Correlation, one of the best known measures of association, is a statistical value ranging from -1 to +1 through zero, expresses a relationship in quantitative form. The relationship is called positive when the two variables change in the same direction, that is, as the value of one variable increases so does the other. On the other hand, the relationship is said to be negative when an increase in the value of one variable is accompanied by a decrease in the value of other variable.

A caution relating to the meaning of a co-efficient of correlation is warranted. The co-efficient of correlation, which is a very useful estimate of relationship, should not be taken as an absolute proof of association among relevant variables in as much as its interpretation depends in a large measure on the size of the sample selected for the study as also on the nature of the data collected. A seemingly high value co-efficient of correlation, say, of 0.80 (±) may really be quite misleading if the standard error indicative of sample fluctuation is relatively large. To take a contrary example, a seemingly low co-efficient of say 0.45 (±) may suggest that the relationship among the variables may well be ignored, but on the plane of reality this may again be erroneous since, the co-efficient of correlation for certain variables may typically be so low that in comparison the above correlation coefficient, i.e., 0.45 would need to be considered relatively quite high for the class of data in question.

However, statistical convention decrees that the co-efficient of correlation ranging from 1 to 0.7 (±) be taken as an indication of 'high' correlation, that ranging from 0.7 to 0.4 (±) as substantial, 0.4 to 0.2 (±) as low and that below 0.2 as negligible.

It also needs to be stressed that a high correlation among two variables does not in itself constitute a proof that they are causally related. A significant correlation between variables, for example, between income and size of family or the size of an educational institution and the performance of the students, is hardly any indication of a causal relationship. Suppose, we were to find that higher income is inversely correlated with the number of issues, i.e., higher the income of parents, the lesser their number of issues (the co-efficient of correlation is, say, –0.8, which is statistically quite high), we shall be wrong and unjustified saying that higher income is the cause of lower fertility. It was pointed out earlier that an inference of causality is warranted only if three kinds of proof, viz., concomitant variation, time order and elimination of any other variable as the determining condition of the hypothesized effect can be secured. In this case, following inferences may possibly be drawn in full consideration of the pronounced correlation evident among the variables of income and number of children: (a) one might be causing the other, (b) both the variables might be the effects of some other cause or causes, and (c) the association may be a mere chance occurrence. Casual inferences can obviously be very surely established in an experimental situation. We have considered this when dealing with experimental designs. In social sciences, it is very difficult to set up experiments, so most of the studies are non-experimental ones. Analytical procedures have, however, been devised to draw inferences about causal relationship in non-experimental studies. We shall consider these procedures later in this chapter.

The social researcher is often interested in estimating the degree of association between attributes, i.e., variables that are defined qualitatively, such as, an association between the sexual attribute and state of anxiety or between nativity and attitude towards a social issue. Basically, the problem of association is one correlation but the association between attributes may not easily become amenable to mathematical treatment as in case of the quantitative measures of variables. A measure of such association among attributes is the co-efficient of relative predictability (RP), which is, in fact, a qualitative correlation co-efficient.

Co-efficient of correlation is calculated to identify the extent or degree of correlation between two variables. It does not mean that their relationship is functional or constant. In other words, correlation in two sets of data need not always be the result of mutual interdependence. Changes in one set of data may be the cause of changes in the other set (of data) and there may be a cause and effect relationship between these two sets. But it is also equally possible that the changes in the two sets of data are the effects of some third factors, which affect both these sets of data.

In such situations the researcher needs to control the effect of a third variable on the bivariate relationship by cross-tabulation or partial table method, which is quite common in the empirical research. However, the method has a serious drawback that limits its use when the number of cases is relatively small. The partial cross-tabulation involves sub-division of the sample into gradually smaller sub-groups. This reduces the size of cell frequency, thus its reliability and validity is questionable.

An alternative to method of control is the partial correlation. This is a mathematical process of adjustment of the bivariate correlation, deemed to nullify the effect of third variable (control variable) on the independent and dependent variables.

However, there is hardly any situation where one independent variable determines the dependent variable. Often, we have situations where a set of independent variables is associated with a set of dependent variables. In other words, more often, several independent variables contribute to the prediction of the dependent variable. Multiple regression is commonly used to estimate the effect of multiple independent variables.

Analysis of Available Data

Data collected by someone other than the researcher for purposes that differ from the researcher are referred to as available data or secondary data. A wide range of such data is available for analysis. For example, governmental as well as non-governmental organisations collect a large amount of statistical data about crime, health, birth rates, death rates and the like. Another form of secondary data are documents in different form of communication in qualitative format. This form of data includes articles of journals, books, magazines, letters, memoranda, diaries, etc. Social work case records and fieldwork records are a rich source of secondary data for social work research. These data in combination with data collected from other sources can make significant contribution to the knowledge base of social work.

Source of Available Data

Data are collected for a number of reasons and much of these data are available to social work researchers. First of all, a major source of statistical data are central, state and local governments that collect data for either administrative purpose or for the purpose of periodical evaluation of their programmes or services. The ministries of Human Resource Development, Social Justice and Empowerment, Labour and Employment, Rural Development, and Municipal Corporations are repositories of vast amount of secondary data. Universities and educational institutions where researches at different levels are undertaken regularly as part of their curriculum are yet another important source of secondary data.

The non-governmental organisations that collect data as required by the funding organisation in the form of need assessment, programme planning and evaluation of programmes/ services for client's services are yet another source of secondary data.

Steps in Conducting Survey

There are several steps in conducting a survey. Some of the major steps are: formulation of problem, defining of research topic, identification of objectives and formulation of hypothesis, review of literature, selection of survey design, selection of population and sample, selection and construction of tools of data collection, collection of data, processing and analysis of data, drawing of inferences and preparation of survey report. Most of these steps have been already discussed in the preceding chapters. Two steps, namely, selection of population and sample and selection and construction of tools of data collection, are crucial in survey research. Therefore, these steps need detailed discussion.

Population

Sometimes, it is not feasible to study a whole group or an extremely large group. For example, social researchers might be interested in learning about the mentally challenged children, mentally ill, prison inmates, street children or some other large group of people. It would be difficult, rather impossible, to study all members of these groups. Here comes a process called sampling, which allows us to study a manageable number of people from the large group to derive inferences that are likely to be applicable to all the people of the large group.

Another reason why we should study a sample is that the results obtained from a sample are more precise and correct than the results from the study of the whole group. Costs involved in studying all units of a large group are yet another factor which compels us to study a small group of people instead. Associated with cost, there are certain other factors too such as time available for the study and accessibility of the units of study. Above all, the point to be kept in mind is, if we can get almost same results by studying a carefully selected small group of people, why should we study the large group at all?

A single unit of study is referred to as an element of population. When we select a group of elements for the purpose of study of a particular phenomenon, we refer to that group of elements as a sample. The aggregate of all the elements that conform to some defined set of definitions is called population. Thus, by the term 'college students of a city', we define a population consisting of all the students studying in various colleges of the city. We may similarly define populations consisting of all the mentally challenged children in the city, all the women workers in a particular slum in a city, all the child workers in a given community less than sixteen years of age who work in hotels, or all the case records in a file. To get the desired information, generally, we study some of the elements rather than all. It is generally much more economical in time, effort and money.

It is presumed that the results obtained from the sample are true of the population as a whole. In reality, this may or may not be true. How closely the sample statistics corresponds to the population depends largely on the way the sample is selected (Kidder, 1981).

For instance, suppose, we want to know what percentage of a population agrees with a statement, 'Child labour should be banned?' We might put the statement to a sample, compute the percentage that agrees, and take this result as an estimate of the percentage of the population who agrees. We can devise a sampling plan that will carry the assurance that our sample estimates will not differ from the corresponding true population parameters by, say, more than 5 per cent; the estimates will be correct within the limit of 5 per cent (commonly known as 'margin of error' or 'limit of accuracy') or 95 per cent of the time (commonly termed as the 'probability' or 'confidence level'). We can similarly devise another sampling procedure, which will produce results within the limits of 1 per cent or 99 per cent of the time.

Sampling Designs

The sampling procedures, which ensure that the sample statistics will be correct within certain limits, are referred to as a 'representative sampling plan'. Here the usage of the word 'representative' does not qualify sample, but sampling plan. A representative sampling plan ensures that the selected sample is sufficiently representative of the population to justify our running the risk of taking it as representative (Kidder, 1981).

Based on this assumption probability sampling makes it possible to select a sample which will be representative. This helps researchers to estimate the extent to which the sample statistics are likely to differ from population parameters. This means, if probability sampling method is used, it is possible to ascertain the size of the sample that will be needed if we want to have a given degree of certainty that their sample results do not differ by more than a specified value from those of the population parameters.

There are a number of sampling techniques which decrease the likelihood of misleading generalizations based on sample statistics. These techniques assure the inclusion of diverse elements of the population in the sample by controlling the proportions of the various types of elements. Alternatively, statistical procedures are used in the analysis of the data.

Another important factor, which affects the representativeness of samples, is data collection procedures used in the study. This is reason why the sample study of a large population can, in practice, produce more valid and reliable results than can a census. For instance, it is always difficult to get skilled interviewers in large numbers to cover widespread area of study. Even if we manage to get required number of skilled interviewers, it is not possible to get anything beyond the most superficial data in a census study. Moreover, the reliability of such data is also not beyond doubts. On the contrary, in a sample study, which requires lesser number of skilled interviewers, not only can we probe thoroughly by spending more time with each respondent but also we can depend on data collected therein. In addition to this, a sample study reduces the large expenses required for census study to a large extent.

Probability Sampling

The 'chance' of being included in the sample is commonly known as *probability*. The probability of an element to be included in a sample can be ascertained on the basis of the theories of probability. The basic difference in sampling methods is between probability and non-probability sampling. The essential characteristic of sampling is that one can specify for each element of the population the chance of being included in the sample. In the simplest case, each of the elements has the same probability of being included, but this is not a necessary condition. What is necessary is that for each element there must be some specific chance that it will be included. This point will be considered more fully in connection with the discussions of simple random samples and stratified random samples.

Major types of probability sampling are: simple random sampling, stratified random sampling and cluster sampling.

Simple Random Sampling

A process that gives each element in the population an equal chance of being included in the sample is termed as simple random sampling. The elements are selected, using a list of random numbers appended with most textbooks of research and statistics. Before using the table of random numbers, it is first necessary to number all the elements in the population to be studied. Then the table is marked at some point and the cases whose numbers come up as one from this point down the column of numbers are taken into the sample until the desired number of elements is obtained. The selection of any given element places no limits on other element being selected, thus making equally possible the selection of any one of the many possible combinations of elements.

Proportionate Stratified Random Sampling

In stratified random sampling, the population is first divided into strata. The strata may be based on a single criterion or on a combination of two or more criteria. In stratified random sampling, a simple random sample is taken from each stratum, and the sub-samples are then joined to form the total sample.

Stratified random sampling can be further divided into proportionate and disproportionate random sampling. In case the researcher is interested in the study of some characteristics of a phenomenon he/she uses a *proportionate stratified random sampling plan.* Of course, this sampling design presupposes that the investigator has some knowledge concerning the population characteristics such as age, sex, marital status etc.

In the sampling plan the sample will have specified characteristics in exact proportion to those same characteristics which are distributed in the population. To understand this sampling plan we will consider the following example.

Let us consider the students of college of social work. The researcher wishes to have proportionate stratified random sample of them taking year of study in the college as basis of stratification.

Let us suppose that the students at this college are distributed as is shown in Table 12.1.

Table 12.1

Distribution of Students According to Year in College

Year	*Population*	*Proportion of Each Class*
BSW I	50	.25
BSW II	40	.20
BSW III	30	.15
MSW I	40	.20
MSW II	40	.20
Total	200	1.00

Further, we suppose that the researcher decides to have a sample of 60 students. First, he determines the proportion of students in each class (as shown in the second column). Then, he calculates the composition of the sample taking each proportion of the stratifying characteristics in the population and multiplying it by the desired size of the sample. Thus, he multiplies 60, the desired sample size by .25, the proportion of BSW first year students in the population or

(60) (.25) = 15

As such, he has to include 15 students from the BSW first year in his sample. This precedence is repeated for each year as described below:

(60) (.25) = 15
(60) (.20) = 12
(60) (.15) = 9
(60) (.20) = 12
(60) (.20) = 12
Sample Size (N) = 60

Table 12.2
Distribution of Students by Proportion

Year	*Sample Break-up*	*Proportion*
BSW I	15	.25
BSW II	12	.20
BSW III	9	.15
MSW I	12	.20
MSW II	12	.20
Total Sample (n) =	60	1.00

After having determined the sample size from each sub-category, the researcher uses simple random sampling for drawing the desired number of elements from each category.

Disproportionate stratified sampling plan is almost similar to proportionate stratified random sampling except that the sub-samples are not necessarily distributed according to their proportionate weight in the population from which they were drawn. It is possible that some sub-samples are over-represented while other sub groups are under-represented.

Let us suppose that the researcher stratifies the population into two sub-strata using sex as the criteria. He would get the following break-up of the population:

Table 12.3
Distribution of Students by Sex

Sex	*No. of Students*	*Percentage*
Male	160	80
Female	40	20
Total	200	100

If the researcher wants to draw a disproportionate stratified random sample of 60 from this population, stratified by sex, then he has to draw 30 from each sub-strata, this means male students (30) will be under-represented and female students (30) will be over-represented in the sample. In other words, disproportionate sampling gives equal weights to each sub-stratum.

There is a clear improvement over simple random sampling when the sampling is based on a stratification of population by sex. With this kind of stratification we get a marked increase in the size of samples that yields statistics very close parameters. On the contrary, a reduction in the size of sample may yield statistics that might deviate widely from the population parameters.

Cluster Sampling

In case the area of study is markedly widespread, large expenses are involved if simple and stratified random sampling is used. For example, in the preparation of sampling frame from the population and in covering the widespread areas by interviewers, a large amount of expenditure is required. The more widely spread the area of study, the greater are the travel expenses, the greater is the time spent in travelling, and hence expensive—and the tasks of administering, monitoring and supervision of the research project and in particular supervising the field staff become more complicated. For the reasons mentioned above and few other reasons, large-scale research studies make use of the cluster sampling methods.

In cluster sampling, first, the whole research area is divided into sub-areas, more commonly known as *clusters*. The simple random or stratified method is used to select clusters. Finally, the researcher arrives at the ultimate sample size to be studied by selecting sample from within the clusters, which is carried out on a simple or stratified random sampling basis.

Let us suppose, for example, that we want to conduct a survey of beggars in urban areas of a state. We may proceed as follows: prepare a list of districts and group them into clusters, and select a simple or stratified random sample from each cluster. For each of the districts included in the sample, list the cities/towns and take a simple or stratified random sample of them. If some or all of the towns/cities thus selected for the sample have more numbers of beggars that can be studied, we may take a sample of these towns/cities in each district. The questionnaires may then be administered to all the beggars in these towns/cities or, if it is desirable and administratively feasible to do so, to a sample of the beggars.

Characteristically, the procedure moves through a series of stages—hence the common term, 'multi-stage' sampling—from more inclusive to less inclusive sampling units until we finally arrive at the population elements that constitute the desired sample.

Non-Probability Sampling

In non-probability sampling, there is no way of estimating the probability that each element has of being included in the sample and no assurance that every element has some chance of being included (Wilkinson and Bhandarkar, 1977). The four important types of non-probability sampling are accidental sampling, quota sampling, snowball sampling and purposive sampling.

Accidental Sampling

Accidental sampling refers to a method of selecting respondents who happen to meet the researcher and are willing to be interviewed. Thus, a researcher may take the first hundred people he/she meets who are willing to be interviewed.

For example, let us consider the situations where a programme director wishes to make some generalizations about the programme in progress, selects beneficiaries who have come to the agency for a service or a community organizer, trying to know how the people feel about health status in that community, interviews available community dwellers like shopkeepers, daily wage earners, barbers and others who are presumed to reflect public opinion. In both the situations, those who are available for study are included in the samples. This is exactly what we call accidental sampling. It is very obvious that the samples so collected are biased and there is no known way (other than by doing a parallel study with a probability sample) of evaluating the biases introduced in such samples. However, in the situation illustrated above, most probably, accidental sampling is the only way out because of the reason that the population parameters of the beneficiaries or the community people are not available with the researcher.

Quota Sampling

Quota sampling insures inclusion of diverse elements of the population in the sample and make sure that these diverse elements take account of the proportions in which they occur in the population. For example, we take a sample from a population with equal number of boys and girls, and that there is a difference between the two groups in the characteristic we wish to study and we fail to interview any girls, the results of the study would almost certainly be extremely misleading generalisations about the population. In practice, elements in small numbers are frequently under-represented in accidental samples. In anticipation of such possible exclusion of small groups, quota sampling ensures inclusion of enough cases from each stratum in the sample. It should be noted here that the major goal of quota sampling is the selection of a sample that is a replica of the population to which one wants to generalize.

Hence, it should be clear that the critical requirement in quota sampling is not that the various population strata be sampled in their correct proportions, but rather that there be enough cases from each stratum to make possible an estimate of the population stratum value (Kidder, 1981: 426). Quota sampling, however, is more or less similar to the earlier described accidental sampling procedure except that it insures the inclusion of diverse elements of the population.

Purposive Sampling

Purposive sampling is based on the presumption that with good judgement one can select the sample units that are satisfactory in relation to one's requirements. A common strategy of this sampling technique is to select cases that are judged to be typical of the population, in which one is interested, assuming that errors of judgement in the selection will tend to counterbalance each other. For example, if a researcher was conducting a study of patients who are not regular in attending out-patient department, it might be desirable to choose patients for the sample from among those who are frequently irregular. Because, the causes of irregularity can be described by irregular patients only. If he selects a random sample, he would have got patients who are regular and that might influence the findings of the study. It is also possible that in a truly random sample, the regular patients would nullify the effects of irregular patients.

Snowball Sampling

Snowball sampling is externally helpful in studying some special sampling situation like getting a sample of drug abusers, or alcoholics or pickpocketeers. In snowball sampling we start with a few respondents of the type we wish to include in our study and who in turn are expected to guide us to get more respondents and so on. Like the rotating snowball, sample increases in its size as we continue to get more units of study. The technique is especially useful in the investigation of sensitive topics mentioned above because this sampling technique depends on sampled cases having knowledge of other similar cases. Another argument in favour of using this sampling technique is that the victims might be hesitant to identify themselves if approached by a stranger but might be friendly to someone who they know and share their experiences or deviant status (Gelles, 1978).

Combinations of Probability and Non-Probability Sampling

If sampling is carried out in a series of stages, it is, of course, possible to combine probability and non-probability sampling in one design. That is, one or more of the stages can be carried out according to probability sampling principles and the balance by non-probability principles.

The investigators may select clusters by probability cluster sampling techniques, but, at the final stage, select the elements as a quota sample. Thus, it is possible to select a probability sample of districts in a state, within each of these districts, a probability sample of towns, and within each of the selected towns, a quota sample controlled for, say, age and sex.

The advantage of such a design is the cost of obtaining cases for the sample. It is relatively inexpensive to select the areas within which the final stage of sampling will take place by probability sampling, and we thereby gain the advantages of probability sampling, at least for the areas. There is some evidence, for instance, that quota samples built up in selected areas are more successful in controlling such variables as socio-economic status than quota samples in which the control of these variables depends on the judgments of the interviewers (Kish, 1965).

The second example of combining probability and non-probability sampling involves the opposite strategy. The investigator takes a probability sample of elements within a non-probability sample of areas. The areas are selected as a purposive sample. For example, a number of districts may be selected on the grounds that they have lower rate of literacy, within each of the 'typical' districts, the investigator selects a probability sample of respondents.

Determination of Sample Size

Determination of sample size is a difficult task. Particularly in social research, where we consider a set of variables, it becomes really difficult to ascertain the size of sample. However, it is possible to determine the size of sample by using a representative sampling procedure.

Based on the assumptions of probability sampling, it is possible to select a sampling procedure which will be representative. This helps researchers to estimate the extent to which the sample statistics are likely to differ from population parameters. This means, if probability sampling method is used, it is possible to ascertain the size of the sample that will be needed if we want to have a given degree of certainty that their sample results do not differ by more than a specified value from those of the population parameters.

There are a number of sampling techniques which decrease the likelihood of misleading generalizations based on sample statistics. These techniques assure the inclusion of diverse elements of the population in the sample by controlling the proportions of the various types of elements. Alternatively, statistical procedures are used in the analysis of the data.

Krejcie and Morgan (1970) have given a table in which no calculations are needed to determine the size of the sample. It is being reproduced as under:

N	*S*	*N*	*S*	*N*	*S*
10	10	220	140	1200	291
15	14	230	144	1300	297
20	19	240	148	1400	302
25	24	250	152	1500	306
30	28	260	155	1600	310
35	32	270	159	1700	313
40	36	280	162	1800	317
45	40	290	165	1900	320
50	44	300	169	2000	322
55	48	320	175	2200	327
60	52	340	181	2400	331
65	56	360	186	2600	335
70	59	380	191	2800	338
75	63	400	196	3000	341
80	66	420	201	3500	346
85	70	440	205	4000	351
90	73	460	210	4500	354
95	76	480	214	5000	357
100	80	500	217	6000	361
110	76	550	217	6000	361
110	76	550	226	7000	364
120	92	600	234	8000	367
130	97	650	242	9000	368
140	103	700	248	10000	370
150	108	750	254	15000	375
160	113	800	260	20000	377
170	118	850	265	30000	379
180	123	900	269	40000	380
190	127	950	274	50000	381
200	132	1000	278	75000	382
210	136	1100	285	1000000	384

Note: N is population size, S is sample of size.

For example, if you want to know the sample size required to be representative of the opinions of 300 social work students, refer table at N=300. The sample size representative of the social work students in this case will be 169. The table is applicable to any defined population.

Construction of Tools for Data Collection

The major objectives of survey research are to (a) collect detailed descriptions of existing phenomena, and (b) examine the data to justify current conditions or practices. This makes the selection and construction of tools for data collection crucial in survey research. Therefore, this step of survey research—construction of tools of data collection—needs detailed discussion. Questionnaire/interview schedule is probably the most widely used tool for obtaining descriptive and evaluative data, such as social background, opinion, attitudes, changes in relations, and the like.

Questionnaire/Interview Schedule

In this section we will discuss the questionnaire/interview schedule as a tool of data collection. First, we will discuss the contents and types of questions followed by the format and sequencing of questions. Next, we will discuss leading, double-barreled, and threatening questions. Finally, the instructions for the investigators will be described.

Content of Questions

Questionnaire/interview schedule enlists questions, which translate the research objectives into specific questions. The questions must also encourage the respondent so that the necessary data is obtained. It is to these two ends that the questions become the focus around which the questionnaire/interview schedule is constructed. One of the major issues involved in formulating the question is its content. The major issues on which questions may be concerned are facts, opinions, attitudes, respondents' motivation, and their level of acquaintance with a research problem. By and large, questions can be classified into two general categories, namely, (1) factual questions, and (2) opinion and attitude questions.

Factual Questions

Factual questions are asked to elicit information from the respondents regarding their background, such as sex, age, marital status, education or income. The following is an example of such a question:

What is your level of education? (please check one)

1. Graduate	( )
2. Intermediate	( )
3. High School	( )
4. Middle School	( )
5. Primary	( )
6. Illiterate	( )
7. Any Other	( )

Other kinds of factual questions are intended to elicit information on the profile of the respondents (sex, marital status, income, work experience, place of residence, nativity etc.).

1.	Name:	__________	
2.	Age in Years: (as on 1st July, 2005)	__________	
3.	Designation:	__________	
4.	Establishment:	__________	
6.	Marital Status :	1. Married	( )
		2. Unmarried	( )
		3. Widow	( )
		4. Divorcee	( )
7.	Occupation:	__________	
8.	Place of Work:	__________	
9.	Salary/Wages:	Rs.________per month	
10.	Religion:	1. Hindu	( )
		2. Muslim	( )
		3. Christian	( )
		4. Any Other	( )

It looks easier to design factual questions. However, many a time, factual questions pose the researcher with problems. In a survey many respondents misunderstood religion as a 'faith/belief' and reported that they do not believe in religion. Similarly, in other research study pertaining to socio-economic status, many failed to mention income out of milch animals, kitchen garden and poultry because they did not consider it as a source of income. Further, most probably, the sources of income are either wages or cash value of crops.

These two examples point to failure of communication system between the researcher and the respondents. A researcher is required to have a clear definition of the concept and is also required to communicate exactly the same to avoid such problems.

Opinion and Attitude Questions

The term 'attitude' refers to the sum total of a person's inclination, prejudices, ideas, fears and convictions about any specific topic. Opinions, on the other hand, are the verbal expression of attitudes (Thurstone, 1928: 33). Thus, a statement such as "child labour should be banned" would reflect an opinion that is against child labour, but an attitude towards child labour would mean a more specific orientation of what a person feels and thinks about child labour.

Attitudes can be described by their content (what the attitude is about), direction (positive, neutral, or negative feelings about the object or issue in question), and intensity (an attitude may be held with greater or lesser vehemence). To one person, child labour may be just of passing interest; to another, it may be of great significance and that person may be ready to join anti-child labour movements.

Questions about opinions and attitudes present more problems in construction than questions about facts. Comparatively, it is simpler to obtain accurate data, for example, whether or not a person is married or single. It can be assumed that the respondent knows whether he or she is married or not. However, questions on opinions or attitudes, assuming that the respondents know, cannot always be made. For example, respondents may not have either positive or negative attitude towards child labour, or if they do, it might be largely latent (Moser and Kalton, 1975:317). Moreover, as there are various aspects or dimensions of attitudes, the respondent may agree with one aspect and disagree with another. This is the reason why attitudes cannot be measured by a single question. For example, if a respondent strongly agrees with the statement "child labour should be banned," this does not imply a broad anti-child labour attitude. This person's agreement may be due to personal circumstances; for instance, the person who may be unemployed thinks that child labour would harm his or her prospect of employment. By using a set of statements, one can reduce the effects of one-aspect responses.

Finally, answers to opinion and attitude questions are more sensitive to changes in wording, emphasis and sequencing than are those to factual questions. This reflects, in part, the multi-dimensionality of many attitudes. Questions presented in different ways sometimes reflect different aspects of the attitude and thus result in different answers.

Formats of Questions

The format of the question and the response categories accompanying the questions are other aspects, which need attention of the researchers. Three types of question formats are discussed in this section: (1) open-ended questions, (2) closed-ended questions and (3) contingency questions.

Open-ended and Closed-ended Questions

Questions in a questionnaire can be either open-ended or closed-ended. In a closed-ended question, respondents are offered a set of answers from which they are asked to choose the one that most closely represents their views. For example, to measure sex discrimination against women in the unorganized sector, the author used, among other questions, the following closed-ended question:

"Are you aware of the Equal Remuneration Act?

(1) Yes (2) No

"Equal remuneration should be given to men and women for same work or work of similar nature."

- Strongly agree
- Agree
- Indifferent
- Disagree
- Strongly disagree

Open-ended questions are not followed by any kind of specified responses, and the respondents' responses are recorded in full. For instance, the question, "What do you personally feel are the most important issues related to child labour, which the government should try to take care of?" is an open-ended question used frequently in questionnaires designed to study public opinion. The advantage of the open-ended question is that it does not force the respondent to adapt to pre-determined responses: having understood the question, one can express one's ideas freely, spontaneously and in one's own language. If the answers to open-ended questions are not clear, the researcher may probe, that is, ask the respondent to explain further or to give reasons for something stated earlier.

The appropriateness of questions depends upon a number of factors. Paul Lazarsfeld (1944: 38-60) suggests the use of the following considerations to determine appropriateness:

1. *The objectives of the questionnaire/interview schedule*: Closed-ended questions are suitable when the researcher's objective is to lead the respondent to express agreement or disagreement with an explicit point of view. When the researcher wishes to learn about the process by which the respondent arrived at a particular point of view, an open-ended question is likely to be more appropriate.
2. *The respondent's level of information about the topic in question*: Open-ended questions provide opportunities for the interviewer to ascertain lack of information on the part of the respondent, whereas closed-ended questions do not. Obviously, it is futile to raise questions that are beyond the experiences of respondents.

3. *The extent to which the topic has been thought tough by the respondent:* The open-ended question is preferable in situations where the respondents have not yet crystallized their opinions. The use of a closed-ended question in such situations involves a risk, that in accepting one of the alternatives offered, the respondent may make a choice that is quite different from an opinion that would have otherwise been expressed had he or she gone through the process of recall and evaluation of past experience.
4. *The ease with which the content of the answer can be communicated by the respondent or the extent to which the respondent is motivated to communicate on the topic:* The closed-ended question requires less motivation to communicate on the part of the respondent, and the response itself is usually less revealing to the respondent (and hence less threatening) than in the case of the open-ended question. The researcher who uses closed-ended questions tends to encounter less frequent refusals to respond.

Contingency Questions

Frequently questions that are relevant to some respondents may be irrelevant to others. For example, the question "Check the most important reasons why you are not going to college" obviously applies only to those intermediate students who are not planning to go to college at all. It is often necessary to include questions that might apply only to some respondents and not to others. Some questions may be relevant only to females and not to males; others will only apply to respondents who are self-employed, and so on.

When a question is applicable to only a sub-group of the sample, it is known as *contingency question.* A contingency question is a special case of a closed-ended question and it is one that applies only to a sub-group of respondents. The relevance of the question to this sub-group is determined by the answer of respondents to a preceding question. For example, in a research study, the preceding question was, "Are you aware of the Act?", the contingency question could be, "If yes, what do you know about it?" The relevance of the second question to the respondent is contingent upon his or her response to the preceding question. Only respondents who responded in the affirmative to the preceding question will find the contingency question relevant. Therefore, the response categories of the preceding questions will be: 1. Yes (answer the following question); 2. No (skip to question 3).

Now, we will discuss some of the formats of response categories of closed-ended questions. The general format is to present all possible responses and of which the respondent has to check the appropriate response. The respondent can either encircle his or her answer or check a box or a blank as in the following example:

What is your marital status?

Married	☐ Married	1. Married
Single	☐ Single	2. Single
Divorced	☐ Divorced	3. Divorced
Widowed	☐ Widowed	4. Widowed

Rating Scale

One of the most common formats for questions asked in survey research is the rating scale. The rating scale is used whenever respondents are asked to make a judgement in terms of sets of ordered categories, such as "agree," "favourable," or "very often". For example: The employers prefer male employees because female employees take more sick leaves and quit more readily:

(1) Agree ( )
(2) Undecided ( )
(3) Disagree ( )

Matrix Question

The matrix question is a method for organizing a set of questions that have the same response patterns. The following is an example of matrix question: In my workplace the following welfare services are provided:

	Yes	*No*	*If yes, then, what do you think about it?*		
			Satisfactory	*Fairly Satisfactory*	*Un-satisfactory*
(1) Crèches and Day Nurseries	( )	( )	-	-	-
(2) Maternity Benefits	( )	( )	-	-	-
(3) Canteen (common)	( )	( )	-	-	-
(4) Canteen (separate)	( )	( )	-	-	-
(5) Rest Place (common)	( )	( )	-	-	-
(6) Rest Place (Separate)	( )	( )	-	-	-
(7) Toilet (separate)	( )	( )	-	-	-

Sequencing of Questions

Once the format of questions is decided, a researcher has to consider the order in which questions are to be placed in the questionnaire/interview schedule. Two general patterns of question sequencing have been found to be most appropriate for motivating respondents to cooperate: the *funnel sequence* and the *inverted funnel sequence.*

It should be kept in mind that questions that are presented first in the questionnaire should put the respondent at ease, and if an interviewer is present, they should help in creating rapport between the researcher and the respondent. Thus, the question in the beginning should be easy to answer, interesting, and it should not deal with sensitive issues. For example, questions about drinking habit or sex life of respondents, if placed at the beginning, in all possibilities, will demotivate the respondents to answer the subsequent questions. It is also suggested that such questions be placed later, for they reduce the respondent's initial motivation to cooperate.

Questions to be Avoided

Leading Questions

A question phrased in such a manner that it appears to the respondent that the researcher expects a certain answer, is commonly known as *leading question*. A question designed to elicit general opinion about work satisfaction might read, "How do you feel about your work?" The same question worded in a leading form might read, "Are you satisfied with your work?" This question makes it easier for respondents to answer *yes* than *no.* In answering *yes,* they are agreeing with the words of the question and are not contradicting the researcher.

As far as possible leading questions are to be avoided if one is looking for objective responses. In some situations, particularly, where leading questions may serve the research objective, leading questions with suitable wordings are used with extra care.

Threatening Questions

Threatening questions refer to behaviours that are illegal or contra-normative or behaviours that are socially deviant and are not discussed in public. For example, questions that inquire about the respondents' gambling habits, drinking habits, child abuse or sexual behaviours are referred to as *threatening questions.* Often, it is necessary to include such questions in studies, which the respondent may find embarrassing and thus difficult to answer.

Though it is suggested to avoid threatening questions as far as possible, in cases where it is necessary to include such questions, it is advised to use a long introduction to the question (or may be indirect question) rather than asking short questions (or direct questions); by an open-ended rather than a closed-ended format; and, to a lesser extent, by letting the respondents pick their own words to talk about the sensitive issues. For example, to know about respondent's drinking behaviour, the following question may be asked: "In the past one year, how often you could not control yourself to become intoxicated while drinking?"

Respondents may be asked to classify their responses into one of the following categories:

Once in three month
Once a month
Once a week
Several times a week
Daily

Double-barreled Questions

When two or more than two questions are included in one question, it is termed as *double-barreled questions*. The following question, included in a survey, is an example:

Women should stay at home and take care of their children and other family members and stop taking up employment outside:

Agree
Depends
Disagree

The above statement includes two separate questions that are joined by the conjunction 'and'.

Such questions might confuse respondents who agree with one aspect of the question—stay at home and take care of children and other family members and not with the other—stop taking employment outside. Many questions that include 'and' are very likely doubled-barreled, hence, it is suggested not to include such questions.

Instructions

While constructing a questionnaire, it is utmost necessary that the instructions must go with each question or with a set of questions. Instructions are required to all such questions that are not self-explanatory. It may be general instruction such as "circle the appropriate category" or very specific instructions that explain how to rank order a set of priorities. The instructions are usually written for the interviewer and thus are often short and concise.

Constructing a Questionnaire: A Case Study

There are many stages involved in the construction of a questionnaire, beginning with the research problem and going through the process of formulating the questions and considering the format and the type of questions to be used.

The questionnaire starts off with respondent number for the person being interviewed as well as his/her personal background, followed by opinion questions on wage differentials. The next part of the questionnaire consists of an attitude question towards wage differentials, followed by opinion questions on work satisfaction in a matrix format. Note also that instructions are provided for the interviewer. Finally, the last section of the questionnaire consists of a set of attitude questions on sex discrimination. To illustrate these, a shortened version of the original questionnaire, which was used to study the attitudes and perceptions related to sex discrimination against women at work, is reproduced below:

QUESTIONNAIRE: AN ILLUSTRATION

RESPONDENT NO:

A Study of Implementation of the Equal Remuneration Act, 1976 in Andhra Pradesh

PERSONAL INFORMATION

1. Name: ____________________
2. Age in Years: ____________________
   (as on 1st July, 2000)
3. Designation: ____________________
4. Establishment: ____________________
5. Level of Education:
   1. Graduate ( )
   2. Intermediate ( )
   3. High School ( )
   4. Middle School ( )
   5. Primary ( )
   6. Illiterate ( )
   7. Any other ( )
6. Marital Status:
   1. Unmarried ( )
   2. Married ( )
   3. Divorcee ( )
   4. Widow ( )
7. Occupation: ________________
8. Place of Work: ________________
9. Salary/Wages: ________________

10. Religion: 1. Hindu ( )
    2. Muslim ( )
    3. Christian ( )
    4. Any other ( )
11. Since how long are you working ________________ (completed years)
12. Were you working before 1996,
    (1) In the same job ( )
    (2) In some other job ( )
    (3) N. A. ( )
13. If in some other, what was the job? ________________ (Designation)
14. When did you take up the present job? ________________
15. Why did you change?________________
16. If you were working before 1996, what was your monthly? salary/wages then? Rs.________________
17. What is your monthly salary/wages now? Rs. ________________
18. Is there any difference of wages between you and a female/male worker having same kind of work as you?
    (1) Yes ( )
    (2) No ( )
    (3) Not sure ( )
    (In case the answer to Q. No.18 is 'No' or 'Not sure', ask Q. No. 21)
19. What do you feel about it?
    (1) Equal remuneration should be given to men, women workers for same work or work of similar nature. ( )
    (2) It doesn't make much of a difference even if we are not paid equal wages. ( )
    (3) Equal remuneration should not be given to men and women workers for same work or work of a similar nature. ( )
20. How much is the difference?
    (1) A great difference ( )
    (2) A little difference ( )

21. After the year 1996 was there any change in your monthly wages/salary?
    (1) Yes ( )
    (2) No ( )
    (3) Don't know ( )
22. If yes what was the change?
    (1) Increased ( )
    (2) Decreased ( )
    (3) N.A. ( )

ATTITUDE TOWARDS EMPLOYMENT OF WOMEN

23. Women's participation in labour work,
    (1) Should be encouraged ( )
    (2) Should be encouraged to a limited extent ( )
    (3) Should not be encouraged ( )
24. Give reasons in support of your answer to the above question. ______________________

AWARENESS OF THE ACT

25. Are you aware of this Act?
    (1) Yes (2) No
26. If yes then what do you know about it?
27. The Act provides for equal pay for equal work for both men and women. What is your opinion about it?
    (1) I'm in favour of it ( )
    (2) I don't care about it ( )
    (3) I'm against it ( )
28. Give reasons in support of your answer to the above question.
29. Is this Act being implemented in your workplace?
    (1) Fully ( )
    (2) Partially ( )
    (3) Not at all ( )
30. In my work place the following welfare services are provided:

	Yes	No	If yes, then, what do you think about it?		
			Satis-factory	Fairly Satis-factory	Un-satis-factory
(1) Crèches and Day Nurseries	( )	( )	-	-	-
(2) Maternity Benefits	( )	( )	-	-	-
(3) Canteen (common)	( )	( )	-	-	-
(4) Canteen (separate)	( )	( )	-	-	-
(5) Rest Place (common)	( )	( )	-	-	-
(6) Rest Place (Separate)	( )	( )	-	-	-
(7) Toilet (separate)	( )	( )	-	-	-
(8) ______________ (Any other, please specify)					

31. If not then what do you intend to do regarding this matter, now that you know about it?

EMPLOYMENT

32. How did you know about this job?
    (1) Relatives ( )
    (2) Friends ( )
    (3) Advertisement ( )
    (4) Employment Exchange ( )
    (5)________________ ( )
    (If any other, specify)
33. Were there other candidates as well for this job?
    (1) Yes ( )
    (2) No ( )
34. If yes, were they:
    (1) All female candidates ( )
    (2) Male and female candidates ( )

35. If there were male candidates as well did your employer show any preference to them while recruitment.
(1) Yes ( )
(2) No ( )
(3) Not sure ( )

36. Did you have a formal interview with your employer at the time of recruitment?
(1) Yes ( )
(2) No ( )
(Note: Formal interview would mean interviewing all the candidates who have come for that particular job, by a Selection Committee who would finally select the best candidate/s from the lot).

37. Does your employer make any discrimination with respect to:

	Yes	No
(1) Nature of work	( )	( )
(2) Duration of work	( )	( )
(3) Wages	( )	( )
(4) Promotion	( )	( )
(5)________________ (If any other, specify)	( )	( )

38. Your employment here is:
(1) Temporary ( )
(2) Permanent ( )
(3) Casual ( )
(Note: Before asking Q.No. (39-43), check the response of Q.No. 6)

ATTITUDE TOWARDS THE JOB

39. Why do you work?
(1) To supplement the family income ( )
(2) To have independent income of one's own ( )
(3) To achieve a position or status of one's own ( )
(4) To utilize plenty of spare time ( )
(5) To be away from the unhappy atmosphere of home ( )

(6) To escape from domestic work and get freedom to mix with people ( )

(7)______________________________ ( )
(Any other reasons, specify)

40. Satisfaction with the job.
    (1) I like the job and would like to continue working ( )
    (2) I like the job but would change if I get some other job ( )
    (3) I hate working here but circumstance force me to do so. ( )

JOB SECURITY

41. How long do you want to work here?________
42. Do you think you can work here as long as you want?
    (1) Yes ( )
    (2) No ( )
    (3) Not sure ( )
43. If no then why?
49. If you quit the present job, how sure are you of getting another job?
    (1) Very sure ( )
    (2) Not sure ( )
    (3) Not at all sure ( )

PROBLEMS FACED

53. As an employee of this organization what are the problems faced by you at work place?
62. How do you think these problems could be solved?

Application of Survey Research

Using the Correlational Study Design of survey research method, this author studied "Sex Discrimination Against Female Workers in Unorganised Sector in Andhra Pradesh". In order to demonstrate the process of survey research, the report is reproduced at the end of this chapter in an abridged form.

Important Terms for Review

- Survey Research Designs
- Source of Available Data
- Correlational Studies
- Co-efficient of Correlation
- Direction of Correlation
- Positive Correlation
- Negative Correlation
- Magnitude of Correlation
- Non-Probability Sampling
- Accidental Sampling
- Limits of Accuracy
- Confidence Level
- Quota Sampling
- Margin of Error
- Purposive Sampling
- Snowball Sampling
- Probability Sampling
- Representativeness of Sampling Plan
- Simple Random Sampling
- Stratified Random Sampling
- Disproportionate Stratified Random Sampling
- Cluster Sampling
- Content of Question
- Format of Question
- Open-End Question
- Closed-End Question
- Matrix Question
- Factual Question
- Opinion Question
- Attitude Question
- Contingency Question
- Loaded Question
- Funnel Sequence
- Inverted Sequence
- Threatening Question

- Double-Barreled Question
- Content Analysis
- Units of Analysis
- Coding Schemes
- Units of Categories
- Coder Reliabilities

Further Readings

Bailey, Kenneth D., *Methods of Social Research*, London: The Free Press, 1978.

Baker, L. Therese., *Doing Social Research,* New York: McGraw Hill, 1988.

Black, James A. and Champion, Dean J., *Methods and Issues in Social Research,* New York: John Wiley, 1976.

Doby, J.T. et al., *An Introduction to Social Research,* London: Harrisburg: Stackpole Co., 1953.

Festinger, L. and Katz, D. (eds.), *Research Methods in the Behavioral Sciences,* New York: The Dryden Press, 1953.

Galtung, John, *Theory and Methods of Social Research,* London: George Allen and Unwin, 1970.

Galtung, John, "Theory and Methods of Social Research: A Plea for Pluralism" in Oyen, Else (ed.), *Comparative Methodology Theory and Practice in International Research,* London.

Gelles, R.J., "Methods for Studying Sensitive Family Topics", *American Journal of Orthopsychiatry*, 48, 408-424, 1978.

Goode, W.J. and Hatt, P.K., *Methods of Social Research,* New York: McGraw Hill, 1952.

Holsti, Ole R, "Content Analysis" in Gardner Lindzey and Eliot Anderson (eds.), *Handbook of Social Psychology*, Mass. Addison Wesley, 1968.

Kerlinger, Fred R., *Foundations of Behavioral Research,* Delhi: Surjeet Publications, 1964.

Kidder, Louise H., *Research Methods in Social Relations,* New York: Holt, 1981.

Kothari, L.R., *Research Methodology,* New Delhi: Vishwa Prakashan, 1985.

Lal Das, D.K., *Practice of Social Research: Social Work Perspective*, Jaipur: Rawat Publications, 2000.

Monette, Duane R. et. al., *Applied Social Research: Tool for the Human Services,* Chicago: Holt, 1986.

Moser, C.A. and Kalton, G., *Survey Methods in Social Investigation,* London: Heinemann Educational Books, 1975.

Nachmias, D. and Nachmias, C., *Research Methods in the Social Sciences*, New York: St. Martins Press, 1981.

Oppenheim, N.A., *Questionnaire Design and Attitude Measurement*, New York: Basic Books, 1966.

Rubin, Allen and Babbie E., *Research Methodology for Social Work*, Belmont, California, Wadsworth, 1989.

Sellitz, G. et. al., *Research Methods in Social Relations,* New York: Holt. Rinehart and Winston (3rd edition), 1973.

Stouffer, S.A., *Social Research to Test Ideas,* New York: Free Press of Glencoe, 1962.

Strauss, Anseln, *Qualitative Analysis for Social Scientists,* Cambridge: Cambridge University Press (photocopies of a major portion of Ch.1 in the library), 1982.

Thurstone, L.L., "Attitudes Can Be Measured," *American Journal of Sociology*, 33 January 1928.

Wilkinson, T.S. and Bhandarkar, P.L., *Methodology and Techniques of Social Research,* Bombay: Himalaya, 1977.

Young, P.V., *Scientific Social Surveys and Research,* Englewood Cliff, N.J.: Prentice Hall (4th edition), 1953.

Review Questions

1. What is survey research design?
2. What is correlational studies?
3. What are the research questions that can be answered by correlational studies?
4. Differentiate between non-probability and probability sampling.
5. What are the advantages of accidental sampling?
6. Under what situations would it be appropriate to use cluster sampling?
7. What are the applications of snowball sampling?
8. What is the meaning of representative sampling plan? Discuss the problem of representativeness.
9. Discuss the merits and demerits of various types of non-probability sampling designs.
10. Discuss some important functions of questionnaire in social research.
11. What are the strengths and weaknesses of open-end questions?
12. Discuss some weaknesses of closed-end questions?

13. What is format of questions? Discuss the format of matrix questions.
14. What are pre-coded questions? Discuss its merits and demerits.
15. How will you analyze the contents of narrative case records to M.A. social work students? Discuss how the results can be used to make the field work more effective.
16. Define the term 'content analysis' and discuss the various steps of content analysis.
17. What is units of analysis? Discuss 'theme' as a unit of analysis.

SEX DISCRIMINATION AGAINST FEMALE WORKERS IN UNORGANISED SECTOR

D.K. Lal Das

Introduction

Inspired by the International Labour Organisation (ILO) Conventions[1] and United Nations Declarations on the Elimination of Discrimination Against Womn[2], the Directive Principle[3] was translated into practice by enacting the Equal Remuneration Act, 1976 (herein after called the Act).The Act aims at providing for the payment of equal remuneration to male and female workers and for the prevention of discrimination on the ground of sex in the matter of employment.

Nevertheless, sex differences in compensation and the discrimination on the ground of sex in the matter of employment continue to exist. What causes the observed differential is more controversial. Working of implementing authorities under the Act may account for much of the differences. It is possible, however, that other factors, particularly, socio-economic characteristics of workers are also responsible. These contending propositions have not been adequately assessed in empirical analysis of wage differential and discrimination on the ground of sex.

Some Research Findings

There have been quite a few micro-studies (Gambhir, 1979; Khanna and Mathew, 1979; Patel, 1982), that show that the disparities in wages/salary of male and female employees for work of similar nature, is part of the general discrimination against women at the work place. Particularly, in unorganised sector, women are invariably paid much less than the males.

What is the relationship between wage differential and regional development? This aspect was studied by the Programme Evaluation Organisation of the Planning Commission (1961). The results show that inter-state variations are quite significant.

According to the studies conducted by Pais (1980), Labour Bureau (1979), Occupational Wages Surveys (1963), with respect of select industries as well as employment, the adoption of the principle of "equal pay for equal work" has discouraged employers from employing women workers profitably. Most probably, one of the reasons for employing women workers was that it was cheaper.

Objectives

The study was conducted to:

(i) to examine the nature and extent of perceived discrimination on the ground of sex male female wage differentials,

(ii) to ascertain the correlates of perceived discrimination and wage differentials, and

(iii) to test the hypothesis that perceived discrimination and wage differentials are associated with regional development.

Concepts

Regional Development: For the purpose of the study, the state of Andhra Pradesh was broadly divided into three major regions, viz., (a) Coastal Andhra; (b) Telangana; and (c) Rayalseema.

Discrimination: Discrimination may be defined as withholding of certain rewards or facilities with regard to employment and matters connected therewith on the ground of sex.

Wage differentials: The term 'wage differentials' refers to the difference in time rate wages of male female workers when work done by men and women is demonstrably identical.

Study Area and Sampling

The study was confined to the three regions of the State of Andhra Pradesh: Coastal Andhra (developed), Telangana (developing) and Rayalseema (underdeveloped). One construction site from each of the three regions was selected for the study. From each construction site 200 respondents were selected. Thus, finally, 600 respondents were selected for the study.

Tools and Methods of Data Collection

Data on wages/salary and personal characteristics were collected from payroll records and employment application forms. For other SECE variables, data were collected by using a pre-tested interview schedule.

Results and Discussion

Nature and Extent of Perceived Discrimination

Table I presents the analysis of perceived discrimination scores (dependent variable). A look at the table shows that perceived discrimination is rated at 74.23 per cent. That is fairly 'high' rating, is clear from two facts. First, on an average, respondents have scored over more than 35 (74.23 per cent of the highest score). Secondly, none of the respondents scored less than 22 (45.83 per cent of the highest score). It is also clear from the above analysis that the respondents differ substantially from one another ($t = 13.66$. $p < .01$) in terms of perception of treatment discrimination.

Table 1

Perceived Discrimination Scores

Perceived discrimination scores	*Frequency*	*Percentage*	*Statistics Used*	*Results*
Low (26-32)	170	28.33	Range Used 48-17	31
			Range Obtained 48-22	26
Medium (33-38)	230	38.33	Mean Score	35.63 (74.23)
			Median Score	36
High (39-48)	200	33.33	Standard Deviation	6.80
			First Quartile	32
			Third	39
Total	600	100.00	t = 13.66	p < 0.01

Correlates of Perceived Discrimination

In order to ascertain correlates of perceived discrimination a set of eight independent variables were considered. Table 2 presents the intercorrelation matrix for the selected variables.

Table 2

Intercorrelation Matrix for the Selected Variables

Variable No.	*X1*	*X2*	*X3*	*X4*	*X5*	*X6*	*X7*	*X8*	*X9*
X1	1.000	0.523	0.260	-0.270	-0.033	-0.298	-0.059	-0.034	-0.317	0.024
X2	0.123	1.000	-0.031	-0.133	0.070	0.092	-0.195	0.227	-0.012	0.262
X3	0.260	0.031	1.000	-0.666	0.196	-0.318	-0.070	0.105	-0.357	-0.040
X4	-0.270	-0.133	-0.666	1.000	-0.162	0.212	0.027	-0.138	0.319	0.036
X5	-0.033	0.070	0.196	-0.162	1.000	-0.121	0.060	-0.147	-0.232	-0.036
X6	-0.298	0.092	-0.318	0.212	-0.121	1.000	-0.134	0.324	0.848	0.448
X7	-0.059	-0.195	-0.070	0.027	0.060	-0.134	1.000	-0.455	-0.153	-0.173
X8	-0.034	0.227	0.105	-0.138	-0.147	0.324	-0.455	1.000	0.198	0.230
X9	-0.317	-0.012	-0.357	0.819	-0.232	0.848	-0.153	0.198	1.000	1.000

'R' Significant at 0.05 = 0.17613
R Significant at 0.01 = 0.22892

X1 = AGE X2 = TOTAL EXPERIENCE

X3 = WAGE X4 = WAGE DIFFERENTIAL

X5 = EQUAL WAGE X6 = REGIONAL DEVELOPMENT

X7 = UNMARRIED X8 = MARRIED

X9 = PERCEIVED DISCRIMINATION

It may be inferred from column one (or row one) of the Table 2 that most of the independent variables are not significantly correlated with one another, which means that

the effect of any independent variable on the dependent variable is likely to be its individual effects and it is not influenced by other independent variables.

In order to ascertain the nature and degree of the influence of independent variables and to quantify the impact of significantly correlated independent variables, technique of regression analysis was applied (Table 3).

Table 3

Regression Analysis of Correlates of Perceived Discrimination

S. No.	*Explanatory Variable*	*Regression Coefficient*	*Beta Coefficient*	*Standard Error*
1	Regional Development	0.676	2.646	0.496
2	Wage	0.158	0.445	0.343
3	Total Experience	0.117	0.340	0.396
4	Unmarried	0.042	-0.300	0.881
5	Equal Wage	0.061	-0.241	0.450
6	Age	0.062	0.139	0.357

Multiple R^2= 0.4011
Multiple R = 0.633

In all, eight variables were included in the regression analysis. Two of the variables did not have any additional impact on the dependent variable beyond what the first five variables had. In other words, two variables turned out to be insignificant as far as discrimination was concerned. Regional development was found to be the most important variable that affected the discrimination. To be more specific, one unit increase in scores of regional development is likely to add 0.68 points to the scores determining the perceived discrimination. In addition to this, wages and work experience were found to be important characteristics of female workers affecting their perception of discrimination.

Nature and Extent of Wage Differentials

The mean of the daily wages for female workers was Rs. 6,47 (Sd = 1.09); for the male workers this mean was Rs 10.35 (Sd = 2,14). these data indicate that the extent of wage differentials between male and female workers. The means were found to be statistically significant (t = 12.514. p <.001). The Rs. 3.88, is large in economic terms. For example, the Rs. 3.88 differentials in daily wages implies an annual (presuming that they get work for 300 days in a year) wage differentials of Rs. 1164.00.4.

Correlates of Wage Differentials

It may be inferred from correlation matrix that most of the independent variables are not significantly correlated with one another, which means that the effect of any independent variable on the dependent variable(wage differentials) is likely to be its individual effects and it is not influenced by other independent variables.

In order to ascertain the nature and degree of the influence of independent variables and to quantify the impact of significantly correlated independent variables, technique of regression analysis was applied (Table 4).

Table 4

Regression Analysis of Correlates of Wage Differentials

S.No.	*Explanatory Variable*	*Regression Coefficient*	*Beta Coefficient*	*Standard Error*
1	Wage	-0.256	-0.4242.	0.240
2	Age	-0.362	-0.475	0.252
3	Unmarried	-0.241	-0.994	0.252
4	Equal Wage	-0.354	-0.817	0.556
5	Total Experience	0.213	0.483	0.522
6	Regional Development	0.133	0.305	0.359
7	Regional Development	0.027	0.045	0.284

Multiple R^2= 0.15424
Multiple R = 0.39273

Of the eight variables studied, daily wages was found to be the most important correlate that affected the wage differentials. The negative co-efficient of the correlate (daily wages) indicates that the increase in the value of this variable is likely to reduce the score measuring the dependent variable(wage differentials). For example, one unit increase in daily wages is likely to reduce the wage differentials by 0.26 points.

Hypotheses

It was hypothesized that wage differentials and perceived discrimination are associated with regional development. The statistical results are reported in Table 6. As is clear from the table, the null hypothesis that there is no association between the wage differentials and regional development can be accepted. Thus the hypothesis that there is a significant association between wage differentials and regional development can be rejected. Thus it can be inferred that the mean wage differentials were not significantly different in the three regions.

It was further hypothesized that the perceived discrimination is associated with regional development. The statistical results are in the direction of the hypothesis (Table 4). Thus, the null hypothesis that there is no association between the perceived discrimination and regional development can be rejected. And the research hypothesis that there is association between perceived discrimination and regional development can be accepted.

Conclusion

In the study an attempt was made to analyse the impact of some socio-economic variables on discrimination on account of sex. As is clear from the data analysed above, except for regional development, the results are non-significant. Specially, perceived discrimination was significantly associated with regional development.

Development brings economic opportunities which in turn raise not only material level of living but also achieve a rise in literacy and inter-systemic contact. Better economic conditions have naturally brought about improvement in workers' education, exposure to the outside world and the general level of living.

However, the impact of development process is not uniform in all regions of Andhra Pradesh. Development has not been an equalizing process either. In fact, it has often generated, perpetuated and accounted for economic and social disparities between different regions and between male and female workers.

Notes

1. The ILO has evolved two such conventions on the subject: (a) Equal Remuneration, 1951, (Convention-100) prescribes equal remuneration for men and women for work of equal value; and (b) Discrimination Convention (Employment and Occupation), 1958, (Convention-111), refers to any distinction, exclusion or preference made on the basis of race, colour, sex, religion or social origin which has the effect to nullifying or impairing equality of opportunity or treatment in employment or occupation.
2. In 1967, the General Assembly of the United Nations unanimously adopted a "Declaration on the Elimination of Discrimination Against Women" which guarantees a broad range of rights to equality in education, work and marriage.
3. Justification for the use of linear probability model can be found in Ladd (1966) and Maddala (1983).

References

Gambhir, G.D. 1979 "Labour in Small Scale Industries", Nagpur University: Diss.

Khanna, K.P. & Mathew, M. 1979 "Women Workers in Unorganised Sector of Coir Industries in India", I.C.S.S.R. Research Abstract.

Labour Bureau 1979 *A Study of Working And Living Condition in Industry*, New Delhi: Ministry of Labour.

Ladd, G. 1966 "Linear Probability Functions and Discriminant Functions", *Econometrics*, Vol. 34. 873-85.

Maddaka, G.S. 1983 *Limited Dependent and Qualitative Variables in Econometrics*, Cambridge: Cambridge university Press.

Pais, H. 1980 "Employment of Women in India", *Indian Labour Journal*, April.

Patel, Vibhuti 1982 "Women and Work" (Mimeographed), SNDT Women's University.

13

Qualitative Research Designs

In qualitative research a researcher takes into consideration the phenomenon as a whole and describes it as it exists. In some situations it is difficult to analyze a phenomenon into various components or variables, which can be measured in quantified terms. In such cases the researcher takes into consideration the phenomenon as a whole and assumes that there is some quality in the phenomenon in its entirety. When the researcher attempts to retain the totality of a phenomenon while verifying propositions regarding it, he/she adopts a qualitative research method. This method of research describes the experiences of people in depth and permits the researcher to record and understand people's perceptions thoroughly. Qualitative research also helps us to examine the nature of human behaviour and experience and social conditions. It permits the researcher to study selected issues, cases or events in depth. While using this method, the researcher seeks to capture what people have to say in their own words.

Qualitative research designs takes into consideration 'detailed descriptions' of situations, events, people, interactions and observed behaviours. These data are also available in the form of 'direct quotations' from people about their experiences, attitudes, beliefs and thoughts. Data in qualitative research are collected through direct observation, participant observation, in-depth interviewing, case studies, recorded documents, open-ended questionnaires and journals.

The validity and reliability of qualitative data depends to a great extent on the methodological skills, sensitivity and integrity of the researcher. Systematic and rigorous observation involves far more than just being present and looking around. Skilful interviewing involves much more than just asking questions. Content analysis requires considerably more insights into the data than reading to see what's there. Thus, generating useful, credible qualitative findings through observation, interviewing and content analysis requires discipline, knowledge, training, practice, creativity and hard work (Patton, 1990: II).

In this chapter, we will discuss three research designs, viz., field study, case study and content analysis.

Field Study

The term 'field study' denotes investigations concerning social phenomena conducted in natural settings. Mostly, field study is identified with the concept of naturalistic inquiry in the areas of 'Anthropology' and 'Sociology'. It has a unique position in the conduct of research in social sciences and has attracted social researchers relatively recently. If a researcher is interested in studying the life of a tribal community, he/she may use field study method to study the problems in their natural settings to find out their actual life situations.

The process of scientific inquiry follows a paradigm of deductive-hypothetico-inductive approach. In other words, the process of scientific inquiry starts with statements of hypotheses, which are arrived at through a deductive process. Then starts the process of testing hypotheses or theoretical questions either in physically controlled situations or through statistically controlled techniques. Objectivity is to be ensured through selection of representative samples, use of standardized tests and instruments, and use of different sophisticated statistical designs for treatment of data and generalizations of findings. On the contrary, field study follows an altogether different conceptual framework which takes into account the following factors:

Multiple Realities

Field studies are based on the basic assumption that there exist multiple realities in social situations which exist in concrete forms. They are perceived by people differently and thus become different mental constructs for different people. In other words, realities are taken to be what people perceive them at a particular point of time. Since social situations keep on changing from time to time, the realities, too, keep on changing. Furthermore, since the realities are context-specific, they cannot be tangible in a generalized form.

Meanings and Interpretations

Researchers favouring field studies emphasize study of meanings given to or interpretations made about objects, events and processes concerning situations. To them, changes in terms of social and behavioural phenomena cannot be identified with the concept of physical movements but by external observation alone. An understanding of human behaviour or a social phenomenon involves understanding of how people see what they are doing or participating in an activity.

Generation of Knowledge

Field studies are aimed at generation of knowledge resulting from the interaction between the researcher and the respondents. The respondents answer the questions put by the researcher in terms of their perception or the meanings they attach to their actions. Moreover, interactions take place between the researcher and his/her respondents to achieve maximum levels of insights concerning the problem under investigation.

Generalization

Field researches do not believe in the process of generalization as propounded by scientists. Field researchers argue that in the process of making generalization, a lot of meaningful information existing in individual units is undermined; hence, knowledge generation must take into account the differences or the real evidence existing in specific situations. That is why, they take into account extreme cases while collecting data.

Human Relations

In the case of human relations several intrinsic factors, events and processes keep on influencing each other constantly. Therefore, it is not possible to identify one-to-one cause and effect relationships in the case of field studies. To field researchers causality in social sciences cannot be demonstrated in the 'true' sense as it is done in the case of physical sciences. Rather, only patterns of plausible influences can be inferred from social and behavioural studies.

Value Systems

Field researchers do not believe in value-free inquiry. They assume the influence of value systems in the identification of problems, selection of samples, use of tools for data collection, the conditions in which data are gathered, and the possible interaction that takes place between the researcher and the respondents. That is why qualitative researchers stress that the researcher's bias cannot be ignored and it must be mentioned in research reports.

Features of Field Study

Some of the unique features of field studies are described as under:

Holistic Approach

Field researchers intend to develop a deeper understanding of a given situation in a holistic fashion. In other words, all possible information concerning all the significant dimensions of the situation under study is gathered with a view to portray the situations in their totality. For example, 'child marriage' cannot be studied in a partial fashion. It has to be studied in a holistic manner taking into account the composite influence of all the socio-economic and cultural factors.

Insightful Inquiry

Field researchers emphasize insightful inquiry, where humans are treated as the sole means of data collection. Qualitative methods like participant observation, informal interviews and discussions, reading of relevant literature, and daily observation notes and diary writing are very often used for fieldwork.

Not a Pre-specific Theory

A researcher goes to the field for data collection without having a pre-specific (*a priori*) theory in mind. Field researchers apprehend that an *a priori* theory restricts the inquiry to those elements which may have been significant prior to developing an understanding of the situation. It blocks the process of holistic enquiry. The field researchers develop theoretical propositions only after interacting with the field. However, it is pointed out by field researchers that there is no insistence on developing theories afresh in each and every inquiry. Experience-based theories in relation to specific situations may act as preliminary guidelines for many naturalistic investigations.

No Pre-specific Design of Study

Prior to fieldwork, field researchers do not make explicit statements on the hypotheses and the conditions in which data are to be collected, analyzed and interpreted. The researcher develops only a broad outline of the study in advance. As the inquiry progresses, appropriate design emerges in the field; hypotheses, mostly in the question form are developed therein; final decisions are taken about the sample respondents/situations during the fieldwork; and experiences gathered through personal insights, intuition, personal images and apprehensions are recast into appropriate procedures for analyses are adopted to study the pattern of relationships on the basis of the specific data collected.

Naturalistic Setting

As stated èarlier, naturalists believe in conducting studies in realistic settings. To them, reality cannot be studied in fragmented and controlled situations. They intend to unfold what happens in realistic situations rather than studying what can happen in controlled situations.

Major Steps in Field Study

Different opinions have been expressed by field researchers about the procedural details of field studies. On the one hand, the radical field researchers believe in non-specification of the processes of conducting a study. They take fieldwork as an almost mystical process which is non-teachable. Accordingly, an investigator can start his/her fieldwork after learning about the relevant substantive theory(ies) and reviewing the empirical results of some field studies related with it.

On the other hand, most experts recommend fieldwork to be made as systematically as possible, retaining the naturalistic status of the study as a whole. This is to smoothen the processes of the conduct of the study. As stated by Erickson (1986), "Preconceptions and guiding questions can be developed beforehand. But, the researcher should not presume to know at the very outset, where specifically the initial questions might lead next". The steps can be organized in the following sequence:

Identification of Broader Questions of Inquiry

First, the researcher is supposed to specify the pertinent issues or questions related to social settings which can be resolved or answered through field study. The main focus of the researcher should be on the specific structure of occurrences rather than general character of any social phenomenon. The issues can be directly linked with improvement of social practices in specific situations. Questions can be raised not only to study the events or facts but also to identify the perspectives of the individuals involved in particular events or processes. As stated earlier, emphasis should be laid on identifying perceptions of individuals regarding their own decisions or contributions to the occurrence of events or processes.

The aim of the social researcher should be to understand the realities by identifying satisfactory patterns in the actions of individuals participating in social activities. For instance, in a social situation, broader questions can be raised, such as, if relationships between a community head and the community are fully interactional, how do people give clear feedback to community head, how do community leaders influence community members or how do the community leader and community people create an atmosphere where most of the community people appear to follow the rulings of the community leader?

The above questions guide the preliminary fieldwork and generate further questions in a given context in the course of inquiry. Besides identifying the broad framework of questions, we must prepare a general outline of the sample population to be contacted or situations to be observed in particular contexts, and draw a sketch of the types of instruments or techniques to be employed for data collection.

Collection of the Data

Once we identify the broad questions for the study, we may make deliberate attempts to identify a full range of variations in the social and the organizational arrangements related to the situations/problems under study. We may start the inquiry in a broader context of the situation before proceeding to investigate specific occurrences of events in a social set-up like a rural/tribal community, or an open in-depth inquiry of functioning of a social institution, we may gather evidence on external social surroundings where the institution functions. This may require us to do an extensive exercise of data collection. After this, we concentrate on in-depth observations or interactions with the situation which is being studied.

Data collection can be carried out in different phases through participant observation. Researcher may introduce himself/herself as one of the members of the social set-up under study. It may be possible that real participants of the system like community leaders, people and head of the community, or head of the social institution can act as observers for conducting the study. We can collect data through all the relevant and available sources and means such as:

(a) study of available literature, records and documents, diaries, pictures, photographs;

(b) interactions with the persons concerned with the programme under study; and
(c) our experiences regarding the situations.

Field researchers make use of purposive sampling of significant situations or behaviours they want to study, as well as the persons they want to interact with. Flexible approaches are followed in the field study to identify:

(a) the situations where participation can take place more intensely;
(b) the persons with whom intensive interaction is required; and
(c) the people with whom casual dialogue is needed.

Even though a broad framework of sampling is chalked out prior to data collection, the actual process of sampling takes place only during fieldwork.

Methods and Tools of Data Collection

Field researchers use different methods and tools for data collection, such as taking notes about an observed situation, using electronic appliances like tape recorders and video cameras, taking photographs and collecting relevant documents and literature on the problem. Planned informal interviews/dialogues with different groups of respondents are conducted and their opinions and perceptions are recorded either during the time of the interview or immediately after the interview. Researchers maintain daily diaries pertaining to the experiences of the field work.

Field researchers maintain separate records regarding (a) what they observe in the situations, (b) perception of respondents about the situations/events, and (c) their own perceptions about the persons and their involvement in the issue under study.

Since there is no hypothesis prior to data collection, data are not manipulated directly to test the hypotheses. However, through scrutiny of daily observation, records and evidence gathered, field researchers identify the emerging themes and patterns, phrases, actions, action sequences, expressed thoughts, feelings, etc. This process helps researchers to identify further the meaningful situations to be studied and also the way in which the complete information can be collected.

Fieldwork can be conducted in different stages. At the end of the first stage of intensive fieldwork, data may be analyzed qualitatively, and previous questions may be refined and arrive at new specific questions for further study. This is the stage where field researchers generate certain context specific hypotheses for minute observation.

Moreover, at this stage, researcher's focus is on a more restrictive range of events within the setting, and he/she begins to look for possible connections or influences between the setting, and its surrounding environment.

Again, researchers return to the field with specific questions/ hypotheses. Since the scope of study is focused at this stage, in-depth interaction concerning the specific questions takes place conveniently. It should be noted that in the final stages of fieldwork, the focus becomes more and more specific along with the development of the working hypotheses.

Data Analysis

In field studies, data are analyzed descriptively. The synoptic views of descriptive data are referred for interpretation. More specifically, the frequency distributions are presented in two or three way contingency tables indicating the patterns of behaviour. Occasionally, we use non-parametric statistical techniques like a Chi-square test, Man-Whitney two tailed tests or rank-order correlation techniques for the identification of certain patterns of relationships in the context of the specific situation under study.

A good field study follows a cyclic process of data collection, generation of hypotheses, examination of data, further generation and/or modification of hypotheses, further data collection and verification till specific research questions are identified and the patterns of refined relationships are arrived at. Moreover, the final analysis of data can provide a ground for identification of specific suggestions for improvement of the system.

Objectivity and Validity in Field Studies

Validity of Findings

Validity of results of field studies has been questioned over and again. It is said that qualitative approaches may bring subjectivity into the study, and the biases of the researcher may not produce reliable results. Moreover, because of subjective interaction, valid knowledge may not be generated. Field researchers have reacted to these questions with force and conviction.

In the recent past, there have been efforts to establish certain standards to check the validity of field studies. The criteria are outlined as follows:

(i) *Credibility*: It pertains to the level of agreement between researcher's data and the interpretations, and the multiple realities that exist in the minds of respondents.

(ii) *Transferability*: It is the quality that makes it possible to derive the accurate meaning of information on interpretation available in specific contexts.

(iii) *Dependability*: It is essentially the stability of information sought and interpretation derived in different situations on a specific issue.

(iv) *Confirmability*: It refers to the possibility of studying the collected data and reaching similar/same conclusions by different researchers.

The qualitative approach is guided by the following principles to enhance the credibility, transferability, dependability and confirmability of the studies:

(a) Sufficient time given to fieldwork can enable one to overcome a variety of possible biases and wrong perceptions, which may appear in one short fieldwork. Moreover, it can help us to identify the salient characteristics of the phenomenon under study.

(b) Continuous observation of typical features can increase the credibility of the study.

(c) Interaction with colleagues helps us evolve suitable designs, share the researcher's anxieties, apprehensions and feeling concerning fieldwork and share with them the growing insights in the field.

(d) A variety of data sources using different investigators with different perspectives can project a consolidated picture of the field easily and can enhance the dependability and confirmability of the data.

(e) Study of the varieties of adequate reference materials like documents, pictures, films, videotapes and audio recordings are essential for increasing the validity of data.

(f) Cross-checking of data and interpretations by some of the respondents can enhance internal validity of the study.

(g) Increasing purposive sampling to collect different instances across a wide range of events can be useful in maximizing the range of information and increasing external validity of the findings.

(h) Substantive description of events in specific contexts can be useful in establishing the reliability and dependability of data and conclusion.

Although the above checks are followed in field studies, there is no guarantee for the validity of a field study. However, such checks can generate a convincing situation regarding the meaningfulness of the study. Unlike a long history of scientific inquiry, which has established clear-cut standards for its validity, field studies have a very recent origin, and is yet to evolve standards to enhance its validity and reliability.

Problems of Observation

The strength of field study lies more in the competence of the field researcher than the methods, tools, techniques and designs of data collection. There are several issues pertaining to the experience and expertise of the field researcher, such as his/her relationship with the group being studied, the ethics involved in the processes of intensive data collection etc. Some of the issues are discussed as follows:

(a) First, it is necessary that only a researcher with a clear understanding of the problem should take up the task of conducting a field study. Since the validity of the field study depends entirely on human approach, it is very important to see 'who' conducts the study and 'how' he/she proceeds with the study.

(b) In cases where researcher acts as a participant observer, there is an apprehension that a stranger who is accepted as an observer may be deliberately informed and invited to observe just because he/she is a stranger. Strangers may notice events that contrast with their expectations. They may affect the behaviour of the group through their influence while assessing this group. The personality traits of the observers and the situations to be studied are the major factors in developing a close affinity between the researcher and the field and making him/her comfortable with the situations.

(c) State briefly, what measures you have to follow to ensure authenticity of data in naturalistic studies.

(d) What kinds of problem do you anticipate if you are to act (a) as an internal observer to observe some of the activities of the institution where you work, and (b) to observe the activities of an outside institution as a participant observer?

Case Study Method

Case studies may include the study of an individual, a family, a community, a social institution, a cultural organization, or a social institution. In the case of studies on communities, a village, a tribe, a slum area or a culture, each can be considered a unit of study.

Whatever the unit of a case study, it is treated as a whole in the context of specific situations. The wholeness is determined through an abstraction of ideas. In one case, an individual's specific behaviour may be perceived as a totality; in another case, a situation consisting of group activities may be treated as a whole. Especially, in social situations, the units under study could be a whole developmental programme, a micro-credit system, a development in a group setting or in an 'individual setting', owing the possibility of using a single method or integration of a number of methods.

Purposes of Case Studies

Usually, case studies are conducted for developing a deeper understanding about intricate relationships existing in the process-aspects of a specific unit(s) through qualitative inquiry. In this context, the case study method is not very different from the approach of field study. So, many a time, the case study method is treated as a kind of field study. For example, the functional aspects of any normal or exceptional institution may be the focus of a case study or any other approach used by the field researchers.

Case studies are conducted with a clinical purpose. They are treated as diagnostic and prognostic measures for clients' treatment. This approach has a psychotherapeutic background. In social research, case studies are conducted for resolving different problems and bringing about improvement in institutions facing such problems.

There can be case studies of biographical type, which aim at giving an account of an individual or tracing the development of an institution through longitudinal and prolonged investigation.

Characteristics of Case Study Method

The methodology of a case study displays certain specific characteristics, viz., continuity in study, completeness, authenticity of data, confidential recording and intellectual synthesis.

Continuity in Study

Continuous and prolonged study of situations is necessary till the underlying factors are explored and plausible patterns of their interaction/relationship identified. For example, the problems underlying the communal harmony cannot be explored in one go. A researcher may have to undertake prolonged inquiries.

Completeness

A case study involves extensive collection of data concerning internal as well as external environment of the unit under study. Data collection continues till the completeness of data is ensured and a complete picture of the unit emerges.

Authenticity of Data

A report of the case study must be based on reliable and valid data regarding the case. Several qualitative techniques such as interviews, observations, survey of records/documents find their appropriate application in case studies. Use of multi-techniques approach to data collection and cross-examination of data through different techniques can take care of the validity and reliability of data. Moreover, since the researcher interacts with the typical situations personally, most of the ethical issues regarding the nature of data, the sample situations, or sample respondents, the nature of interactions etc., emerge during the inquiry.

Confidential Recording

The necessary data, involving personal and ethical issues like relationships, confidential records, documents about the institution etc., must be handled tactfully and every care must be taken to maintain their secrecy.

Intellectual Synthesis

Since a case study involves several methods and tools during inquiry and deals with all significant situations concerning the unit, appropriate synthesis of the data is necessary to depict the uniqueness of the unit and to explore significant relationships. As such, field researchers need theoretical sophistication, insightfulness and writing skills to do justice and prepare a case study.

Main Steps in a Case Study

Most researchers treat case study method as one of the forms of field study. Therefore, the case study method follows the same steps as are followed in the case of field study. However, the following steps are considered to be very significant:

Selection of a Case for Study

The first step in case study is the identification and selection of a case for investigation. By and large, it depends on the following:

- Whether the study of a normal situation is with a view to developing deeper insight in the phenomenon? or

- Whether the study is to solve the problems of a typical institution? or
- Whether the study is to identify the underlying factors contributing to the excellent performance of an institution?

Once the case is selected, then the researcher needs to determine the status of the case. For this, several pieces of preliminary information are collected about the background of the case through the already available sources.

Data Collection

The next step in a case study is data collection. In the process of collecting data about the case, researcher may make use of qualitative techniques like observations, interviews, open-ended questionnaires, survey of record/documents, etc. In most cases, the preliminary data is collected through personal interaction with the situation under study.

Analysis of Preliminary Data

Through systematic analysis of the preliminary data, the researcher identifies the more complicated situations or problems, and raises pertinent questions about the factors affecting the problem/ situation. In the case of clinical case study, the researcher may state various hypotheses about the solutions/problems.

Study of the Case

Further study is conducted for only those specific questions or factors which are identified through the analysis of the preliminary data. Intensive investigations about these specific issues/ problems are conducted through prolonged observations, informal and formal interviews, questionnaires, cross-examination of different documents and records etc. At the end of this, analysis and interpretation of data begins. In fact, in a case study, the process of data collection, its analysis and interpretation go on in cyclical order till answers to the questions arising in the course of investigation are found and a portrait of the case emerges through investigation.

Follow-up

Repeated inquiries should be made regarding the reliability of the data collected during the study. Such investigations give us feedback on the strengths and weaknesses of the answers. If we find them unreliable, the researcher should conduct further studies to arrive at valid and reliable data with regard to the case.

Scientific Nature of Case Study Method

There have been criticisms against the case study method for lack of scientific approach. One criticism is that the case study method is useful in the exploration of knowledge related to a single unit, but it does not have scope to test hypotheses or confirm any evidence.

However, this limitation of the case study method cannot undermine its meaningfulness in the process of generating knowledge. Even though the case study method is viewed as a kind of field study, this accommodates the process of hypothesizing in a manner different from that of the survey and the experiment methods.

Generating Hypotheses in the Case Study Method

Hypotheses in the case study method are generally found in the form of questions or statements related to the unit of study, which are tested or confirmed qualitatively in the given context of investigation.

Generalization of Case Study Findings

A researcher studying a case would primarily have the purpose of understanding that particular case in its entirety and, hence, he/she may not be concerned with extending his/her understanding to other cases. However, such an understanding may take the form of further hypotheses which could be tested through other investigations.

There are possibilities of considering the findings of a case which may be significantly similar to another case studied at a later stage. There are situations where studies of different cases can be useful in developing a new trend. The issues concerning the objectivity and reliability of the case study method are similar to those of the naturalistic method already discussed in the preceding section.

Content Analysis

In the preceding chapters we have discussed about analysis of data collected from primary sources. In this chapter, we will discuss content analysis as a method of analyzing the secondary data.

Content analysis is a method of analyzing data collected by some one other than the researcher for different purposes. One can analyze the content of letters, diaries, newspaper articles, minutes of meetings, and the like, hence, the name content analysis.

Broadly defined, content analysis is "any technique for making inferences by systematically and objectively identifying specified characteristics of messages" (Holsti, 1968: 601). Objectivity refers here to an analysis that is pursued on the basis of explicit rules that enable different researchers to obtain the same results from the same messages or documents. In a systematic content analysis, the "inclusion or exclusion of content is done according to consistently applied criteria of selection; this requirement eliminates analyses in which only materials supporting the investigator's hypotheses are examined" (ibid: 598).

Content analysis is a method of analyzing secondary data, such as field records, articles published in journals or newspapers, letters, diaries, etc. It consists basically of coding, tabulating and analyzing of content of data obtained through secondary sources. For example, we might analyze the fieldwork reports of students to see if certain types of students have more knowledge base in social work than do others. Or, we might review the dissertation submitted by students to examine the methodological characteristics of the dissertations in term of nature and source of data and research design. Content analysis is particularly well suited to the study of communications and to answering the basic questions of communication research. "Who says what to whom, why, how, and with what effect (Rubin and Babbie, 1989)?"

Secondary Data

Data collected by some one other than the researcher for purposes that differ from the researcher are referred to as secondary data or available data. A wide range of such data is available for analysis. For example, governmental as well as non-governmental organizations collect a large amount of statistical data about crime, health, birth rates, death rates and the like. Another type of secondary data is documents in different forms of communication in qualitative format. This type of data includes articles of journals, books, magazines, letters, memoranda, diaries etc. Social case records and fieldwork records are a rich source of secondary data for social research. These data in combination with data collected from other sources can make significant contribution to the knowledge base of social sciences.

Sources of Secondary Data

Secondary data are collected from a number of sources and much of these data are available to social researchers. First of all, a major source of statistical data is central, state and local governments that collect data for either administrative purpose or for the purpose of periodical evaluation of their programmes or services. The ministries of Human Resource Development, Labour and Employment, Rural Development, and Municipal Corporations are repositories of vast amount of secondary data. Universities and educational institutions, where researches at different levels are undertaken regularly as part of their curriculum, are yet another important source of secondary data.

The non-governmental organizations that collect data as required by the funding organizations in the form of need assessment, programme planning and evaluation of programmes/ services for client's services are yet another source of secondary data.

Purposes of Content Analysis

The contents of documents and other material are analyzed for different purposes. They may be analyzed by their characteristics, causes and effects. Accordingly, specific purposes of content analysis are categorized as under (Sellitz, et. al., 1973: 334-35):

(a) *Purpose of ascertaining the characteristics of content:*
— To describe trend in communication-content;
— To trace the development of scholarship;
— To disclose international differences in the communication of content;
— To compare media or 'levels' of communication;
— To audit communication-content against objectives;
— To construct and apply communication standards;
— To aid technical research operations;
— To expose propaganda techniques;
— To measure 'readability' of communication materials; and
— To discover stylistic features.

(b) *Purpose of ascertaining the causes of content:*
— To identify intentions and other characteristics of the communicators;
— To detect the existence of propaganda;
— To determine the psychological state of persons and groups; and
— To secure political and military intelligence.

(c) Purpose of ascertaining effects of content:
— To reflect attitudes, interests, values of populations;
— To reveal focus of attention; and
— To describe attitudinal and behavioral response to communications.

It should be remembered that any single study might have one or more of these purposes.

Sampling in Content Analysis

It is often impossible to analyze all documents or communications pertaining to the subject selected for content analysis. For example, if a researcher wants to analyze social work syllabi to see if certain schools have more content on women's issues than do others, it would not be possible to go through the syllabi of all the schools. Usually, then, it is appropriate to select a few schools and analyze their syllabi.

For example, if a researcher is interested in analysis of the contents of TV programme on women's issues, the first task will be to define the universe. Obviously, it would not be possible to cover all the channels of TV. Thus, it would be proper to select a few channels and then draw from each channel a random sample of programmes covering women's issues.

Content analysis has same serious limitations so far as its reliability and validity is concerned. Theoretically, the methods of analysis and quantification should be so clearly defined that different researchers would arrive at the same conclusions when analyzing the same documents. But, reliability is something that can be realized at the cost of the quality of analysis of the documents. Just counting the number of times a word appears in documents in a specified period of time does ensure reliability but this is only a very superficial type of analysis, because the same word carries different meanings in different contexts. The basic method of increasing reliability of classification is to specify clearly the characteristics of statements rather than words that are to be placed in a given categories and to use many examples drawn from the documents being analyzed to illustrate what kind of statements are to be considered as representing a given category.

Steps in Content Analysis

The steps in content analysis are:

(i) Selection of the topic to be analyzed.
(ii) Selecting the media from which data are to be analyzed.
(iii) Constructing a coding scheme.
(iv) Deciding the sampling plan.
(v) Deciding the coder's reliability.
(vi) Analysis of data.

The first step in content analysis is to select a topic to be analyzed. For example, one might decide to analyze the status of women or one might select the subject of persevere portrayal of elderly people. The next step is to select the media from which the observations/recording are to be made. The important issue here is the selection of media that are typical or representative of what is available. In the third step, the categories are coded. The categories can range from simple dichotomous system in which presence or absence are noted to several mutually exclusive categories in which differentiations are made on a range of phenomena such as the marital status of the portrayed character and physical background.

Sampling units of analysis is other step. The task here is to choose either to code every reference to the context in question or to select discrete events through method of sampling. For example, one might select all articles covering the topic published in a journal over a period of 20 years or one-fourth of the articles on the issue under study over a period of 20 years. In the next step, a researcher trains his coders to get the highest order of reliability of content analysis. Reliability of content analysis becomes more important when the inferences are made for generalization. Lastly, we analyze the data. In most of the cases analysis of data is presented in a summary form. However, inferences of content analysis with the help of numbers and percentages become very specific and clear.

Units of Analysis

The units of analysis commonly found in content analysis is a word, a theme, a major character, or a sentence or a paragraph. Out of these units of analysis a single word has been considered as most convenient unit of analysis because coding the presence or absence of certain words in documents can be accomplished easily and with high degree of reliability. The pre-condition for using a single word as unit of analysis is that the single word has to qualify as a valid indicator of the measurement of the phenomena.

The theme as a unit of analysis refers to the major subject matter of an article or a document. An article can be characterized as having a primary theme. Article of journals, for example, can be characterized on the basis of status of women or community development as major themes. Main character as unit of analysis is tuned to document a cast of characters such as movies and television programmes.

The fourth unit of analysis is sentence in paragraph. Social work student's responses preceded and followed by social work educators comment can be coded as congruent or incongruent. Such comments or responses often contain more than one idea and this may make the comments and responses more difficult to classify while maintaining the categories mutually exclusive and intercoder reliability.

Coding Schemes

The most important phase in content analysis is to develop a coding scheme that can be used in analyzing the documents. Coding schemes vary according to the documents being studied and research question of the study.

Coding categories should be exhaustive and mutually exclusive. When it is possible to put every relevant element of the document into a particular category, it is called as exhaustive. On the other hand, if a particular element of the document falls into one and only one category, we call it mutually exclusive.

Application of Content Analysis

Using the method of content analysis, Vijayalakshmi, et. al. reviewed 194 articles published in *The Indian Journal of Social Work* between 1971 and 1990 and identified the trends in content, subject area and methodology of research articles. In order to demonstrate the process used in content analysis, the article is reproduced at the end of this chapter in an abridged form.

Important Terms for Review

- Qualitative Research
- Field Studies
- Validity and Reliability of Field Studies
- Problems of Observation
- Case Study
- Purpose of Case Study
- Authenticity of Data
- Content Analysis
- Source of Available Data

- Units of Analysis
- Coding Schemes
- Units of Categories
- Coder Reliabilities

Further Readings

Bailey, Kenneth D., *Methods of Social Research,* London: The Free Press, 1978.

Baker, L. Therese, *Doing Social Research,* New York: McGraw Hill, 1988.

Cook. Thomas D. and Charles S. Reichardt (eds.), *Qualitative and Quantitative Methods in Evaluation Research,* Hills: Sage, 1979.

Doby, J.T. et al., *An Introduction to Social Research,* London: Harrisburg: Stackpole Co., 1953.

Engstorm, G.A., "Research Utilization, the Challenge of Applying Social Research", *Welfare in Review,* Vol. B, No.1, 1970.

Erickson, F., "Qualitative Methods in Research on Teaching" in Merlin C. Wittrock (ed.), *Handbook of Research on Teaching,* Third Edition, London: Collier Macmillan Publishers, 1986.

Festinger. L. and Katz. D. (eds.), *Research Methods in the Behavioral Sciences,* New York: The Dryden Press, 1953.

Galtung, John, *Theory and Methods of Social Research,* London: George Allen and Unwin, 1970.

Galtung, John, "Theory and Methods of Social Research: A Plea for Pluralism" in Oyen, Else (ed.), *Comparative Methodology Theory and Practice in International Research,* London.

Goode, W.J. and Hatt, P.K., *Methods of Social Research,* New York: McGraw Hill, 1952.

Holsti, Ole R., "Content Analysis" in *The Handbook of Social Psychology,* edited by Gardner Lindzey and Eliot Anderson, Mass. Addison Wesley, 1968.

Kerlinger, Fred R., *Foundations of Behavioural Research,* Delhi: Surjeet Publications, 1964.

Kidder, Louise H., *Research Methods in Social Relations,* New York: Holt, 1981.

Lal Das, D.K., *Practice of Social Research: A Social work Perspective*, Jaipur: Rawat Publications, 2000.

Monete, Duane R. et. al., *Applied Social Research: Tool for the Human Services,* Chicago: Holt, 1986.

Moser, C.A. and Kalton, G., *Survey Methods in Social Investigation,* London: Heinemann Educational Books, 1975.

Nachmias, D. and Nachmias, C., *Research Methods in the Social Sciences*, New York: St. Martins Press, 1981.

Rubin, Allen and Babbie E., *Research Methodology for Social Work*, Belmont, California, Wadsworth, 1989.

Sellitz, G. et. al., *Research Methods in Social Relations,* New York: Holt, Rinehart and Winston (3rd edition), 1973.

Strauss, Anseln, *Qualitative Analysis for Social Scientists,* Cambridge: Cambridge University Press (photocopies of a major portion of Ch.1 in the Library), 1982.

Young, P.V., *Scientific Social Surveys and Research,* Englewood Cliff, N.J. Prentice Hall (4th edition), 1953.

Wilkinson, T.S. and Bhandarkar, P.L. *Methodology and Techniques of Social Research,* Bombay: Himalaya, 1977.

Review Questions

1. What is qualitative research?
2. Discuss the objectivity in qualitative research.
3. Discuss the authenticity of qualitative data.
4. What are the problems of observation?
5. What is a field study?
6. How will you analyze the contents of narrative case records? Discuss how the results can be used to make the field work more effective.
7. Define the term 'content analysis' and discuss the various steps of content analysis.
8. What is units of analysis? Discuss 'theme' as a unit of analysis.
9. What is coding in content analysis?
10. What is coder's reliability?

TRENDS IN ARTICLES PUBLISHED IN *THE INDIAN JOURNAL OF SOCIAL WORK*, 1971-1990

B. Vijayalakshmi, B. Devi Prasad and K. Visweswara Rao*

The major research expectation of the content analysis was to document research trends; more specifically, trends in the content and methodology of research articles published in *The Indian Journal of Social Work*, over a time span of 20 years.

Methods

All the research articles published in *The Indian Journal of Social Work* between 1971 and 1990 constituted the universe for study. The unit of analysis for the review was an article.

In order to control the cyclical trends because of publication of special issues or fluctuations in the research priorities, all these articles were listed by the name of first author and serially numbered. In all, 813 articles were published during January 1971 through December 1990. The universe is divided into two time frames, that is, 1971-80 (430 articles) and 1981-90 (383 articles) and a proportionate stratified random sampling method was used to select samples from each time frame separately. In view of the constraints of time and manpower, 194 articles (23.86%) were selected for the study.

Classification of Categories

The following categories were used in the analysis:

1. Background characteristics of authors which comprised:
   - gender
   - rank
   - institutional affiliation
   - geographical location
   - writing collaboration of the authors of articles
2. The research articles were classified into the following categories:

* Dr. (Mrs) B. Vijayalaksmi and Dr. B. Devi Prasad are Professors in Social Work, and Dr. K. Vishweswar Rao is Reader in Social Work, Department of Social Work, Andhra University, Visakhapatanam, Andhra Pradesh.

- Source (primary, secondary, and so on) and nature of data (quantitative, qualitative, and so on).
- Nature of the article (empirical and non-empirical).

Empirical

Under this subject category the following sub-categories were adapted for coding purposes:

(a) Experimental: Studies primarily concerned with cause-effect relationships through the use of experimental designs.

(b) Quantitative-descriptive: Studies having as their purpose, through the systematic collection of data, simple delineation's or assessments of phenomena, evaluation or isolation of key variables.

(c) Exploratory: Studies that have as their purpose the formulation of questions for subsequent research and the development of hypotheses, clarification of concepts or the enhancement of an investigator's familiarity with the phenomenon or setting for more precise future research.

(d) Case study: Studies that involve in-depth consideration of one person, group, project, institution, agency or any other entity with intensive investigation of the factors that contributed to the characteristics of the case.

Non-Empirical

This category included the articles that discuss research either in general terms or draw implications from one or more studies or those articles concerned with the development or testing by empirical means of research technique or a measurement device.

Coder Reliabilities

The analysis was carried by going through the articles as per the article-reading schedule prepared by using the above categories. Firstly, the article-reading schedule was applied to a prior sample of 30 articles by two coders (the second and third authors) independently. An inter coder reliability test, was used to find out the reliability between coders for the different categories used in the study. The results showed a high rate of agreement between the two coders on characteristics of research articles, author's background, and areas of research. However, coding the articles with regard to research design and source of data showed some variation. The definitions of categories were revised and a high level of agreement was obtained later.

Source and Nature of Data

It is found that majority of the articles was based on primary data and was of a quantitative nature, followed by a few qualitative articles and studies based on secondary data. However, it can be seen that the percentage of articles based on primary data and quantitative studies showed a downward trend during 1981-90.

Empirical Orientation

It can be seen that more than half of the sample articles published in *The Indian Journal of Social Work* during the period under study is empirical in content. The empirical category includes articles that come under four sub-categories, namely, experimental, quantitative-descriptive, and exploratory and case studies. A trend analysis of the proportion of empirical articles and non-empirical articles for the period indicated a slight upward trend for both the categories. However, appearance of non-empirical articles showed a noticeable rise in percentage as compared to the empirical articles published during the period.

Research Design

Survey research was found to be the most frequently reported design in the sample articles and a majority of the articles reported the use of questionnaires and interviews as methods of data collection. Use of survey research design indicated a descending trend in the second decade, while articles using observation, and unobtrusive techniques involving archival data such as government documents, census reports and clinical records showed an increase in the percentage over the two decades. While articles employing experimental and quasi-experimental designs appeared during 1971-80, the same were conspicuously absent during 1981-90.

Studies based on evaluative research designs were reported during both the decades and the proportion of evaluation studies showed an increase over the two time frames. However, single subject research designs, which are becoming popular in social work practice research, have not been reported in the articles of the study sample.

Quantification

The trend towards quantification in social science research is a well-recognised fact. Articles in the study sample were examined to get some notions about the nature of the data and the kinds of statistical analysis employed. To obtain a picture about the trend pertaining to quantification, a four-fold classification was devised. Roughly, 48 per cent of the total sample articles employed some sort of statistical analysis, which ranged from ordering of data in percentages to the use of descriptive and inferential statistical analysis. The remaining 52 per cent of articles were discussions or studies whose data do not reflect any sort of statistical analysis.

From this perspective, an examination of sample articles in the present study revealed that articles dealing with topics on Family, Child and Social Work were in the large number (19.6 per cent during first decade and 20.6 per cent during the second decade). While Community Development took second place next in the order during the first decade, articles in the area of Personnel Management and Labour Welfare took second place during the second decade. However, the percentage of articles published in these specific areas indicated a decline over the two decades. Articles in Criminology and Corrections, and Medical/Mental Health Settings figure in a considerable percentage in the first decade, though the proportion of articles published in the former area indicated a downward trend as compared to the latter.

An attempt was made to analyse the study sample regarding the presence of articles devoted to women's issues. For the purpose of this study, women's issues were defined as topics that acknowledge the unique status of women and their problems as spouses, mother, clients and workers. For example, rape, abortion, and wife abuse were some of the issues that were included in this category.

The analysis revealed that less than 15 per cent of the articles published in *The Indian Journal Of Social Work* during the sample period were devoted to women's issues. The percentage of articles that focused on women's issues registered a slight increase, that, from 13.7 per cent in the first decade to 16.3 per cent (n=15) in the second decade.

Conclusions

It is evident, in this review of articles, that incorporation of methodological improvements to better the quality of research is necessary. There is a need to refine both the conceptual foundations and methodology of social science research. It is encouraging to see that a considerable number of social work educators contributed articles to the journal and more so during the second time period (1981-90). The practitioners and educators should be able to use research as a tool to measure practice effectiveness, improve intervention skills used by them and to refine methodology measuring the outcomes. This is necessary as the evidence from the study suggests that these functions in general did not manifest in the content of the articles. The review further indicates a slight increase in the articles based on qualitative data over the two decades. Qualitative designs provide detailed data and facilitate an understanding of the subjects' point of view with flexibility in studying social life (Chandwick *et al*. 1984). There is a need to strengthen research approaches in this direction.

14

Evaluation of Research Project

Every research, based on data, is concluded by presenting its results in the form of a report. The reporting of results of a research depends on the purpose, with which it was undertaken. A study might have been conducted for various reasons, such as a personal research, for award of a degree, an article for publication in a journal, a paper to be presented in a national or an international conference, or a project funded by an agency, and so on.

Research studies are required to follow a scientific process. When it is reported, it follows certain conventions and formats for maintaining parity in reporting and for easy grasps by readers. Therefore, it is imperative to develop a paradigm or a scientific method for evaluating research reports.

Research studies can be classified into three categories, namely, (a) Research Studies, Assignments or Papers for Training, (b) Research Studies or Analytical Papers for Problem Solving, and (c) Research Studies for Generation of Knowledge.

Research for Training

The purpose of research projects, especially at the post-graduate and doctoral levels, is training (Rubin and Babbie, 1989). The dissertations for Master's, M.Phil. and Ph.D. degrees are intended to train students in research, and diagnostic research basically aimed at problem solving. The research studies or analytical papers, where the new vistas of knowledge, come under the third category, that is, knowledge generation.

Another purpose of conducting research is training in research methodology. This is quite true for the research projects linked with various programmes of education or training.

Building the Rationale

The first chapter of a research report is the introduction. This is the chapter from where one can learn about the purpose for which the study was undertaken. Whenever a researcher tries to support his/her view about a phenomenon, there is a likelihood of biases (Mukhopadhyay, 1981). Many a time, the researchers or authors get emotionally involved and bring in a bias, which is easy to detect.

To identify any biases in research study one has to look into the researcher's efforts in collecting data and thematic literature. For example, a particular area of research may have quite a range of references and the studies might contradict one another in terms of findings. Of these, the researcher may choose only such studies that support his/her point of view instead of referring to the contradictions. As a reviewer, we may first like to identify if there is any bias, the extent of the bias and its likely impact on the research process and findings. The second important point for evaluation is the kinds of arguments being built up to justify the relevance of the study. To evaluate an introductory chapter we have to see if the problems or topic selected is relevant, important, timely, researchable, and within the competence of the researcher.

While presenting the review of literature a researcher should touch upon the introduction justifying the research, methodological details and findings and their implications. But, most researchers or authors present the findings only. Very few researchers look into the findings as well as the research methodology in their reviews. From the perspectives of findings, major objectives of a review are to: (a) find gaps in research, (b) identify the areas of overlap, and (c) identify contradictions. As an evaluator, we need to check out whether the researcher has indeed identified gaps, overlaps and contractions. However, within that broad framework, we may have to make a qualitative assessment about how effectively the researcher has argued the cases of gaps, overlaps and contradictions.

There are at least three basic patterns of reviewing literature. The first and the most elementary pattern is where a researcher presents the findings of a study against the name of the researcher in one paragraph. The second paragraph refers to another and the third to yet another researcher and so on. In such a case, the researcher does not interlink one study with another.

In the second type of review of literature a researcher refers to a particular set of findings and provides a few references of those who contributed to that particular finding in brackets. In this case, the researcher basically clusters studies around a finding. Still, he/she does not compare any two sets of findings.

In the third pattern a researcher develops a conceptual framework of his/her research in a particular field. The conceptual framework is built on the previous research study. Fitting it into a conceptual framework allows him/her to compare and contrast issues and findings, identify the gaps, overlaps and contradictions and also derives methodological implications.

Obviously, the three patterns are in a taxonomic structure. As such, as an evaluator of a research report, we would award higher credit to the researcher who uses pattern three and least to the one who resorts to pattern one for reviewing research literature.

Objectives and Hypotheses

It is important to examine whether the researcher has raised very clearly the questions to which he/she is looking for a solution. These questions should be explicit and the researcher should categorically put down them on paper. This set of questions can be converted into objectives. Objectives are the foundation of a research project. Eventually, the objectives guide the entire process of research study. The major attributes of well-written objectives are the following:

- *Clarity of expression and direction*: The objectives must have been stated clearly enough to indicate what the researcher is trying to investigate. It is equally important to avoid overlaps while stating objectives.

- *Measurability*: The objectives must be stated in a manner that they are measurable; in case of qualitative research it should be possible to at least codify the data and information so that assessment can be made whether the objectives have been achieved or not.
- *Comprehensiveness*: The objectives provide the guiding framework for a research project. Hence, the statement of objectives should be comprehensive enough to cover each and every aspect of the research study. In other words, nothing should be outside the purview of the stated objectives.
- *Judiciousness*: Another important attribute is the judiciousness in, and justifiability of, choosing and stating objectives. For example, many young scholars, in their post-graduate dissertations and doctoral theses, mention "recommending future research" as one of the objectives. In all fairness, this is not feasible. Similarly, in a short time-bound project, an objective that actually calls for sustained and long-term study becomes less feasible.
- Thus, an evaluator, while evaluating the objectives, needs to examine clarity of expression, measurability, and comprehensiveness of the objectives and judiciousness in choosing and stating them.

An important task of the evaluator in the case of research study is to check whether the researcher has provided sound back up from the previous research and findings and important theoretical analyses to justify his/her formulation of hypotheses. For the purpose of evaluation, it is important to examine whether the choice of hypotheses was logical, whether the researcher has adequately argued out his/her case and whether the hypotheses are testable, and are clearly indicating one-to-one relationships between two (or more) variables.

Selection of Research Design

There are several research designs that can be chosen by a researcher to achieve the research objectives and test the hypotheses. While evaluating a research report, it is important to assess whether the chosen design is competent to respond to the research objectives and questions laid down. For example, if the objective is to test the impact of a board treatment to a group of clients, it has to follow an experimental design. Similarly, if the objective is to assess the status of certain psycho-social variables in a given sample of population, it would require survey designs (Rubin and Babbie, 1989). Within survey designs, if the purpose is simply to describe their status and not to compare them with any standard norm or not even develop a norm, the design can be descriptive.

Hence, in evaluating research, it is necessary to check the choice of appropriate research design against the objectives. Another means of evaluating the applicability and appropriateness of the research design is to check it against the hypothesis. If the hypothesis to be tested is formulated in terms of relationships, the study has to adopt a survey design, by which relationships can be tested. Compared to it, if the hypothesis is to test the performance of two different groups against a particular type of treatment, the research design has to provide for that opportunity by adopting an experimental design. Depending on the nature of the groups, the treatment, the size of the sample and also the nature of that experiment, one would adopt a pre-experimental, quasi-experimental or true experimental design.

Thus, an evaluator of a research report needs to examine the appropriateness of the choice of research designs vis-à-vis the research objectives. The details of the design, too, have to be evaluated. Equally important is the argument put forward by the researcher in deciding the research design.

Choice of Variables

Choice of variables is an important step in a research project. There can be at least three sets of variables, namely, independent, dependent and control variables. The important point to evaluate in the choice of variables is the formulation of the dependent variables. This is particularly important in experimental research where the impact of other variables on the criterion variable is assessed.

Since the research makes a meaningful contribution, it is important to choose the independent variables depending upon more than one consideration. Of the considerations is the existing knowledge on the basis of previous research, which shows that certain types of variables are indeed related to and predict the variables are the criterion variable. The second important consideration is the assumption of the researcher—that there are particular sets of variables which are likely to be related to the dependent variables.

The third set of variables is the control (Nachmias and Nachmias, 1981). These are often ignored in research, although these actually intervene and influence the relationship between the independent and the criterion variables. On the basis of the research literature, the researcher is expected to identify such variables that are likely to influence the relationship under test.

Besides the identification and classification of the variables, it is also important that variables are measurable. Further, all variables may not have standard definitions. In such a case, it is expected that the researcher shall provide operational definitions and also indications of their measurability.

Hence, an important consideration in evaluation is how meticulously the variables have been identified and classified under the three categories mentioned above. The second important consideration in this case is whether the researcher has provided operational definitions of at least such variables that do not have a standard meaning in the literature. The third important consideration is whether there are clear indications of the measurability of variables.

Research Instruments

There are several research instruments, such as psychological tests, achievement tests, questionnaires, opinionnaires, information blanks, inventories, interview schedules, and so on. For the purpose of evaluating a research report, the important consideration is whether the instrument chosen or developed is appropriate for measuring the variables or not. The points to be borne in mind while evaluating research instruments are the following:

1. Whether the researcher has chosen an instrument that can actually measure the variables.
2. Whether the research instrument has been picked up from an existing stock or has been constructed by the researcher. In case of the former, whether the researcher has checked its validity and reliability. In case the researcher has used the instrument on his/her own, has care been taken to pre-test the tool.
3. Besides these three criteria, research instruments can be examined from the angle of language, communication, provision of recording response by the respondents, and so on.

Sample

With respect to the sample, the major issues that need to be considered are sample size, sampling technique and type of sampling. The size of the sample depends on the nature of objectives of a research project and the research design. For example, in case of rigorous experimentation, it is difficult to handle large samples. Also, it is not necessary. Similarly, for surveys and such other status studies, samples have to be large. There has to be an optimum size of sample beyond which it is waste of research resources. What is to be considered is whether the sample size has been scientifically determined.

What is important is the technique of choosing a sample. There are several techniques of choosing a sample, namely, randomization, stratified randomization, clustering and so on. In case of exploring a new phenomenon primarily for understanding and learning, one may use purposive sampling. Since it is a purposive sample, it is obviously not randomized. It does not have the value of generalization but can be used for generating the first set of information. The important point is to check whether there is a case for using purposive sampling. A random sample is often quoted as the ideal sample; it is necessary for generalization and the creation of new knowledge. However, a modified version like stratified randomization is used in social research. It provides a sound basis for generalization. The important point to check here is whether the researcher has identified the right and relevant criteria for stratification and sub-stratification of the population, and then developed a sampling frame to choose a stratified random sample.

It is also important to look into the argument that is put forward by the researcher, justifying the method of selection of the sample. There are studies where the researcher starts with a particular sample size, but ends up with a considerably reduced one. Say, for example, beginning with a stratified large sample, the researcher ends up with a small sample by default or with a residual sample. This may require a change in the statistical analysis of the data.

An evaluator needs to carefully evaluate the explanation provided by the researcher and the way he/she purports to cope with it.

Data Collection and Analysis

The quality of the outcome of a research depends on the quality of data itself. In turn, the quality of data is determined by the procedure of data collection. The indication of the quality of data lies in the dependability of the information collected from the sample. The worst case is when a researcher manipulates the responses by filling research instruments himself/herself. While it is difficult to catch such unprofessional research behaviour, it does generate a pattern that is unlikely to produce results. Other important problems associated with data collection are on-the-spot collection that provides a definite return of responses, but not necessarily quality responses because the respondent is likely to respond mechanically. In the second type, where the researcher sends the instrument by mail or leave it to the respondent to respond, there is a large amount of loss because only a small percentage of the prospective respondents respond. The data thus generated are not of the pre-determined sample but of the positive type of respondents in the sample, may be we can call it the default sample.

Generally speaking, in a research exercise that requires primary data, it is better to collect the data personally and in case of secondary data, it is important to check the sources of data and their trustworthiness. The points to check here are whether the researcher has categorically recorded the details of data collection, such as, whether research instruments were administered personally or by a representative or by mail and whether sources and authenticity of secondary data were checked, and the kind of problem that the data might have in terms of quality.

Data analysis can be either qualitative or quantitative. However, a large majority of research depends on quantitative methods and statistical procedures. A major point in evaluating a research study is to see if quantitative analysis is used where objectives and hypotheses do not demand a quantitative analysis. Similarly, whether the researcher has chosen a qualitative technique where it was not required at all.

Within quantitative research, statistics can be parametric or non-parametric. The point for evaluation is whether the researcher has justified the choice of the broad option between parametric and non-parametric tests. The size of the sample is another determinant in choosing the statistical tests as a small sample often warrants non-parametric tests. Within the parametric and non-parametric tests there is a wide range of options. Whether the researcher has chosen a right test is another important point to consider. For example, within the application of simple central tendencies, it has to be seen whether the researcher has used mean where it is indeed the appropriate application or whether he/she has mechanically used a mean where a median or a mode would have been the more appropriate choice.

Findings and Implications

The final outcome and, hence, the value of a research project lies in its findings, that is, results and their interpretation. The findings are presented not only in the descriptive form but also in the form of tables and graphic representations. The evaluator needs to examine whether a table or a graph has been used whenever it was required. Similarly, if a table or a graphical presentation has been provided, it has to be seen whether it has been given a title and followed up with an explanation. The second important point to check is whether the researcher has related the graphic presentation with the corresponding tabular presentation and ensured that there is no contradiction between the two.

Along with the results, it is necessary to provide an interpretation and implications of the results. In order to do so, a researcher often refers to previous studies to derive support for his/her findings. He/she is also expected to reflect previous studies that contradict his/her findings. The important issue of evaluation here is to critically examine the way a researcher interprets the findings. That is whether the interpretation has been related to introductory chapter where the researcher built up the rationale for his/her research and whether the argument built up in each chapter is adequately reflected in the interpretation of the results. In other words, this is where an evaluator examines the analytical skill of a researcher, the skill of extrapolation, the skill of observing and explaining relationships between two or more variables, and so on.

Summary and Conclusions

The chapter on summary and conclusions provides a quick glimpse of the entire project. Brevity with comprehensiveness is the rule of the game for this chapter. An evaluator often examines within the small space of a summary how a researcher has built the rationale, how he/she has documented the objectives, hypotheses, research methodology and findings.

Referencing

Referencing is an important skill. Most researchers flounder at this item—they lack both the skill and the seriousness of purpose. It is easy to check because there are some definite internationally recognized formats. One comes across many research theses where a researcher mentions only the authors and the names of the books and skips the place, publisher and even the year of publication, little realizing that an evaluator or a future reader of the thesis would not be able to refer to any book or study without the details about the publisher and the year of publication. At the very elementary level, it is necessary to check whether all the information has been provided. Secondly, it has to be checked whether the information provided is in one of the standard forms.

Annexure

Last but not the least, an important component of the research report is annexure. Annexures usually contain the research instruments, sampling frame, and instructional material that might have been used for experimentation, and so on. Annexures are also serialized. The main purpose is that an evaluator can check the actual quality of the material that has been used by the researcher. Annexures need to be fully documented and also serialized as indicated in the content of the research report. Thus, the checkpoints are the comprehensiveness and serialization of the annexures.

There are a few other simple indicators that also determine the quality of a research report. These are:

1. Language and expression including correctness of syntax and spelling.
2. Typing, word processing and printing of a report.
3. Margins, line spacing and font type and size.
4. Placement of tables, diagrams, illustrations and graphs.
5. Binding and overall get up.

Research Studies for Problem Solving

The second category of researches is primarily for problem solving. Different types of research have been undertaken for this purpose. Most relevant among the problem-solving types of research is the intervention research, where a specific intervention is designed, tried out and evaluated to assess exactly the extent of alleviation of the problem. This is the highest form of social research. The other types of problem-solving research are the evaluative and diagnostic types. The main objective of this type of research analysis is to diagnose the causes of a problem, assess the magnitude and provide an action plan to solve the problem.

The methodological rigour of this kind of research is as important as we have mentioned in the previous section. Intervention research deals with the application of research methods and skills in social work theory and practice. In other words, social work practice is a scientific practice using various research methods, tools and techniques. Therefore, while we evaluate research in social work or social work research, we have to keep in mind whether the research studies, analytical or assignment papers in question

1. enhance the knowledge base of social work,
2. assess the effectiveness of social work intervention,
3. suggest alternate intervention,
4. innovate intervention, and
5. evaluate the outcomes of interventions.

For other types of research such as for problem solving research that is evaluative and diagnostic, following points may be looked into:

1. relevance and magnitude of the problem,
2. the quality of the solution identified,
3. replicability of the approach,
4. sustainability of the solution, and
5. transferability of the experience.

Research Studies for Knowledge Generation

The third type of research studies is for knowledge generation. In assessing a research report from the angle of knowledge generation, we will have to begin with the assessment of the methodological component. In this case, it becomes all the more important because without the right methodology, the results—the basis of new knowledge—will not be dependable. In the research parlance generating knowledge implies generalizability. Generalizabilty depends on the sophistication of the research design, control of variables and the level of confidence (in statistical terms), on which a phenomenon can be predicted. This requires very serious methodological rigour.

Beyond methodological considerations, there are several other areas for the evaluation of research studies intended to generate knowledge. One important component of evaluation is the researcher's own understanding and assessment of the existing knowledge in the field of his/her own research. This is often indicated in the introductory chapter and the review of literature carried out by the researcher or author. However, two factors are important: coverage of theoretical literature dealing with the conceptual paradigm proposed by the researcher/author and/or one of the existing conceptual paradigms. Both these exercises should lead to identification of the strength or weakness of the conceptual framework as much as the contradictions, gaps and the overlaps in research findings. This is precisely why the evaluation of higher forms of research becomes necessary.

The second aspect to be evaluated in this case is the new contribution made by the researcher whether the research or study has brought in any new findings in the concerned area of research. The new findings have to be adequately supported with tests of validity and reliability and the feasibility of the solutions. What is to be checked is whether the research methodology adopted by the researcher had taken adequate precautions to test the reliability and validity of the findings.

Finally, it is the generalizability of the findings that contributes to knowledge generation. In assessing a research report of this category, this particular aspect needs to be carefully considered. In doing so, some of the alternative mechanisms would be examined whether the researcher/author corroborates his/her findings and also justifies the claims of the new addition to the knowledge system.

Research reports follow certain conventions and formats for maintaining parity in reporting and for easy grasps by readers. Therefore, it is imperative to develop a paradigm or a scientific method for evaluating research reports. To evaluate a research report, the following questionnaire can be used:

Questionnaire for Evaluation of a Research Report

1. Introduction
   - (a) Is there any bias? Yes/No
   - (b) If yes, what is the extent of the bias? Extensive/some/little
   - (c) Are the related areas of education (the field concerned) laid out? Yes/No
   - (d) Whether the problem selected is appropriate? Yes/No
   - (e) Whether the problem is relevant? Yes/No
   - (f) Whether the problem is important? Yes/No
   - (g) Whether the problem is researchable? Yes/No
2. Review of literature
   - (a) Whether gaps have been identified? Yes/No
   - (b) Whether overlaps have been identified in the review? Yes/No
   - (c) Whether the contradictions have been identified in the review? Yes/No
   - (d) What is the level of the review? Level 1/Level 2/Level 3/Level 4
3. Objectives and hypotheses
   - (a) Are objectives stated clearly? All/Some/None
   - (b) Are objectives measurable? All/Some/None
   - (c) Are objectives comprehensive? All/Some/None
   - (d) Are objectives judiciously chosen? All/Some/None
   - (e) Are the hypotheses logical? All/Some/None
   - (f) Are the hypotheses logical? All/Some/None
   - (g) Are the hypotheses stated clearly? All/Some/None
4. Research design
   - (a) Whether the choice of research design vis-a-vis the research objectives are appropriate? Yes/No
   - (b) Whether the details of the design are given? Yes/No
5. Variables
   - (a) Whether the variables have been rightly identified? All/Some/None
   - (b) Whether the variables have been Operationally defined? All/Some/None

(c) Whether the variables are measurable? All/Some/None

6. Research instruments

(a) Whether the instrument selected can measure the variable? Yeş/No

(d) Whether the instrument has been constructed or adopted? Constructed/ Adopted

(c) Whether the feasibility of the instrument has been tested? Yes/No

(d) Is the language used in the research instruments comprehensible? Yes/No

7. Sample

(a) Is the size of the sample appropriate? Yes/No

(b) Is the technique of choosing the sample appropriate? Yes/No

8. Data collection and analysis

(a) Whether the research instruments are administered? Personally/by a Representative/ by Mail

(b) Whether the secondary date are authentic? Yes/No

(c) Whether the right kind of test is chosen? Yes/No

9. Referencing

(a) Whether all the information is provided in the references? All/Some/None

(b) Whether information provided is in the standard form? All/Some/None

(c) Whether the reference are indexed? All/Some/None

10. Annexure

(a) Whether the annexure are comprehensive? Yes/No

(b) Whether the annexure are serialized? Yes/No

11. Findings and implications

(a) Whether the findings are in descriptive form or in tables? Description/ Table/Graphs

(b) Whether the tables/graphs have appropriate titles? Yes/No

(c) Whether the tables/graphs have been explained? Yes/No

(d) Whether the findings have been related to the introductory chapter? Yes/No

12. Summary and Conclusions
    Whether the summary presented is comprehensive? Yes/No
13. General indicators
    (a) Are there typing mistakes? Many/Some/None
    (b) Whether the gap between the lines is sufficient? Yes/No
    (c) Whether the placement of tables/graphics/illustrations is proper? Yes/No
    (d) Whether the margin left is sufficient? Yes/No
    (e) Whether the binding is proper? Yes/No

Further Readings

Bailey, Kenneth D., *Methods of Social Research*, London: The Free Press, 1978.

Baker, L. Therese, *Doing Social Research*, New York: McGraw Hill, 1988.

Black, James A. and Champion, Dean J., *Methods and Issues in Social Research*, New York: John Wiley, 1976.

Kidder, Louise H., *Research Methods in Social Relations*, New York: Holt, 1981.

Kothari, L.R., *Research Methodology*, New Delhi: Vishwa Prakashan, 1985.

Lal Das, D.K., *Practice of Social Research: Social Work Perspective*, Jaipur: Rawat Publications, 2000.

Monette, Duane R. et. al., *Applied Social Research: Tool for the Human Services* Chicago: Holt, 1986.

Nachmias, D. and Nachmias, C., *Research Methods in the Social Sciences*, New York: St. Martins Press. 1981.

Rubin, Allen and Babbie E., *Research Methodology for Social Work*, Belmohf, California: Wadsworth, 1989.

Review Questions

1. What is research for training?
2. What is research for knowledge generation?
3. What is problem-solving research?
4. What is format of research report?
5. What are the patterns of review of literature?
6. What are the general indicators of a research report?

Appendices

Appendix A

Level of Measurement and Statistical Tests-1

Measurement level of first variable	*Single variable procedure*	*Two-variable (bivariate) procedure*			
		Measurement level of second variable			
		Dichotomy	*Nominal (c categories)*	*Ordinal*	*Interval and ratio*
Dichotomy	Proportions, percentages, ratios	Diff. of prop., Chi-square, Fisher's exact test, f, Q, Tb lb,	...	...	...
Nominal (r categories)	Proportions, percentages, ratios	Chi-square, V,C,T, Tb lb	Chi-square, V,C,T, Tb lb	...	...
Ordinal	Medians, quartiles, deciles, quartiles deviations	Mann-Whitney, runs, Smirnov, signed-ranks	Analysis of variance with ranks	Rank-order correlation, Kendall's tau, gamma, rs, dyz	...
Interval and ratio	Means, medians, SD	Difference of means	F test, E2, intraclass correlation	...	Correlation and regression

T-Tschuprow's
V-Cramer

Appendix B
Levels of Measurement and Statistical Tests-2

Type and Number of Samples

Levels of measurements	*Single sample*	*Two related samples*	*Two independent samples*	*More than two independent samples*	*Correlational measures*
Nominal	Chi-square one-sample test		Chi-square test for independent samples with two subclasses	Chi-square test for more than two subclasses	Phi co-efficient, Ylue's Q
Ordinal	Kolmogorov-smirnov one-sample test	Sign test, Wilcoxon matched-pairs signed-ranks test	Mann-Whitney U test Wald-Wolfowitz runs test		Spearman rank order correlation
Interval and ratio		Paired t-test,	T-test for independent samples	Analysis of variance	Pearson product moment correlation co-efficient

*Each column lists those statistical tests and correlational measures that are often used by human service workers along with the required level of measurement for each procedure.

Measurement level of first variable	*Single variable procedures*	*Two-variable (bivariate) procedure*			
		Measurement level of second variable			
		Dichotomy	*Nominal (c categories)*	*Ordinal*	*Interval and ratio*
Dichotomy	Proportions, percentage, ratios	Difference of proportions, chi-square, Fisher's exact test, Ø, Q, Tb, lb	...	...	...
Nominal (r categories)	Proportions, percentages, ratios	Chi-square, lb	Chi-square, lb	...	...
Ordinal	Medians, quartiles, deciles, quartile deviations	Mann-Whitney, runs, Smirnov, signed-ranks	Analysis of variance with ranks	Rank-order correlation, Kendall's tau, gamma, rs, dyz	...
Interval and ratio	Means, median, standard deviations	Difference of means	Analysis of variance, intraclass correlation	...	Correlation and regression

Bibliography

Abram, M., *Social Surveys and Social Action*, London: Heinemann, 1950.

Ackoff, R.L., *The Design of Social Research,* Chicago: University of Chicago Press, 1953.

Bailey, Kenneth D., *Methods of Social Research*, London: The Free Press, 1978.

Baker, L., Therese, *Doing Social Research,* New York: McGraw Hill, 1988.

Barlow, D.H., and M. Hersen, "Single-Case Experimental Designs: Uses in Applied Clinical Research", *Archives of General Psychiatry*, 29 (1973), 319-325.

Bennel, Carl et. al., *Evaluation Experiments*, New York: Academic Press, 1975.

Bhatt, Anil and A. Subramaniam, "Directing Program, Evaluation towards the Field Worker: An Experiment", *Management in Government*, Vol. XVI, No. 3, 1984.

Black, James A. and Dean J. Champion, *Methods and Issues in Social Research,* New York: John Wiley, 1976.

Blalock, H.M., *Social Statistics*, Auckland: McGraw Hill, 1988.

Bloom, M., "Challenges to Helping Profession and the Responses of Scientific Practice", *Social Service Review,* 52, 584-595, 1978.

Bloom, M. and J. Fischer, *Evaluating Practice: Guidelines for the Accountable Profession*, Englewood Cliffs, N.J.: Prentice Hall, 1982.

Broadbeck, May (ed.), *Readings in the Philosophy of Science*, New York: The MacMillan, 1968.

Campbell, D.T. and J.C. Stanley, *Experimental and Quasi-Experimental Designs for Research,* Boston: Houghton Mifflin, 1963.

Chapin, F.S., *Experimental Design in Sociological Research,* New York: Harper, 1974.

Cohen, Yehezkel, "Some Critical Reflections on Participatory 1982, Research" *Convergence,* 15, (3): 77-79, 1953.

Cook, Thomas D. and Charles S. Reichardt (eds.), *Qualitative and Quantitative Methods in Evaluation Research,* Beverly Hills: Sage, 1979.

Dasgupta, Sugata, "Social Work Research" in *Encyclopaedia of Social Work,* New Delhi: Government of India, 1977.

De Geyndt, W., "Five Approaches for Assessing Care", *Hospital Administration*, Vol. 15, No. 21, 1970.

Doby, J.T. et al., *An Introduction to Social Research,* London: Harrisburg: Stackpole Co., 1953.

Elhance, D.N., *Fundamental of Statistics*, Allahabad: Kitab Mahal, 1984.

Engstorm, G.A., "Research Utilization, the Challenge of Applying Social Research", *Welfare in Review,* Vol. B, No. 1, 1970.

Epstein, I. and T. Tripodi, *Research Techniques for Program Planning, Monitoring and Evaluation*, New York: Columbia University Program, 1974.

Fansel, David, "Services to and by the Real People", *Social Work,* 34, 195-196, 1980.

Festinger, L. and D. Katz (eds.), *Research Methods in the Behavioral Sciences,* New York: The Dryden Press, 1953.

Freemen, H. and C. Sherwood, "Research in Large-Scale Intervention Programme", *Journal of Social Issues,* Vol. 21, No. 11, 1965.

Freud, J.E., *Modern Elementary Statistics,* New Delhi: Prentice Hall, 1977.

Galtung, John, *Theory and Methods of Social Research,* London: George Allen and Unwin, 1970.

Galtung, John, "Theory and Methods of Social Research: A Plea for Pluralism" in Oyen, Else (ed.), *Comparative Methodology Theory and Practice in International Research*, London, 1978.

Garret, H.E., *Statistic in Physical and Education,* Bombay: Vakils, 1966.

Gelles, R.J., "Methods for Studying Sensitive Family Topics", *American Journal of Orthopsychiatry,* 48, 408-424, 1978.

Gingerich, W. and W. Feyerherm, "The Celeration Live Technique for Assessing Client Change", *Journal of Social Service Research,* 3, 1, 99-113, 1979.

Glaser, E.M. and S.H. Taylor, *Factors Influencing the Success of Applied Research: A Study of Ten NIHM-Funded Projects,* Los Angeles: Human Interaction Research Interaction Research Institute, 1969.

Goel, S.L. and R.K. Jain, *Social Welfare Administration,* New Delhi: Deep and Deep, 1988.

Goode, W.J. and P.K. Hatt, *Methods of Social Research*, New York: McGraw Hill, 1952.

Gopalan, V., *Evaluation of Social Welfare Program, Evaluation of Social Welfare in India V-I,* Ministry of Welfare, Government of India, 1987.

Gupta, S.P., *Statistical Methods*, New Delhi: S. Chand, 1980.

Hart, E. and M. Bond, *Action Research for Health and Social Care: A Guide to Practice*, Buckingham: Open University, 1995.

Holsti, Ole R., "*Content Analysis*" in *The Handbook of Social Psychology*, Gardner Lindzey and Eliot Anderson (eds.), Mass. Addison Wesley, 1968.

Hopps, J.G., "Services to and by the Real People", *Social Work*, 34, 195-196, 1989.

House, E.R., *Evaluating with Validity*, Beverly Hills, California, Sage, 1980.

Jacob, K.K., *Methods and Fields of Social Work in India*, Bombay: Asia Publishing, 1965.

Jain, S.C., *Application of Social Research in Developmental Projects*, Baroda: Baroda Citizens Council, 1982.

Jayaratne, Srinika and Rona L. Levy, *Empirical Clinical Practice*, New York: Columbia University Press, 1979.

Jayaratne, Srinika, Tony Tripodi, and Engene Talsama, "The Comparative Analysis and Aggregration of Single Case Data", *Journal of Applied Behavioural Sciences*, 1, 24, 119-28, 1988.

Kerlinger, Fred R., *Foundations of Behavioural Research,* Delhi, Surjeet Publications, 1964.

Kidder, Louise H., *Research Methods in Social Relations,* New York: Holt, 1981.

Kish, Leslie, *Survey Sampling*, New York: 1965.

Khinduka, S.K., *Social Work in India,* Allahabad: Kitab Mahal, 1965.

Kothari, L.R., *Research Methodology*, New Delhi: Vishwa Prakashan, 1985.

Krishef, Curtis H., *Fundamentals Statistics for Human Services and Social Work*, Boston: Duxbury Press, 1987.

Lakatos, Imre, *The Methodology of Scientific Research Programmes,* (Vol.1) Cambridge: Cambridge University Press, 1978.

Lal Das, D.K., *Practice of Social Research: Social Work Perspective*, Jaipur: Rawat Publications, 2000.

Levin, M.H., *Costeffectiveness: A Primer,* New Delhi: Sage, 1985.

Lundberg, G.A., *Social Research*, New York: Longman, 1946.

Lynn, Lvons V. and Morris (eds.), *Programme Evaluation,* London: Sage, 1978.

McTaggart, R. (ed.), *Partcipatory Action Research: International Context and Consequences*, New York: State University of New York Press, 1997.

Micheal, J. and Associates, *Evaluating Your Agency's Programme*, London: Sage, 1982.

Mill, J.S., *A System of Logic*, New York: Longmans (8th edition), 1930.

Miller, D.C., *Handbook of Research Design and Social Measurement*, New York: David McKey Co., 1964.

Mishan, E.J., *Cost-Benefit Analysis: An Informal Introduction*, London: George Allen and Unwin Ltd., 1971.

Mohsin, S.M., *Research Methods in Behavioural Sciences*, Calcutta: Orient and Longman Limited, 1984.

Monette, Duane R. et al., *Applied Social Research: Tool For the Human Services*, Chicago: Holt, 1986.

Moser, C.A. and Kalton, *Survey Methods in Social Investigation*, London: Heinemann Educational Books, 1975.

Mullen, E.J. et al. (ed.), *Evaluation of Social Intervention*, San Francisco: Jossey Bass, 1972.

Nachmias, D. and C. Nachmias, *Research Methods in the Social Sciences*, New York: St. Martins Press, 1981.

Oppenheim, N.A., *Questionnaire Design and Attitude Measurement*, New York: Basic Books, 1966.

Ostle, B. and R.W. Mensing, *Statistics in Research*, New Delhi, Oxford, 1975.

Panadikar, A. Pai (ed.), *Program Planning and Management in Development Administration in India*, Delhi: The Macmillan, pp. 69-70, 1974.

Paul Choudhary, D., *Social Welfare Administration*, Delhi: Everest Press, 1962.

Paul Choudhary, D., *Training Methodology and Management*, New Delhi: Sterling, 1962.

Philip, A.E. et al., *Social Work Research and The Analysis of Social Data*, Oxford: Peragon Press, 1975.

Polansky, N.A. (ed.), *Social Work Research*, Chicago: The University of Chicago Press, 1975.

Posova, E.J. and R.G. Carey, *Programme Evaluation Methods and Case Studies*, NJ: Englewood Cliffs, Prentice Hall, 1985.

Ramachandran, P., "Social Work Research and Statistics" in *History and Philosophy of Social Work in India*, Bombay: Allied Publishers, 1968.

Ramchandran, P., "Research in Social Work" in A.B. Bose (ed.), *Encyclopaedia of Social Work in India*, New Delhi: Government of India, p. 386, 1987.

Reid, W., "The Social Agency as a Research Machine", *Journal of Service Research*, 2, 11-23, 1978.

Report of the working group on *Evaluation in the State Planning Commission Government of India*, 1964, New Delhi.

Rossi, H.P. and W. Williams (ed.), *Evaluating Social Programs: Theory. Practice and Politics*, New York: Seminar Press, 1972.

Rossi, P. and H. Freeman, *Evaluation: A Systematic Approach*, Beverly Hills: Sage, 1982.

Rubin, Allen and E. Babbie, *Research Methodology for Social Work*, Belmohf, California: Wadsworth, 1989.

Sanders, D.H. et al., *Statistics: A Fresh Approach*, New Delhi: McGraw Hill, 1975.

Schneirer, M.A., *Programme Evaluation: The Organizational Context*, Beverly Hills, California: Sage, 1980.

Sellitz, G. et al., *Research Methods in Social Relations*, New York: Holt, Rinehart and Winston (3rd edition), 1973.

Service, A.I., S.J. Mantal, and A. Reismen, "System Evaluation of Social Agencies", in *System Approach and the City*, M.D. Mesorovic and A. Reisman (eds.), Amsterdam: North Holland Publishing, 1972.

Shah, V.F., *Research Design*, Ahmedabad: Rachna Prakashan, 1977.

Sjoberg, G. and B. Nett, *A Methodology of Social Research*, New York: Harper & Row, 1968.

Stouffer, S.A., *Social Research to Test Ideas*, New York: Free Press of Glencoe, 1962.

Strauss, Anseln, *Qualitative Analysis for Social Scientists*, Cambridge: Cambridge University Press (Photocopies of a major portion of Ch.1 in the Library), 1982.

Suchman, E.A., *Evaluative Research: Principles and Practice in Public Service and Social Action Programmes*, New York: Russel Sage Foundation, 1967.

Tilly, Charles, *Big Structures. Large Processes and Huge Comparisons*, New York: Russell Sage Foundations, 1982.

Thomas, E.J., "The BBESDAS Model for Effective Practice", *Social Work Research and Abstract*, 13, 12-16, 1977.

Thomas, P.T., "Social Research" in *Encyclopaedia of Social Work India*, New Delhi: Government of India, p. 294, 1977.

Thurstone, L.L., "Attitudes Can Be Measured," *American Journal of Sociology*, 33 (January 1928).

Trecker, H.B., *Group Process in Administration*, New York: Womens Press, p. 308.

UNDP, *Human Development Report*, New York: Oxford Press, 1993.

Van Maanen, John, *Varieties of Qualitative Research,* New Delhi: Sage, 1982.

Weiss, Carol, *Evaluation Research Englewood,* Cliffs N.J.: Prentice Hall, 1972.

Werner, W.B., *Objectives of Social Curriculum of the Future,* New York: Council on Social Work Education, 1959.

Wienback, R.W. and A. Rubin (eds.), *Teaching Social Work Research: Alternative Programs and Strategies,* New York: Council on Social Work Education, 1980.

Wilkinson, T.S. and P.L. Bhandarkar, *Methodology and Techniques of Social Research,* Bombay: Himalaya Publishing, 1977.

Yin, Robert K., *Case Study Research Design and Methods,* Applied Social Research Methods Series, Vol. 5, New Delhi: Sage, 1982.

Young, P.V., *Scientific Social Surveys and Research,* Englewood Cliff, N.J.: Prentice Hall (4th edition), 1953.

Index